CW01020175

HISTORIC CARRIAGE DRAWINGS

(Series Editor: David Jenkinson)

VOLUME THREE:

NON-PASSENGER COACHING STOCK

In memory of Smokey Bourne

Compiled by Peter Tatlow
in association with the LMS Society

A collection of many LSWR and three Midland non-passenger coaching stock vehicles are gathered in the goods yard at Swanwick, Hampshire between Fareham and Southampton (LSWR) in late June/early July circa 1910. Strawberry fruit is in the process of being loaded from some horse drawn carts for conveyance to market, while other carts wait on the approach ramp for their turn. (G Warburton collection)

We would like to extend our sincere thanks to those many draughtsmen and photographers (past and present) whose work we have been delighted to incorporate in this book. The names of the draughtsmen are shown in the Contents List and the photographers with each caption.

Note: Unless stated otherwise, all drawings in this book are reproduced at a scale of 4mm to 1 foot.

Published by Pendragon Partnership, PO Box No 3, Easingwold, York, YO61 3YS

Designed by Peter Tatlow, Godalming and Barry C Lane, Sutton-in-Craven

Text in Times Roman by the Editor

Printed in England by Amadeus Press Ltd, Huddesfield, west Yorkshire

British Cataloguing-in-Publication Data: a catalogue reference for this book is held by the British Library

ISBN No 1 899816 09 7

Contents

Contents (continued)

Key to draughtsmen

TWB	Smokey Bourne	MEML	Mike Lloyd	IRS	Ian Smith	GW	Graham Warburton
EDB	Eric Bruton	RM	Roger Marsh	WDS	Willie Stuart	JW	John Watling
NHC	Nick Campling	KRM	Ken Morgan	PT	Peter Tatlow	AW	Arthur Whitehead
RC	Ray Chorley	MP	Mike Peascod	LT	Len Tavender	AWHLW	Alistair Wright
TLJ	Trevor Jones	DPR	Don Rowland	EBT	EB Trotter	U/k	Unknown
BCL	Barry Lane	IGS	Ian Sadler	RET	Ray Tustin		

In Memoriam – TW (Smokey) Bourne: 1934-1995

This book is dedicated to the memory of the late 'Smokey' Bourne. He was a founder-member of the LMS Society in 1963 and remained a very active member until his untimely passing at the early age of 61 years in March 1995. He became well-known and greatly respected for the range of articles he contributed to railway model and prototype magazines over a long period, particularly in the specialist area of Non-Passenger Coaching Stock, and railway road motor vehicles. Whilst he was a hard-back book author in 1983 - joint author of *LMS Road Vehicles* - he never got round to committing his knowledge nor the extensive collection of drawings, photographs and information he amassed on NPCS vehicles from the many railway companies, into hard-back print.

Following Smokey's passing, his widow, Muriel, entrusted his NPCS records to the LMS Society, and from the initial discussions to determine storage arrangements, it was decided to honour his memory by publishing this NPCS volume.

Railway operations in model form are intended to reproduce what actually happened on the prototype railways, and it is due to the likes of Smokey Bourne and a number of others, that much of the historical information on NPCS prototypes has been preserved for modellers and future generations. The work of such people will continue to help modellers produce accurate representations of the original vehicles, and it is to this objective that this book is dedicated.

Smokey Bourne was a tireless researcher, and whilst much of this volume is from his records, I would like to express sincere thanks to a number of other people who, from their own NPCS records, have allowed many of the gaps to be filled. Finally, on behalf of Muriel Bourne, I would like to express sincere thanks to Peter Tatlow, current Chairman of the LMS Society, for his work in bringing this project to fruition, and to the publisher for agreeing to bring the material to the bookshelves.

I trust that the contents of this volume will inspire you, the reader – also the modeller perhaps – to build models to add further interest to your chosen railway prototype scene.

HN Twells OBE,
Hon. Secretary, LMS Society
August, 1999

One of the few innovations in non-passenger coaching during the grouping period was the introduction of tank wagons for the conveyance of milk in bulk from the producers in the countryside to the users in major conurbations - see page 112. All four of the grouping companies used them. Here LMS Stanier 5P5F 4-6-0 No. 5377 is seen with a milk train in 1937. The first two vehicles are six-wheelers, followed by a pair of four-wheelers and another six-wheeler with a LNWR bogie brake van bringing up the rear. (JF Hull, HMRS collection AAE126)

Series Editor's Introduction

In introducing this, the third in the Pendragon series of historic carriage drawing compilations, it is once again my pleasure and privilege to contribute some of the essential background information which, in a number of cases, touches upon matters which those who have been more directly involved with the preparation of this particular volume would probably be too modest to mention themselves.

In the first two volumes, I explained how this series started as an expansion of a single book of LMS/LNER carriage drawings which Nick Campling and I had put together way back in the late 1960s. For this reason, the first two volumes of the new survey included much which had gone before, albeit being supplemented with augmented text plus a few new drawings, together with the all-essential pictures which were not offered in the 1968-9 survey. This third book, however, although following that general approach in terms of both narrative and picture coverage, moves onto totally new ground in a number of ways which warrant further explanation.

Firstly, I am delighted to be able to say, without serious risk of contradiction, thanks to the unstinting support of more helpful folk than I care to think about, that although some of it has been seen in the transient form of magazine or specialist journal publication, the whole of the material in this book has never before been offered in permanent hard back form.

Secondly, and unlike the previous two volumes, we have deliberately chosen to offer a subject which is by way of being cross-company in its coverage. Its inspiration stems from the particular man to whom the book is dedicated. He was largely, but not exclusively of LMS persuasion in the context of his own primary interests, but the subject of his research was more like that of freight vehicles in the sense that most of the vehicles themselves could be seen system wide. It thus seemed far more logical this time to go for a thematic rather than a company approach.

Thirdly, and more practically speaking, because of the very nature of the vehicles covered, it has been possible to design the whole book in the conventional 'portrait' form rather than the landscape format which the previous two volumes exhibited. But mindful of the fact that modellers will (we hope) find this book to be of value, we have continued with the 'wipe-clean' form of cover presentation. Lastly in this context, largely because the subject matter itself is not well covered in print, we thought it expedient to extend the narrative parts to encompass rather more of the nature and operation of the vehicles concerned than was the case in the first two volumes.

That this is possible at all is largely through the herculean efforts of the compiler of this particular volume, Peter Tatlow, who has also made a number of considerable offerings from his own drawing board. It is no small task to bring together the work of so many individuals in a coherent way and to him and his many collaborators in this particular volume (who are named elsewhere), I offer my very sincere thanks. No series editor could have been better served.

As before, I should state that it is not our intention to offer a comprehensive history within these pages, nor a manual of drawings which the full size railway restorer could use. We will be content if our efforts serve to provide enthusiasts in general (and modellers in the smaller scales) sufficient information either to whet their appetites for more serious research or to make reasonably accurate representations of what were undoubtedly a most fascinating group of vehicles.

Finally, I trust that I shall be forgiven if I conclude by adding my personal comments regarding 'Smokey' Bourne to those already offered on previous and subsequent pages. He was a friend of mine, though I never knew his 'given' first name(!), and although I think he would have been the first to admit that he was no more than a self-trained draughtsman (as, indeed am I), such was his dedication to the investigation of what was, when he started out, relatively uncharted water, that he found sufficient time to divert attention from his first love (a modelling bench whose output was both prolific and authoritative) to make his own drawings of many of those vehicles which had first attracted his interest.

I doubt if any of his and my generation (leave alone those much younger) would have known half as much about non-passenger coaching stock had it not been for his catalytic efforts a generation ago. Sadly, he never finished all the drawings to which he had set his mind, but I like to think that he would have been pleased at the way in which his original inspiration has finally appeared in the shape of this book.

I can therefore think of no better way to make the point than to quote (opposite) his own words on the subject, written in the early 1970s when both he and I were almost thirty years younger.......

David Jenkinson
Series Editor, February 2000

The following comments were offered by way of introduction to a series of magazine articles on NPCS by the late 'Smokey' Bourne in 1973.

Before commencing, it would be as well to explain the apparent contradiction in the terms non-passenger and coaching stock. In essence, it is simply the designation given to vehicles built to coaching stock specifications but used to convey anything but passengers. So far, so good, but it becomes more difficult when the term coaching stock specification has to be defined. Frankly, I cannot, as yet, do this; no matter on what basis I start; with any railway; there are numerous contradictions. So, if anyone can shed light on the subject, I would be most pleased to hear. In the interim, I am pressing on with my own research, deciding between goods vehicles and non-passenger coaching stock – purely by instinct.

My instinct is of little use to readers who do not possess it, of course, and the best I can do - lacking a set of finite specifications - is to explain why this class of vehicle came into being at all.

As soon as railways began running passenger trains faster than freight trains, there were people about who would pay better than freight rates to have their goods conveyed on passenger trains at the improved speeds. Such profitable business could not be turned away and goods were conveyed by train. Now, I do not know if anyone tried tying the un-sprung freight stock of those early days to a passenger train and then running it at speed, but suspect that someone did. The resulting derailment brought about the building of sprung freight stock. Here was the origin of the hybrid and, subsequently, non-passenger coaching stock which always had a better chassis design than purely freight stock. As train speeds rose, however, speed restrictions were imposed on shorter wheelbase vehicles, be they non-passenger coaching stock, or freight stock.

It cannot have been long after the beginning of railways that the use of non-passenger coaching stock was enlarged from adding a few vehicles to a passenger train to the running of complete passenger trains composed exclusively of such vehicles. The most obvious examples are the fish and Royal Mail trains, but there were others. It does seem, however, that most parcels traffic and milk traffic vehicles were tacked on to passenger trains until just before the First World War. It was about that time the LNWR seemed to have taken the lead in trying to segregate, as far as possible, the three classes of traffic - passenger, passenger rated goods and freight.

My interest in these vehicles stems from observations made at the Central Goods Yard, Birmingham in the early 'fifties. This yard was the loading and marshalling point for the parcels traffic and, in those days, the variety of vehicles used was fantastic. The choice of locomotives also was considerable; ranging from 3F 0-6-0s to Royal Scots. Since those days, I have been set on the idea of modelling these top rated freight trains which as Parcels or Perishable trains (composed entirely of non-passenger coaching stock) quite literally have a higher line priority than an express passenger train. The combination of interest and modelling experience should have resulted in models being built but, unfortunately, there is very little information available. I, therefore, decided to research the subject myself and have accumulated as much information as is available from my fellow members of the LMS Society, their friends, my friends and, indeed, anyone who has been able to help. I am still in need of a lot of information but I had a flying start with the LNWR vehicles and am in a position to put forward a fairly comprehensive picture of that company's stock. These vehicles should be of special interest to any model maker, for they were used on long distance traffic generally and it is quite likely that one of the type could turn up far from home on foreign metals, even down the most remote branch line. They can be run in parcels or perishable trains, tacked on to passenger trains or slipped in to goods.

GW 4-6-0 Saint class Princess Eugenie *passes Southam Road and Harbury station in 1936 with a class C parcels train. The cosmopolitan nature of non-passenger coaching stock workings is exemplified by the presence of a Southern Railway four wheel utility van at the head, followed by two empty coaches and a string of Siphon milk vans behind. (JAGH Coltas)*

Compiler's Introduction

Once it was decided to consider the publication of a book devoted to non-passenger coaching (npc) stock, it became apparent that the material that Smokey Bourne left was in itself insufficient in quantity and was not sufficiently representative in its coverage for a book of this nature. There are of course several examples of bogie passenger brake vans and Post Office vehicles in *Historic carriage drawings – Volumes 1 and 2, LNER and LMS* respectively, together with a small selection of other npc stock of the GN and NER/LNER in the former. Nonetheless, to broaden the selection therefore, additional material has been collected from a wide range of sources and new specially prepared.

Its preparation could not have been undertaken without the whole-hearted support of members of the LMS Society. Material assistance has been provided by Gordon Coltas, John Edgington, Bob Essery, Niall Ferguson, Bernard Holland, Barry Lane, Mike Peascod, Don Rowland, Jim Smellie, Arnold Tortorella, Nelson Twells, Graham Warburton, David White and Alistair Wright, together with former members Ken Morgan and Arthur Whitehead. I have been further assisted with support my fellow members of the LNER Study Group. In particular Nick Campling, John Edgson, Tony Evans, Pete Hall, Jim Hay, Terry Henderson, Murray Hughes, Roger Marsh, Kevin Tong, Wilf Wells and Harry Wilson have made material and information available from their archives. Of equal value has been the encouragement of those from the Historical Model Railway Society and G&SWR Association, including Peter Bunce, Richard Casserley, Ray Chorley, David Goodwin, John Lewis, Mike Moreton Lloyd, John Quick, Stuart Rankin, Ian Sadler, Len Tavender, John Watling and David Williamson. Others who have contributed in some way include Steve Banks, Mike Fish, Robin Peover and Marshall Shaw, together with Slater's Plastikard Ltd. Individual photographers are acknowledged in the captions, whilst the names of draughtsmen are given in the contents list. We are grateful to them all and thank them for their assistance in making this book possible.

Peter Tatlow, Chairman of the LMS Society
December 1999

Loading Ford saloon motor cars, possibly at Dagenham, into a string of covered carriage trucks at an end loading dock. The leading truck is an ex-G&SWR 25 foot long milk and motor car van. Note the doors folded back at both ends. (G&SWR Association)

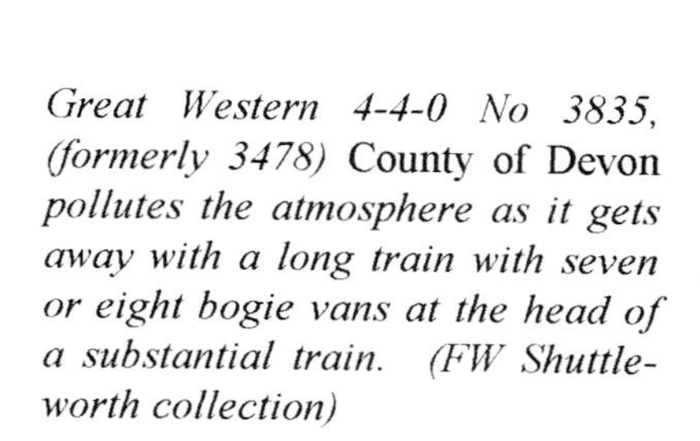

Great Western 4-4-0 No 3835, (formerly 3478) County of Devon *pollutes the atmosphere as it gets away with a long train with seven or eight bogie vans at the head of a substantial train. (FW Shuttleworth collection)*

The Nature and Operation of Non-Passenger Coaching Stock

Ex-Midland Railway 4-4-0 Johnson No 499, rebuilt by Fowler, Class 2P, with tall chimney, bogie brakes and Ramsbottom safety valves, at the head of a parcels train on the Up Slow line ¾ mile north of Mill Hill station soon after 1928. The eight vehicle train is largely made up of MR/LMS types, starting with a 45 foot bogie clerestory full brake, followed by two six wheel outside frame fish vans, four further six wheel vans and a 50 foot passenger brake van in the rear. (GR Grigs, P Tatlow collection)

In the very early days railways carried minerals usually associated with mine workings or quarries. Later public railways developed as conveyors of both passengers and goods, including of course minerals. In due course priority was given to passengers, who were then transported in trains separately from goods and minerals. Certain classes of valuable and perishable goods, however, could attract a premium fare for transit by passenger train and initially this would have been accommodated in the guard's van. Whilst this continued until recent times, as traffic developed, vehicles were designed for specific uses, such as the conveyance of mail; parcels; luggage; newspapers; horse drawn and later motor road vehicles; theatrical scenery; aeroplanes; horses; valuable cattle; hounds; fruit; fish; game; meat; yeast; and milk.

In the early days of railways, the specification for the construction of passenger vehicles was little different from that for goods, if not minerals. As speed and distance of travel grew and public expectations increased, so the construction of carriages improved, particularly once the Government insisted on the installation of automatic brakes on passenger trains. It then became no longer acceptable to add ordinary goods vehicles for the speedy conveyance of valuable goods at passenger rates. This led to the classification of non-passenger coaching stock built to a standard to permit their inclusion in passenger trains.

In the early days of an infrequent service, trains would consist of a combination of various classes of coach and vans, as necessary to meet the demands of the traffic, and this continued in many cases until recently. Only on heavily trafficked routes did the train devoted solely to non-passenger vehicles come into use. Some such traffics were entirely predicable and include mail, newspapers, parcels and milk with regular vehicles identified for their use. Others, such as traffic in fish and meat, although reasonably regular might fluctuate in volume and in such cases vehicles would be added or removed from the trains as required. Fruit on the other hand is wholly seasonal, whilst horse, valuable cattle, pigeons and hounds traffic will in part have been to accord with the races, shows, markets and hunt meetings, when appropriate vehicles will have to be on hand and sent to the departure station as required.

The movement of larger predictable traffic will have been met by the running of a specific mail and/or parcels, milk, fish and newspaper trains. Other smaller regular traffics were allowed for by the attachment of appropriate vehicles to the necessary train. Details of both of these will have been published in the periodic printed passenger train marshalling arrangements and vehicle circuit diagrams. Some companies even went to the trouble to devise and

GN 2-6-0 Gresley K2 class No 1645, later LNER No 4645, built in 1914 heads a parcels train at Holme, south of Peterborough, in 1923. A NER six wheel passenger brake leads two unidentified vans and a GN bogie milk brake etc. (LGRP, courtesy P Tatlow collection)

print instructions for the loading and stowing of parcels traffic etc, which indicated predetermined areas within the van for each destination along the route. This was no doubt carefully planned as the result of experience over the years to afford the maximum efficiency in loading and unloading. Fluctuations in volume of certain traffics, particularly at prior to Christmas, will have been catered for by drawing upon a pool of spare vehicles as the need arose by local arrangement. Care will have of course to be taken to ensure that surplus empty vehicles were returned to a point where they were likely to be needed next.

The demand for vehicles for entirely random traffic will have been met from a pool kept at appropriate points on the system. When sufficient notice was given, arrangements will have been published in advance in the weekly special traffic notice. The odd one or two vehicles, therefore, were often added to the front of the most convenient passenger train and the train marshalling arrangements often refer to the possibility and sometimes state the preferred position and order within the train. Larger volumes may have required the provision of a locomotive and brake van with staff for the running of a special train. The working timetables often include provisional Q paths for the possible running of ocean liner expresses and boat trains dependent on the tide, and where appropriate these paths will have been used in part or whole. Some companies ran regular horse and carriage trains on their main lines to clear such random traffic. They were also often used to move carriages to and from their main works for repair and overhaul.

A special case was at the location of race courses and the larger horse trainers. Here a series of the latest horseboxes would be allocated to the nearest station for use as required and often boxes would be allocated to specific trainers with their names and home station painted thereon.

Former LSW 4-6-0 H15 class, now BR No 30490, heads the 7.02pm Waterloo to Bournemouth parcels train up the 1 in 338 bank between Clapham Jct and Earlsfield in June 1949. Numerous examples of the ubiquitous Southern four wheel and bogie vans make up the majority of this train with a leavening of a couple of equally common LMS passenger brake vans. (JAGH Coltas)

Liveries

Liveries of Pregrouping Companies:

Caledonian: Dark purple lake with yellow lining edged in a fine vermilion line and medium chrome yellow lettering, the initials CR being shaded lower left in vermilion.

Cambrian: Bronze green bodies. Black solebars and running gear. 3½ inch gold lettering shaded dark blue below and lighter blue to the right and highlighted in white. Feathers in gold and shaded.

Furness: Ultramarine for the body sides and ends, as used for the lower panels of passenger carriages. Lining is thought to have been either white or yellow.

GC: Varnished teak with black underframe and when freshly out-shopped white roofs. Lettering was in gold or yellow around 4½ inches high.

GE: Varnished teak with gold or straw yellow lettering shaded in black to the lower right. The roof and its fittings were white with the section between the rain strip and eaves sometimes painted dark grey. The underframe was black, together with iron fittings on the body, although the wheel centres were varnished teak and the Westinghouse brake hose white. As the teak finish deteriorated due to staining, a teak coloured paint was used. From February 1919 a crimson lake livery was adopted by the GE with a serif style lettering.

GNS: Crimson lake sides, ends and solebars with ironwork picked out in black and yellow lettering. Brake vans were white from the waist panels upwards with the panels lined round in pale yellow and below the waist was crimson lake, similarly lined in yellow, with the ends lake. Just below the waist panels a 1½ inch vermilion line separated the two basic colours. Ironwork and running gear was black and roof pale French grey. Lettering was in gold or yellow, shaded with bright red.

Highland: Olive green with yellow lettering and black underframe, see *A Register of Highland Railway Liveries*, by Howard Geddes and Eddie Bellass, HMRS/Pendragon, 1996.

LB&SC: Varnished mahogany with gilt lining and gold lettering shaded red, vermilion brake ends, white roofs.

LC&D: Varnished teak, gold letters shaded red.

LNW: Black below solebars, chocolate-brown body (plain, not milk chocolate), varnished wood louvres and grey roof. The varnished louvres do not seem to have lasted very long; perhaps just one or two repaints and then they were painted brown. Lettering was plain yellow. For details see *LNWR liveries* by Ted Talbot, Philip Millard, George Dow and Peter Davies, HMRS, 1985.

L&SW: Coach brown all over the body, ends, solebars and buffer beams with black running gear and buffer heads and a white roof, with gilt lettering. A new livery was introduced from 1921 onwards with green sides, black ends and underframe and a white roof. For further details see *HMRS livery register No 3 – LSWR and Southern*, by Len Tavender, HMRS, 1970.

LT&S: Varnished teak with red ends to brake vans.

L&Y: The L&Y livery was a tan upper half over carmine lake lower, lined orange, with dark umber ends. The company initials and running number were applied in gold leaf serif coach lettering with an outer white line with an inner red border. Where transfers were not available, lettering was sign written in golden orange to match the transfers.

Metropolitan: Varnished teak with the Company's coat of arms based on City of London, together with the counties of Middlesex, Buckinghamshire and Hertfordshire.

Midland: Crimson lake, from which the LMS's first livery style was derived. For further details see *Midland style* by George Dow, HMRS, 1975.

MSWJ: Crimson lake with white roofs and lettering, later yellow shaded black. Black running gear.

NB: Maroon sides with black ends and underframes and plain gold lettering.

NE: For details of the crimson lake livery and lettering see *North Eastern Record, Volume 2*, HMRS, 1997.

Rhymney: Prior to 1907: brown, darker than GW, with white, tending to cream with age, panels above waist, with ½ inch wide lining, gilt or chrome yellow shaded lower right in red lettering, monogram and crest. Post 1907: dark red all over with ¼ inch wide gold or chrome yellow lining to panels and lettering as above, but monogram replaced by letters RR. Black underframe and fittings for both livery periods.

S&DJ: Dark blue with black mouldings lined on both sides with 1 inch vermilion lines and 1 inch mid-chrome yellow lines. Lettering was in gold leaf, shaded left and below in red with the company crest a little above dead centre. Later this may have given way to something less elaborate, probably unlined dark blue with the lettering and, maybe, the crest. In 1930 the S&D stock was shared out between the LMS and Southern railways. See also *Midland style* by George Dow, HMRS, 1975.

SE and **SE&C**: Crimson lake, see David Gould's *Bogie carriages of the South Eastern & Chatham Railway*, Oakwood Press 1993 for details.

Taff Vale: Carriages were pale cream for the waist, upper and eaves panels with yellow lining edged with fine vermilion line. Below the waist and ends dark was chocolate. Lettering was in gilt shaded lower right in red. The underframes were black, the roof white. Other vehicles were dark brown lake sides and ends with black underframes, white roof and yellow lettering.

WCJS: Dark chocolate brown, lined yellow until about 1916, with grey roofs, slate waist panels and black running gear. The louvres were varnished wood. For further details see *A register of West Coast Joint Stock* Richard Casserley and Philip Millard, HMRS, 1980.

Liveries of the Grouping Companies:

Item	LMS	LNER	GW 1920-47	SR
Body sides	Crimson lake lined in black, sometimes omitted, edged with pale yellow until 1934. Simple lining on luggage and parcels vans from 1934	Brown including solebars. Varnished teak for LNER built corridor PBVs & TPOs lined if fitted with gangways until 1940	Brown	Sage/olive green lined yellow and black. Malachite green unlined from 1938
Body ends	Crimson lake, black from 1937	Black	Brown	Black
Roofs	Black and/or grey	White, grey from 1940	White, grey from 1941	White
Running and brake gear	Black	Black. Wheels teak with white rims	Black	Black
Other ironwork	Black	Black except solebars	Black	Black
Wheels	Black	Teak brown with white rims	Black	Black, with white rims until 1938

Insignia - Letter and numeral sizes

Company title	3 inch high LMS in serif style on sides at waist height, 4 inch white LMS on CCTs & OCTs from 1936	18 by 12 inch where practical, 4 by 3 inch from 1936, high white initials NE on sides	25 inch until 1920, after 16 inch yellow initials on sides & ends, shirt button GWR from 1934 on sides, 5 inch GW on sides from 1936 & 3inch from 1942	Gilt shaded black 3¼ inch. Straw 4 inch from 1938. 12 inch white on SCVs until 1936
Running numbers	3 inch scroll towards RH end, 3 inch white on CCTs & OCTs from 1936	5/4 inch white with prefix where appropriate	5 inch, 3 inch from 1942	3¼ inch gilt shaded black
Tare weight	3/2 inch white	3½/3 inch white	1 inch white italic	Plate on ends
Wheel base	2 inch white	2½ inch white	2 inch	2 inch white
XP	4 inch	4 inch white	4 inch	4 inch white
Vehicle code	2 inch	5 inch white	5½/4½ inch	3¼ inch yellow

Notes:

LMS: Npc stock was fully-lined from 1923, but this soon gave way to unlined lake body with coach lettering. The door waist-panels were slate and used as chalk boards. In 1923 each pregrouping company was allocated a block of numbers in the LMS's npc list and each type of vehicle renumbered in their previous order as one continuous sequence. In 1932 all coaching vehicles were renumbered in blocks by type and age. For further details, see *LMS coaches – An illustrated history 1923-1957* by David Jenkinson and Bob Essery, OPC, 1969.

LNER: Npc stock was renumbered in separate series by type of vehicle. Several carried a prefix to indicate the type, eg MCK, BOK, LCK, LLCK, XCK and BCK for various carriage trucks, together with SC for special cattle vans. Passenger brake vans were renumbered in 1943. For further details see *Historic carriage drawings – Vol 1, LNER and constituents* by Nick Campling, Pendragon 1997.

GW: For further details, see Jack Slinn's *Great Western way*, HMRS, 1978.

SR: The brake handles were white and the door handles polished brass. For further details see *HMRS livery register No 3 – LSWR and Southern*, by Len Tavender, HMRS, 1970.

BR: Carmine was applied to the body sides from 1949 with black ends and underframe etc and grey roof. Lettering was in straw gill sans font with the regional letter E, M, S or W added as a prefix to the company number. Crimson lake was used for the body sides from 1956, except that green, including the ends in some cases, was restored on the Southern Region from July 1956. Matt blue and white lettering was introduced in 1967.

Glasgow & South Western Six Wheel Passenger Brake van

Designed by James Manson, ninety one six wheel passenger brake vans were built between 1894 and 1907 to diagram 16 and frequently to be found at one, if not both, ends of G&SW trains to provide accommodation for the guard and passengers' luggage. Fitted with automatic vacuum brake gear and initially all lit by gas, many were subsequently converted to electric lighting. Stoutly built, repairs to panelling in later years were often carried out in match boarding. Many survived in departmental service on the LMS and BR until the early 60s, examples being DM284290 and DM297291– Engineer Inverness; DM297295 – MPD tool van at Kyle of Lochalsh; 297247 and 297264 – Pooley weighing machine van; and 297267 – tool van at Perth.

Glasgow & South Western Railway six wheel passenger brake van built in 1898, seen here as LMS 34239. (WO Steel collection, courtesy RJ Essery)

PROTOTYPE DETAILS

Built	G&SW No	LMS 1st No	LMS 2nd No
1894	37-40	6995-8	34228
1895	31-4, 41-4/9, 60/8	6989-92/9-7002/7/18	34231
1896	35, 57/8, 66	6993, 7015/6/22-7	-
1897	45, 53/4/6	7003/11/2/4	34235-7
1898	26, 46-7/8-50/2, 61-4	6984, 7004-6/8/10/19-22	34231/8
1899	1, 59, 67	6959, 7017	34243
1900	2-10, 117-20	6960-8, 7074-77	34245-48
1901	11-18, 121-5	6969-76, 7078-81+?	34251-55
1902	19-24	6877-82	34260-62
1903	69	-	-
1904	70-77	7030-7	-
1905	78-84	7038-40+?	34274
1906	85-7	7045	-
1907	88-91	7046-9	34279-81

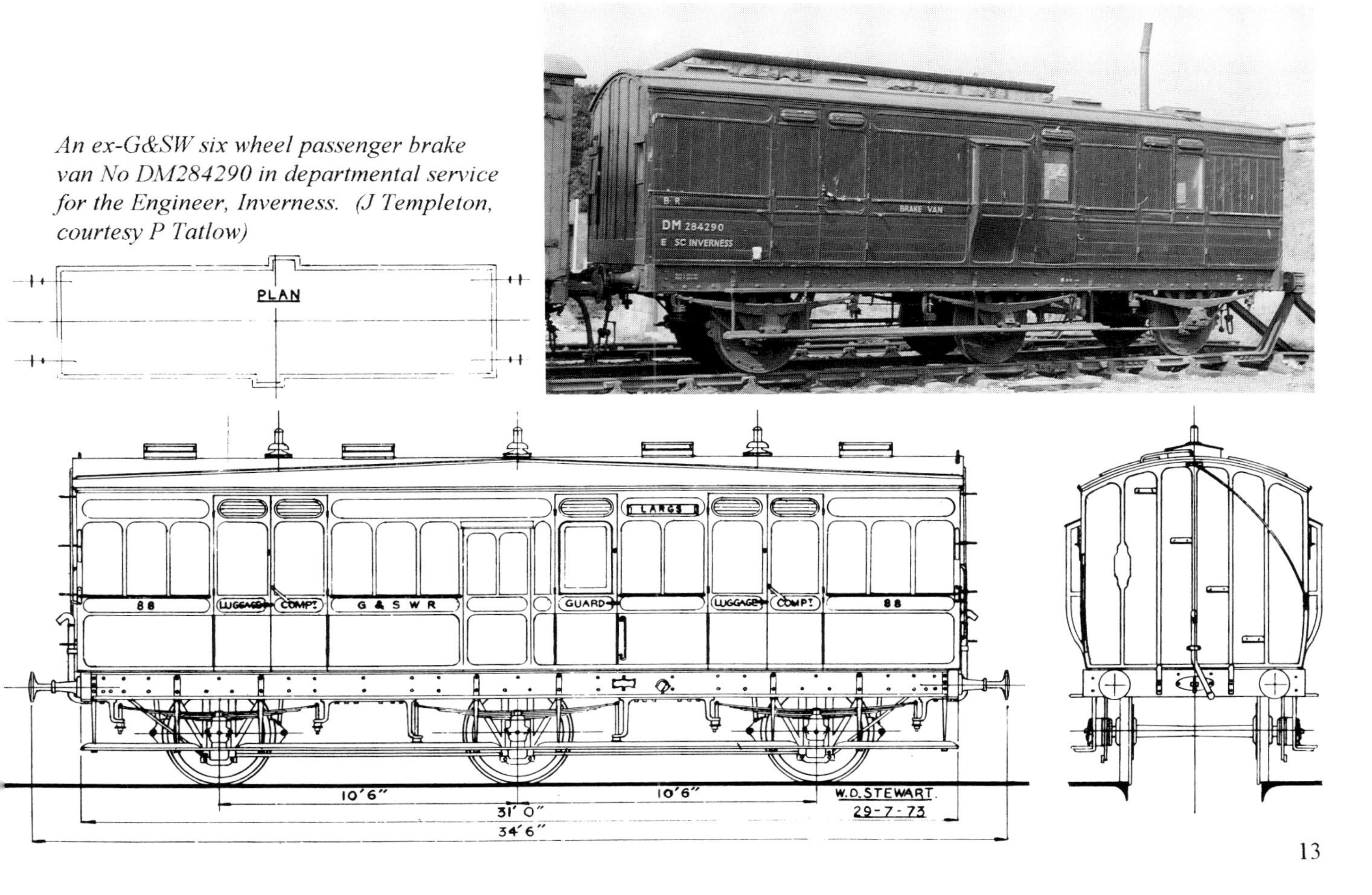

An ex-G&SW six wheel passenger brake van No DM284290 in departmental service for the Engineer, Inverness. (J Templeton, courtesy P Tatlow)

Highland Railway 46ft 8in Bogie Passenger Brake Van

These panelled bogie passenger brake vans were introduced by Highland in 1904. From 1907 the body sides and ends were vertically planked and drop-lights in the double doors were added. All were dual braked and steam pipes were added from 1912. Initially they were gas lit, but were converted to electric lighting from 1916. Repairs during their life led to panelling of the sides, but not ends, being replaced by vertical planking and sheet metal covering to the duckets; the removal of the lower foot boards, leaving a short length on the outer end of the bogies.

Towards the end of the LMS era a number, including 33692 and 33696, were rebuilt as a Beatties bread vans for a steady passenger train traffic of city steam-baked bread supplied to rural Scotland. The conversion consisted of stripping out the guard's equipment and fitting a four-spoked hand brake wheel of about 18 ins dia. below the solebar. The upper foot board was removed between the double doors. No 33695 was sold to the LNER in February 1943 and numbered 301 for similar traffic. It was finally withdrawn in May 1947.

PROTOTYPE DETAILS

HR Nos	Builder	Year	LMS 1st No	LMS 2nd Nos	Ext't
69-72	Pickering	1904	7432-5	33692/3	13/62
73-76	Inverness	1907	7436-9	33694-7	9/54
77	Inverness	1909	7440	33698	U/k

HR passenger 46ft 8in vertically planked brake van, in its latter days as No 33694, built at Inverness in 1907. (P Tatlow collection)

An unidentified formally panelled van built in 1904, at Oban in service as a bread van. Note the panelled ends, hand wheel and the reduced upper footboards. (I Peddie)

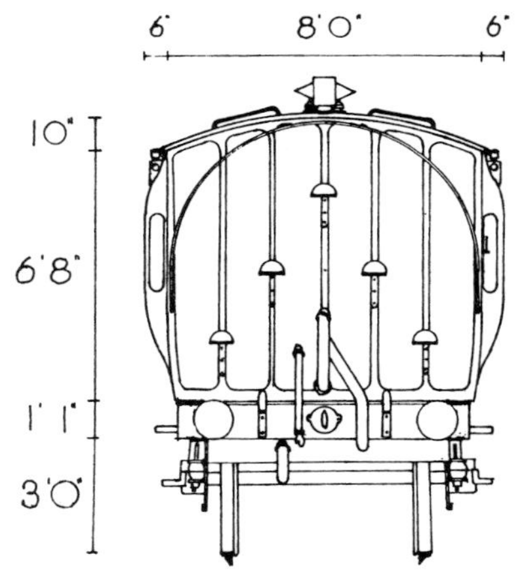

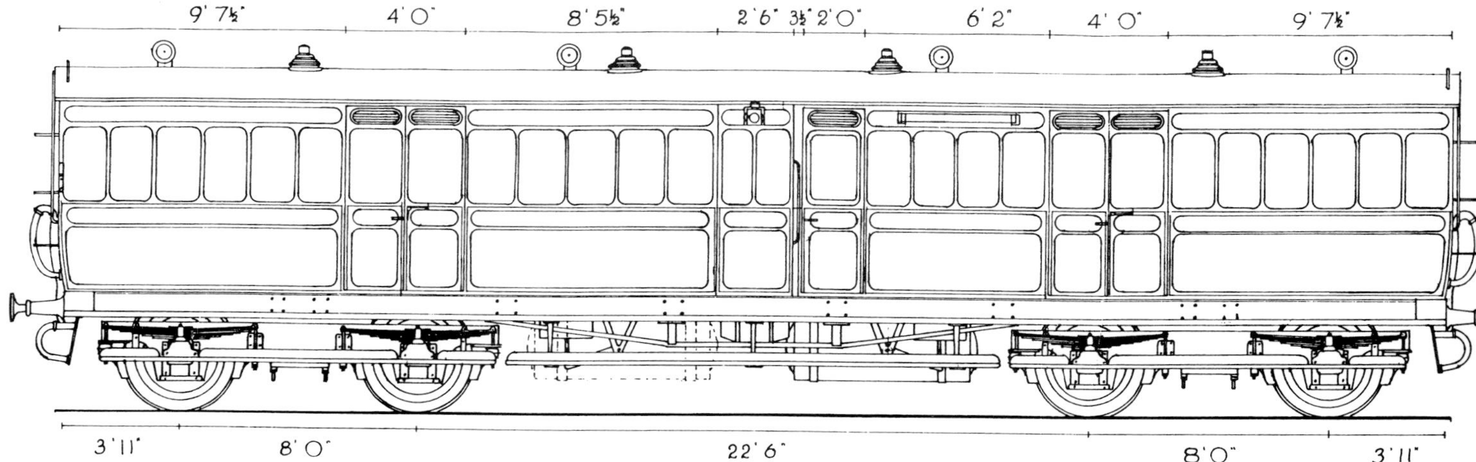

Highland Railway Bogie 37ft 9in Passenger Brake Van

During the period of shortages and inflation following World War 1, the Highland railway's need for some passenger brake vans was met by the expedient of rebuilding three redundant 38 foot bogie post office mail vans, Nos 5, 6 and 10, at Lochgorm in 1919. Six of these are thought to have been built around 1889 originally on six wheel underframes, but the three converted had previously been mounted on bogies. The rebuilding seems to have consisted of removing the original panelling and re-cladding in the current HR fashion of vertical match boarding with the addition of side lookouts for the guard. The beading on the ends, however, still exhibit the Jones style of vertical rectangular panels. The LMS first renumbered the vans 7371, 7372 and 7375, the last also receiving No 33691 in the 1933 renumbering scheme. Withdrawal dates are not known, but No 33691 survived into the mid 1950s. Photographs suggest that at first they were used on the line to the North from Inverness.

As no clear photograph of these in Highland days has come to light so far, it is not possible to be precise about details. As far as is known standard LMS livery for NPC vehicles was applied. It is possible No 33691 received BR's carmine livery.

HR 38 foot bogie passenger brake van No M33691 at Birmingham New Street on 5 May 1954. (SNJ White collection)

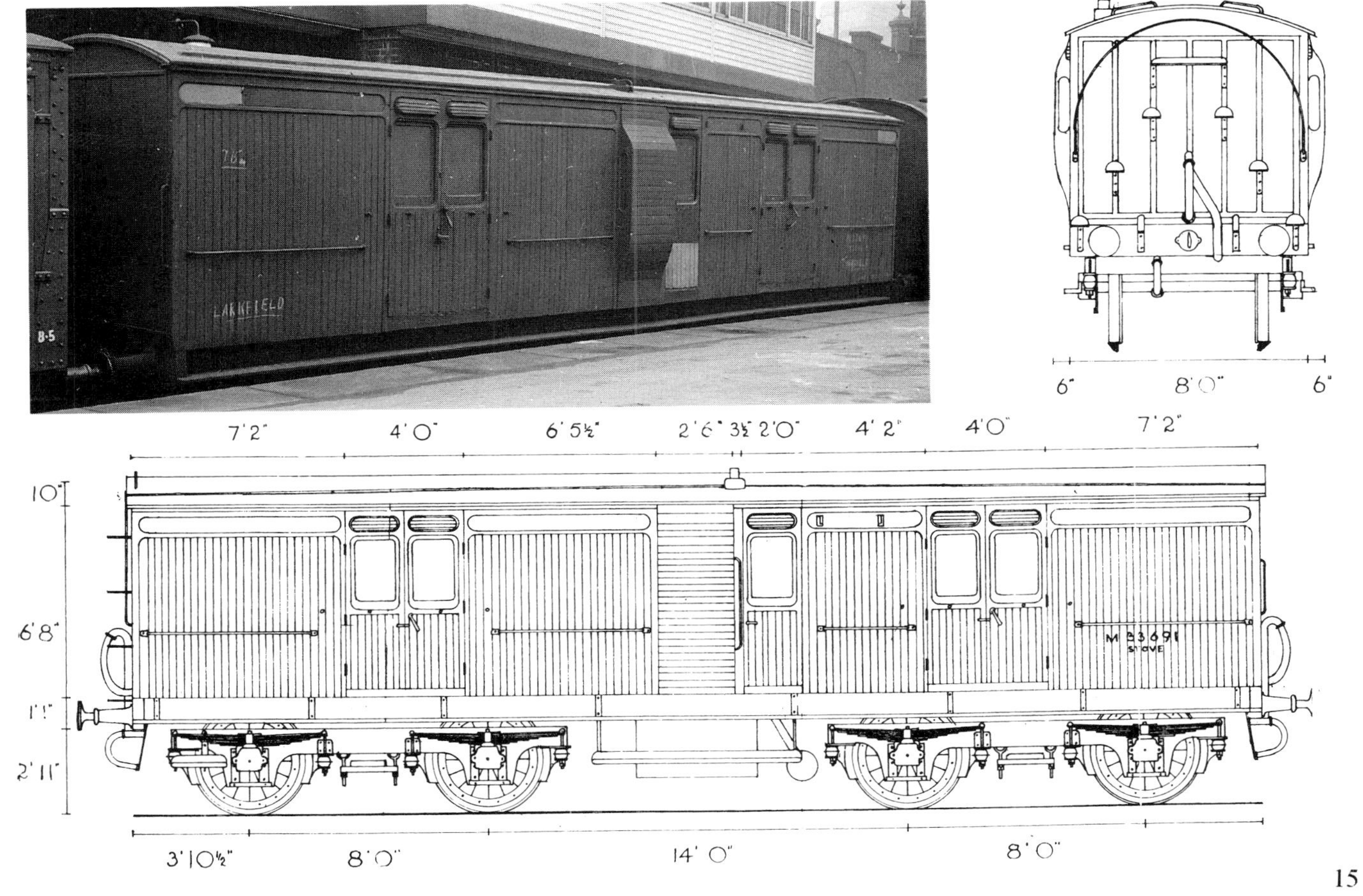

Another view of No M33691 in the 'Coffee Bay' at Birmingham New Street. It is just possible to discern Iracier axlebox covers on the original print. (JE Cull)

LMS Six Wheel Passenger Brake Van

Later well known as Stove Rs, these six wheel passenger brake vans were unusual in that they were fitted with gangway connections, which led one to assume that they were intended for more than mere local or parcels trains. The first six wheel passenger brake vans built by the LMS, at Wolverton, were not introduced until 1932 and were among the first to Stanier's Period III style. The bodies included horizontal beading above and below the windows and along the bottom edge. There were two diagrams, D1796 and D2000, but there were few differences. All the vehicles built to the first had torpedo roof ventilators, narrow double doors and initially carried the fully lined livery, whereas some of the latter had shell ventilators and were out-shopped in the plain livery. They also had wider doors and internally the hand brake was repositioned.

It was only during the war that guards began to request stoves to keep them warm when not marshalled in a passenger train with steam heating. Once fitted, they, and other similar vehicles, became known as Stove Rs.

PROTOTYPE DETAILS

Diag	Lot	Year	LMS Nos
1796	664	1932	32900-32924
	669	1933	32925-32974
2000	1091	1938	32975-32999
	1262	1940	33000-33019

LMS six wheel passenger brake van No M33000 of Lot 1262 to diagram 2000 built in 1940, as altered to a STOVE R, in the early days of British Railways. (SNJ White collection)

By the early 1960s alterations and repairs show their effect on the appearance of No M32905M to diagram 1796 at Euston. The end steps and grab rails have been removed as a precaution following electrification and the beading is incomplete and repositioned. (MS Welch)

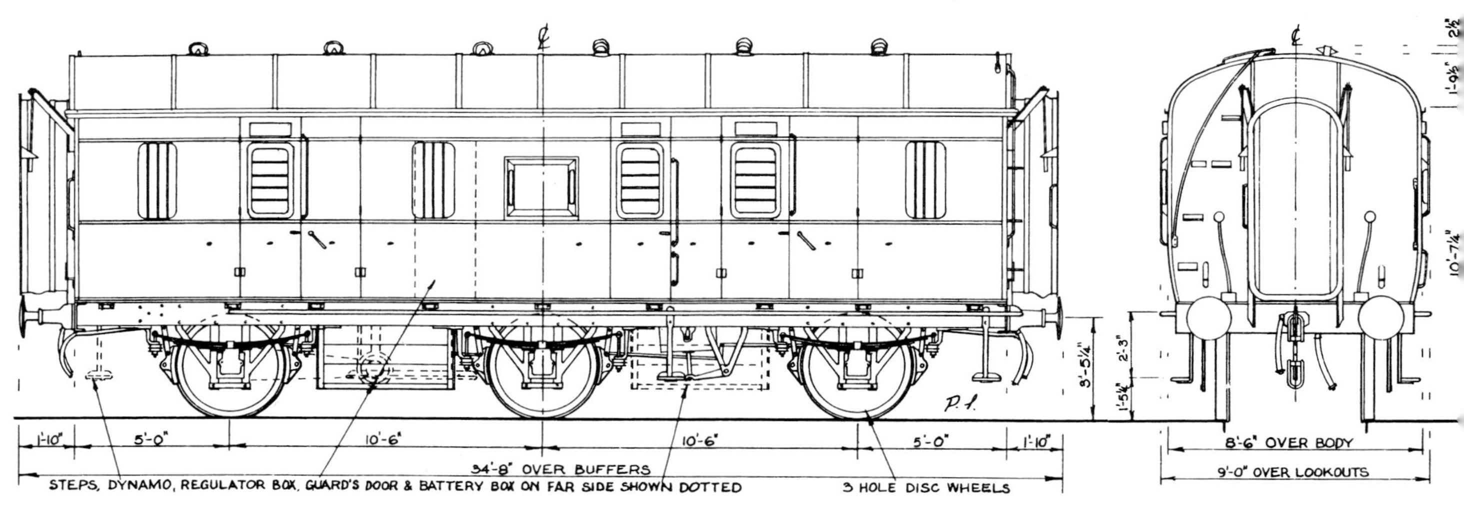

LNWR standard Four and Six wheel underframes

Much LNWR npc stock was built on one of the two chassis shown in the drawings. The solebars and buffer beams for both chassis originally utilised wood, but sections of either bulb angle or channel, the latter with the flanges facing both inwards or outwards, were subsequently substituted for the solebars. Also shown are two types of axlebox and the later type guard irons with tie rods. Earlier vehicles had guard iron outside the springs and solebars and a detail drawing is included when appropriate.

On the four wheeler depressing the brake lever on the side shown reacts through the pivot on a dog-clutch principle to raise the first link which, in turn, operates through the pin and slot joint to raise the second link, turning the transverse shaft anticlockwise. There is a drop arm from this shaft with a slip connection to the power brake rodding. The transverse shaft on the other side of the vehicle is connected directly with a brake lever of the same size and shape as the one drawn. The two intermediate links are not present on the other side. The hand brake on the six wheeler consists of two independent brake levers, each connected directly with a drop arm and slip connection to the power brake rodding. Only one pair of wheels is braked by the hand brake in every case.

The end elevations are correct for almost all vehicles designed for end loading, ie open and covered carriage trucks. The two 'T' shaped pieces partially hidden by the buffers are the fixed plates and supports which form a track for wheeled vehicles to be end loaded or unloaded. The Westinghouse steam and vacuum pipes are shown in the dropped position. For vehicles with 'dead ends' they are, of course, often mounted in the normal position with the bottom ends more or less level with the bottom edge of the buffer beam.

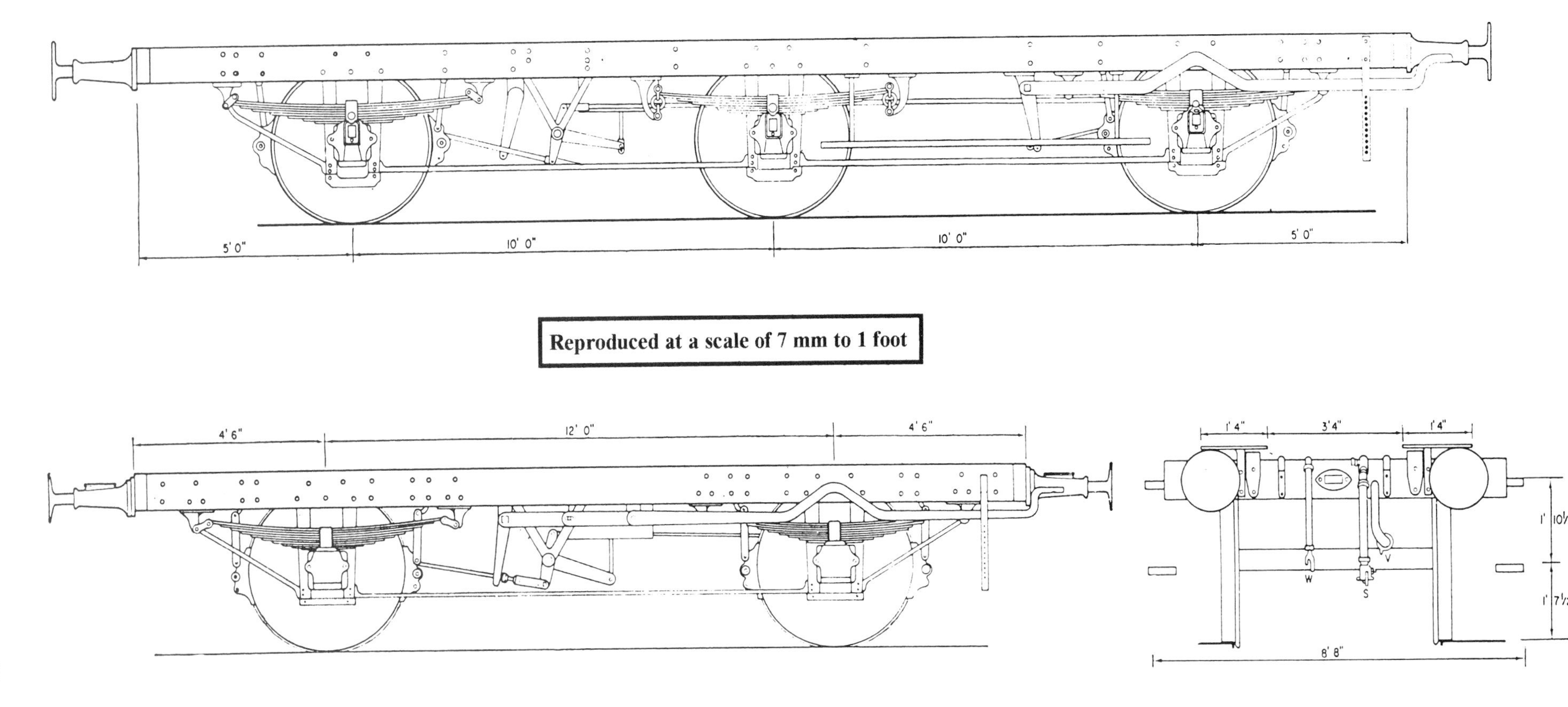

LNWR 32 foot Six Wheeled Milk Traffic Brake van to Diagram 384

These six wheel vans, built in 1907 for use in milk trains, were unusual in having corridor connections. Although the chassis is a different length to standard LNWR six wheel underframe shown above, the detail is applicable adjusted to the new wheelbase. It is presumed that when built the corridor connections were provided to allow the guard to pass through on passenger trains to enable him to check tickets.

The vans probably received the full two-colour LNWR passenger livery for they were fitted corridor connections.

During service with the LMS they would have been fitted with stoves and labelled 'Stove R'. Under BR this would have become 'Stove BGZ'. The only external difference is a small stove pipe chimney poking through the roof. Later, when fitted with stoves, these vehicle would have been used almost exclusively on parcels and perishables trains and fitted freights, but rarely as part of a passenger train. When gas lamps were removed and replaced with electric lights, standard accumulators were substituted for gas cylinders on the underframe.

LNWR 1st Nos	LNWR Nos 2nd	LMS 1st Nos	LMS 2nd Nos	Extinct by
752 to 791	8752 to 8791	2791 to 2829	33442 to 33479	1957

Former LNW six wheel milk brake van as LMS 2nd No 33461. Note the corridor connections, cove shaped roof profile and battery boxes. Two of the four top lights appear to have been obscured. (HMRS collection V1237)

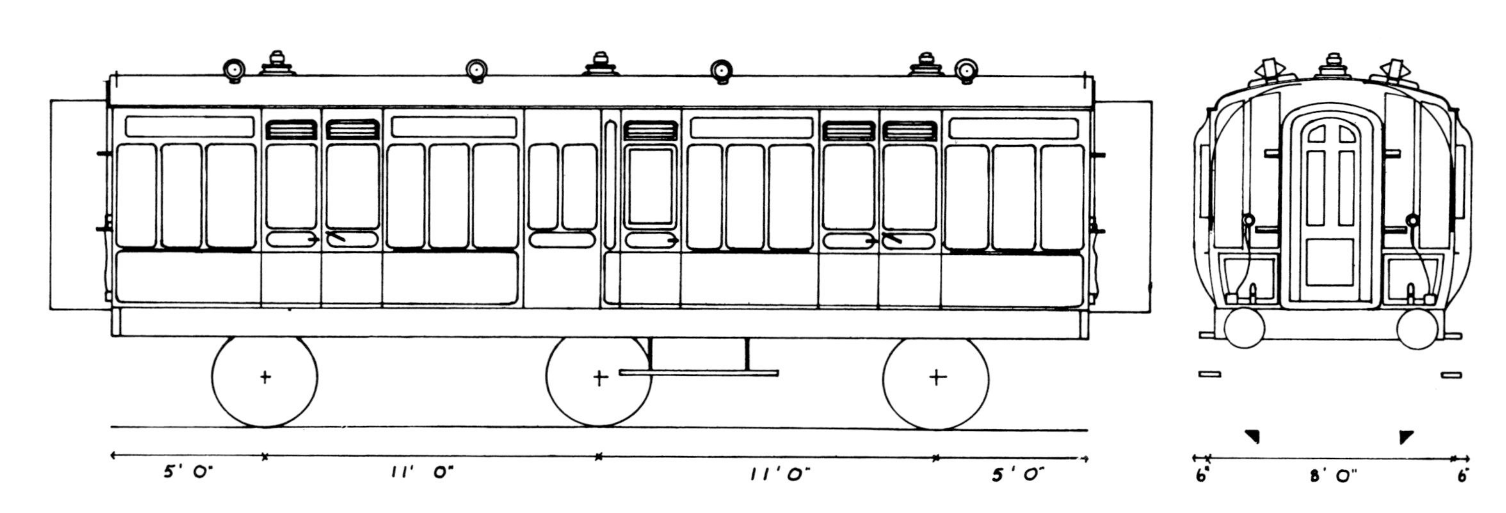

LTSR Four Wheel Passenger Brake Van

A diagram of train formations published in *The Engineer* (1911) shows an 1881 rake with a 'birdcage brake' at both ends, each brake with three pairs of side doors. Most full brakes are open from end to end, but this one was divided as three compartments by two solid partitions, these being positioned under the ends of the birdcage. Between the centre door and one partition there was a full width locker which the guard could use a seat or a platform to aid his seeing through the top lights. A hand brake wheel, situated above the locker, could only be applied comfortably while standing in the higher position.

All but No 17 of these vans survived to be taken over by the Midland Railway in 1912. One was often seen on the Romford branch. Over the years they underwent several modifications, including the provision of a generator, battery boxes and power brakes. More radical rebuilding involved the removal of the 'birdcage' and the provision of a ducket in lieu, as shown in the revised side elevation. The other side of the vehicle would have been a mirror reverse, because Tilbury duckets were opposite each other. Steps and handrail were added to one end and a short grab handle to the other. On the rebuilt version the guard's door opened inwards and was provided with a grab handle at either side.

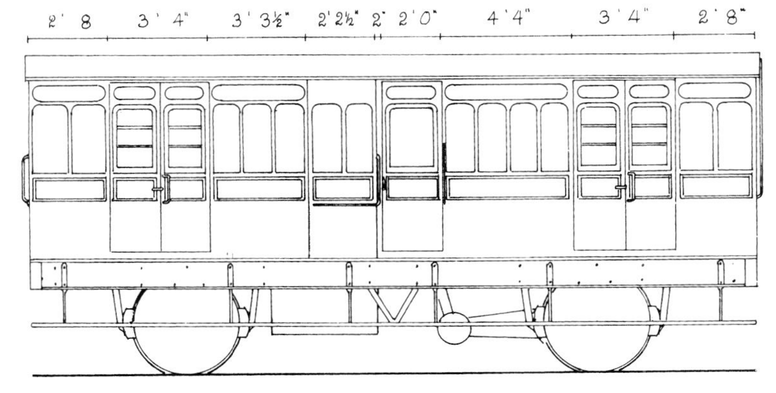

LT&SR four wheeled passenger brake van No 5 as rebuilt with side duckets in lieu of a roof lookout and electric lighting, yet retaining side chains. (RJ Essery collection)

PROTOTYPE DETAILS

LT&S Nos	Built	MR/LMS (2nd) Nos	Ext't
1-6	1877	165-8/70-2	1929
7-10	1883	174-7 (33931)	5/38
11-17	1886	178/87/93/4, 202/6	1930

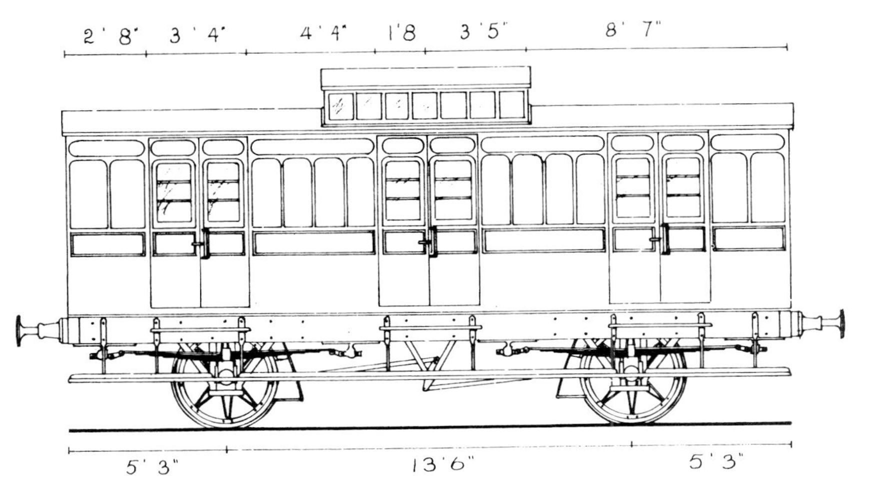

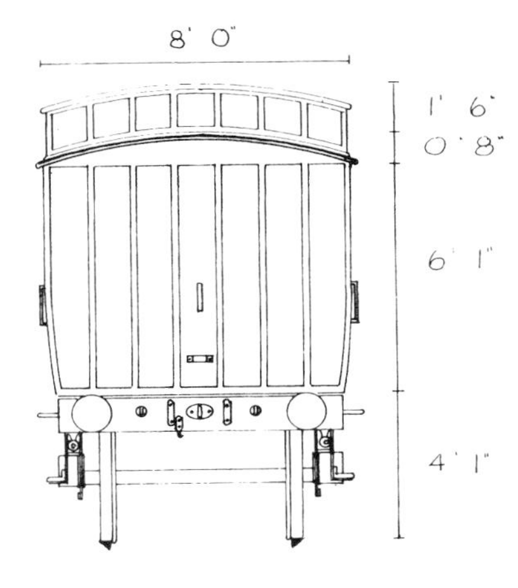

MR 31 ft Passenger Brake Van

The layout of these vehicles follows very closely the layout of the earlier square panelled, clerestory design, except that it has been restyled and built to the latest profile. There is one feature which does reflect a change of policy, however; early vehicles- and most Midland non-passenger coaching stock had 7 foot springs, but these vehicles and some other contemporary types only had 5 foot springs. The shaded panels represent slate, used as chalking boards on the prototype. Both side elevations were identical,. The guard's door is to the right of the lookout and opened inwards.

Throughout the life of these vehicles in revenue service the livery was crimson lake, first lined Midland, then semi-lined or plain LMS and, finally, BR. These vans were still in revenue service in the middle 1950 and retained the full-length footboards and most of the panel beading.

Ex-MR PBV in departmental service at Kettering as No 021683. Note the boarding repairs to the panelling. (RJ Essery)

Built	MR Nos & LMS 1st Nos	LMS 2nd No	Ext't
1913	120/82/4, 226, 309, 409, 509/16/20/1/9/30	34145-34156	12/53
1913/4	188/90, 201/5/17/25/47/58, 417, 523/4, 637	34157-43168	2/57

Midland Railway six wheel passenger brake van No 521 to diagram 530A built in 1913. (Roger Carpenter)

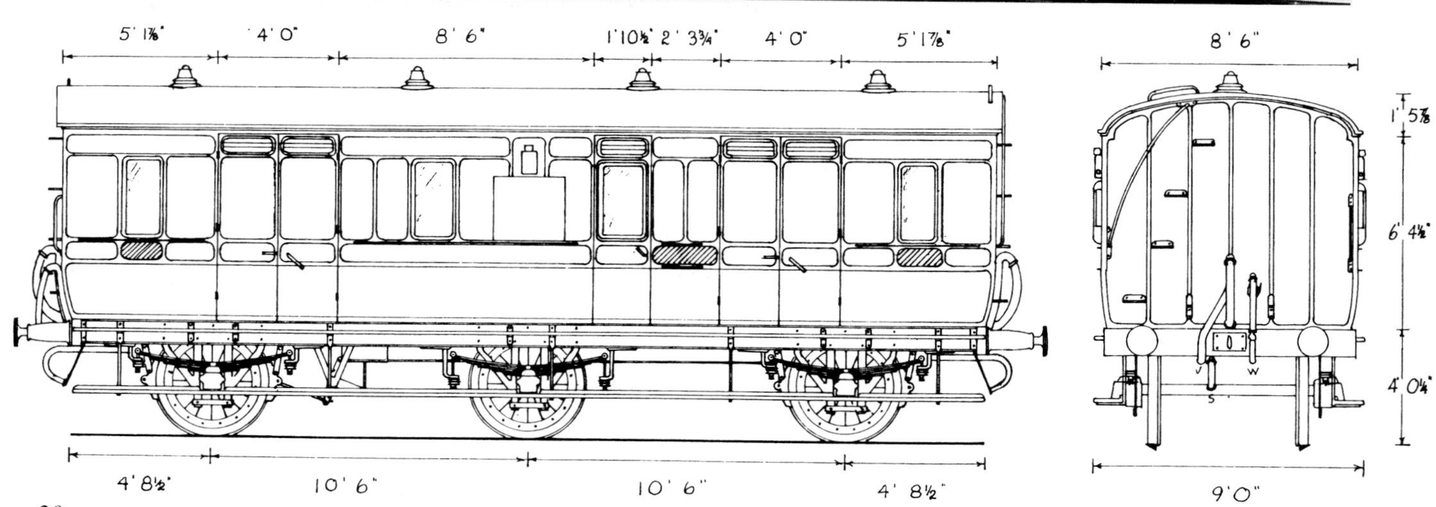

GNS Six Wheel 27 foot Passenger Brake Vans

Seven six wheel passenger brake vans were built in 1893, as shown in the main drawing. These were later allocated Nos 727-733 by the LNER and assigned to Diagram 57s (Code 7026). Another eighteen were supplied between January 1897 and December 1898. These were similar but had the guard's ducket on the extreme end of the body and had louvered ventilators in the doors, see scrap view. Diagram 58s shows a tare weight of 11 tons 15 cwt and a load capacity of 4 tons. LNER Nos were 734 to 751 and it was given the telegraphic code 7027. They were extinct by 11 December 1948, although some passed into departmental service. They were dual braked and lit by oil and, later at least some by electricity. All are believed to have had 10 spoke wheels. The draughtsman – IR Smith – seems to have overlooked the necessary brake gear!

GNS six wheeled passenger brake van in early LNER days as No 736. (Real Photographs)

An ex-GNS six wheeled passenger brake van in departmental service as No DE 320010 for the Signal & Telegraph Department at Edinburgh Waverley. Note the horizontal over-cladding to the lower panels, typical of the Scottish Region departmental stock during early BR days, the ladder carried between the step boards and replacement disc wheels. (Photomatic, courtesy RAS Marketing)

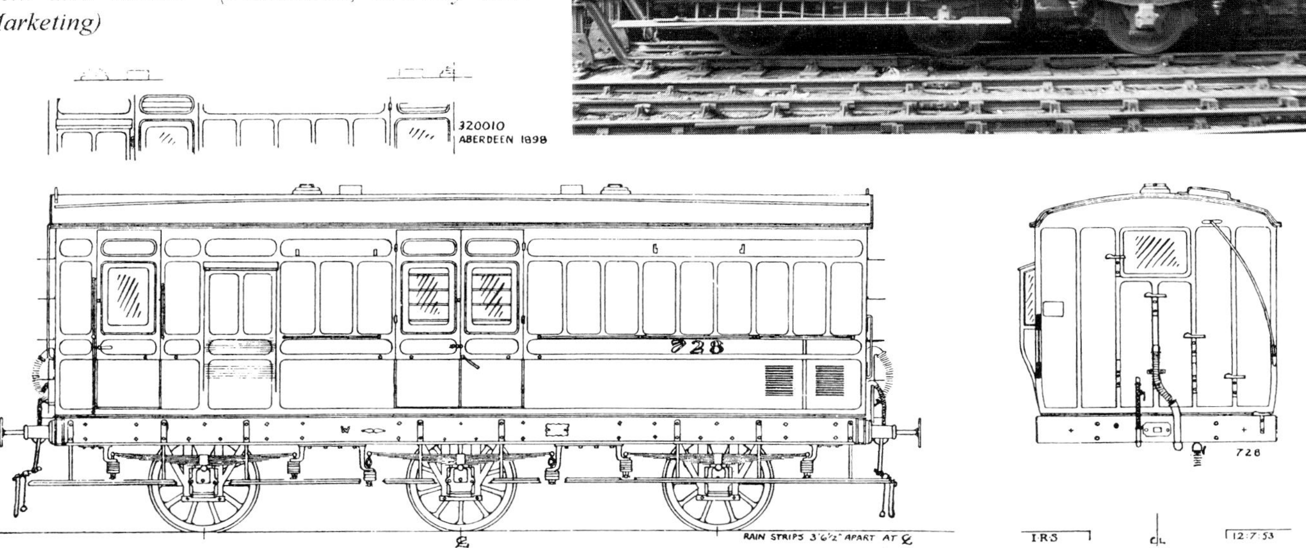

LNER Four Wheeled Brake Vans

In 1928 the LNER introduced four wheeled 5 ton 32 foot long passenger brake vans for use on the GE Section to Diagram 120 with steel underframe, outside W irons and body in the Gresley style. The withdrawal in 1932 of ex-GNR Howlden four wheel coaches of generally similar length led to the re-use of their timber frames for the production of further vans in the same style for use on other sections. Vehicles to diagram 120 were fitted with fold up racks for the conveyance of 40 baskets of racing pigeons.

PROTOTYPE DETAILS

Diag	Built at	Year	Length (ft-in)	1st Nos	2nd Nos
120	Stratford	1928	32-0	6801-6829	70194-70222
120	Stra'd & York	1929-30	32-0	6830-6850	70223-70240
120	York	1930	32-0	6851-6854	70247-70250
120	York	1930	32-0	767-771	70241-70245
170	Darlington	1933	31-8⅝	5228-5245	70304-21
170	Darlington	1935	31-8⅝	5255-5260	70322-27
176	Darlington	1933	31-11⅝	4140-4, 1224-7	70328-34/6
177	Darlington	1933	31-10½	5246-9	70337-40

In BR days 32 foot long four wheeled brake van to Diagram 120 No E70212, built at Stratford in 1928. (Paul W Bartlett collection)

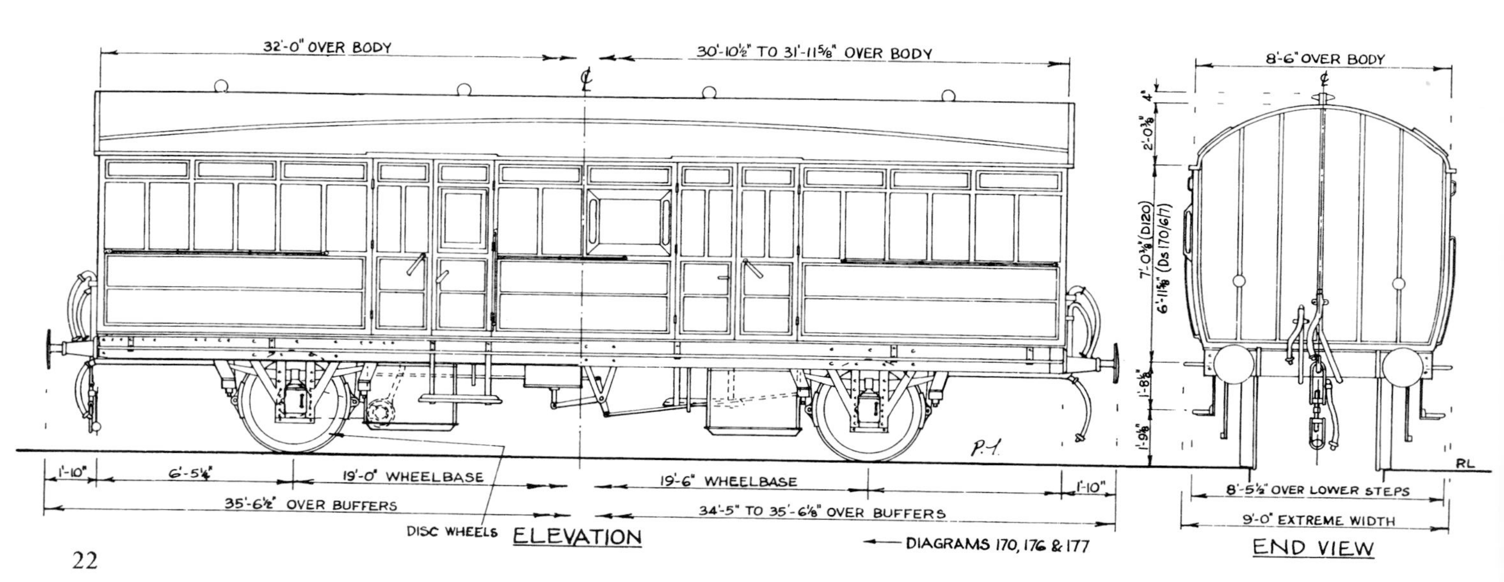

NER Six Wheel Passenger Brake Vans

The NER produced passenger brake vans of various types over the years. 171 of the last version were supplied between December 1908 to 1922, and were followed by seven more for the LNER to a slightly different design in 1924/5. Modellers should note from the plan view that one end had a light in the two outer panels on each side, while only the outer panels had lights at the other end. Early batches were gas lit, while later on the dynamo, cell box and break in the foot board on both sides were located at the end in which there were four lights. Vacuum cylinder between the middle and axle towards the other end and double brake blocks were fitted to the outer axles only. Instead of the timber ogee guard's ducket, later vans had a plain steel lookout. These vans survived well, the last few being withdrawn at the end of 1962. Later in life some were converted into milk vans. Not dissimilar luggage vans to Diagram 185 were also produced without a separate guard's door from 1911, fitted with shelves expressly for pigeon baskets. Examples of both types were converted in 1918 to covered carriage trucks to Diagram 215 for the conveyance of aeroplanes.

As per usual NER practice numbers are entirely random, including 214, 259 and 2139. A full list with details of their duties and alterations will be found in an article by IG Sadler in *The North Eastern Express*, Volume 21, No 87 for May 1982.

Six wheel passenger brake van No E214E was built for the NER in August 1922 with metal guard's lookout and is depicted here as a milk van, in BR livery at Oxford on 13 March 1957 and was withdrawn in September 1961. (HC Casserley, courtesy RM Casserley)

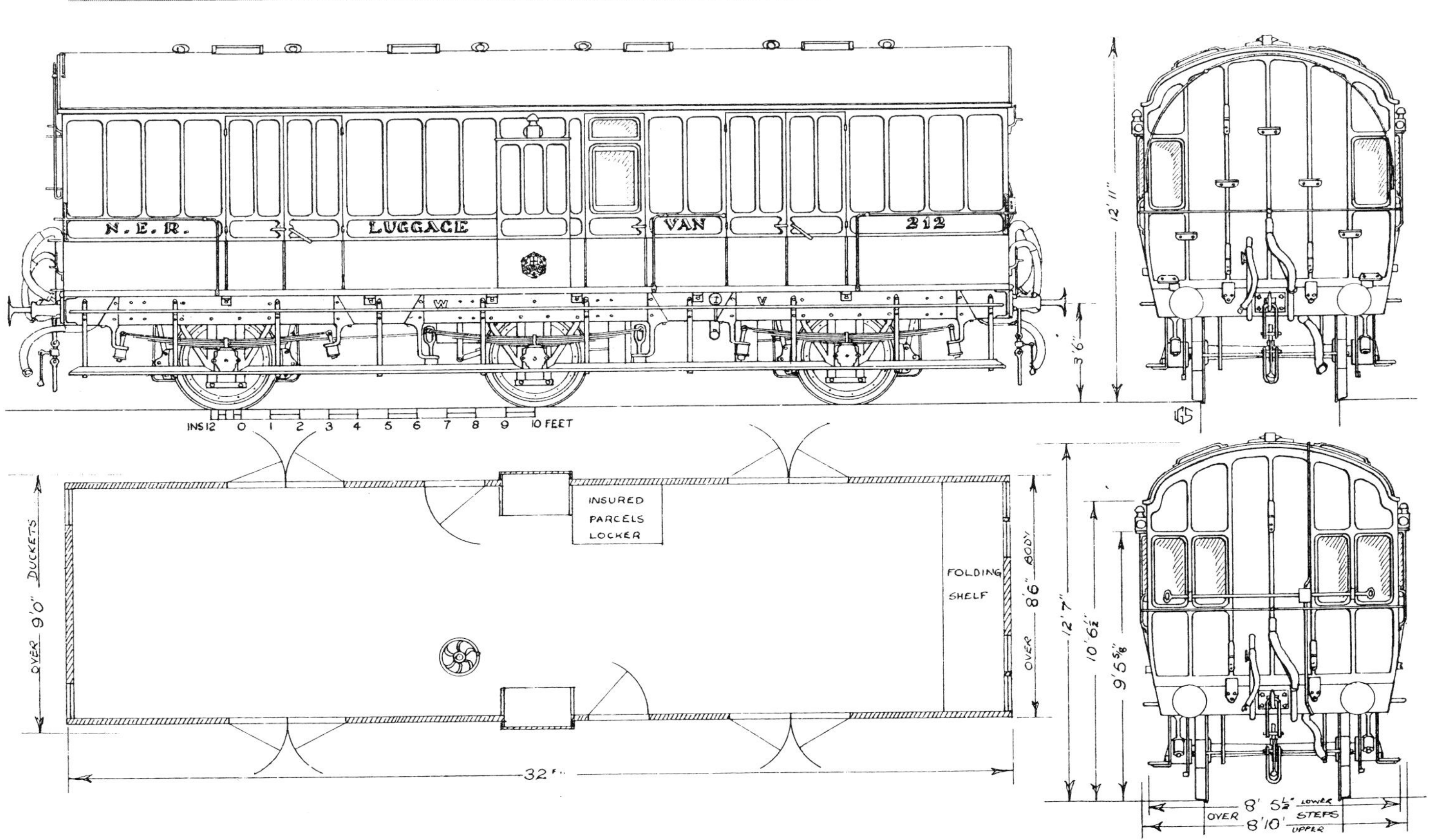

Great Western 40 Foot Passenger Brake Vans

Two Double Doors

Diagrams K1, K2 and Lots 469 and 532 of K4 were built for broad gauge, mounted on 7 foot wheel base trucks, and converted to standard gauge and renumbered during 1892. Diagram K1 was oil lit and had no drop lights in the double doors. All diagrams had panelled ends and three centre roof profile, except Lots 255, 258 and 288/312/383 which were originally an arc profile. However those to diagram K1 were built 10 foot wide, only to be reduced to 8 foot on conversion resulting in a hybrid roof style. The body of Lots 382 was 7ft 6in high, rather than 7ft 3in, and some had an arc (A) roof profile, while others were elliptical (E). No 879 received a new underframe in Nov 1902 with 8ft 6in wheel base bogies at 23ft 6in centres (K3). Bulls-eyes lens for internal lamps were fitted to the top of the lookouts during 1903 to 1908, only for them to be removed by 1916. All are believed to have had the external doors to their dog lockers removed around 1912-4. During 1920s some vans to diagrams K1, K2 and K4 were altered to parcels vans by the removal of the lookouts to become diagrams K32, K28 and K30 respectively. K11s were as K4, but with 8ft 6in bogies.

PROTOTYPE DETAILS

Diag	Lot	Built	BG Nos	NG Nos	Bogies/ crs (ft-in)	Ext't by
K1	255	1882	137-138	881-882	6-4/ 23-2	9/31
	258	1882	139-142	883-886		12/32
K2	288	1884	146-151	887-892	6-4/ 23-2	9/32
	307	1884	-	633-638		8/32
	312	1884	156-165	893-902		7/32
	382	1887(A)	172/3/7-80	903/4/8-11	6-4/23-2	7/38
	382	1887(E)	174-6/81	905-7/12	8-6/23-6	10/30
K4	413	1888	-	671-690	6-6	11/36
	469	1889-90	188-197	913-922		'36
	485	1889-90	-	747-781		5/51
	532	1890	206-210	923-927		9/35
	550	1890-91	-	1001-1050		10/47
	683	1893	-	1058-1061		7/35
K11	812	1896	-	1066-1068	8-6	8/40

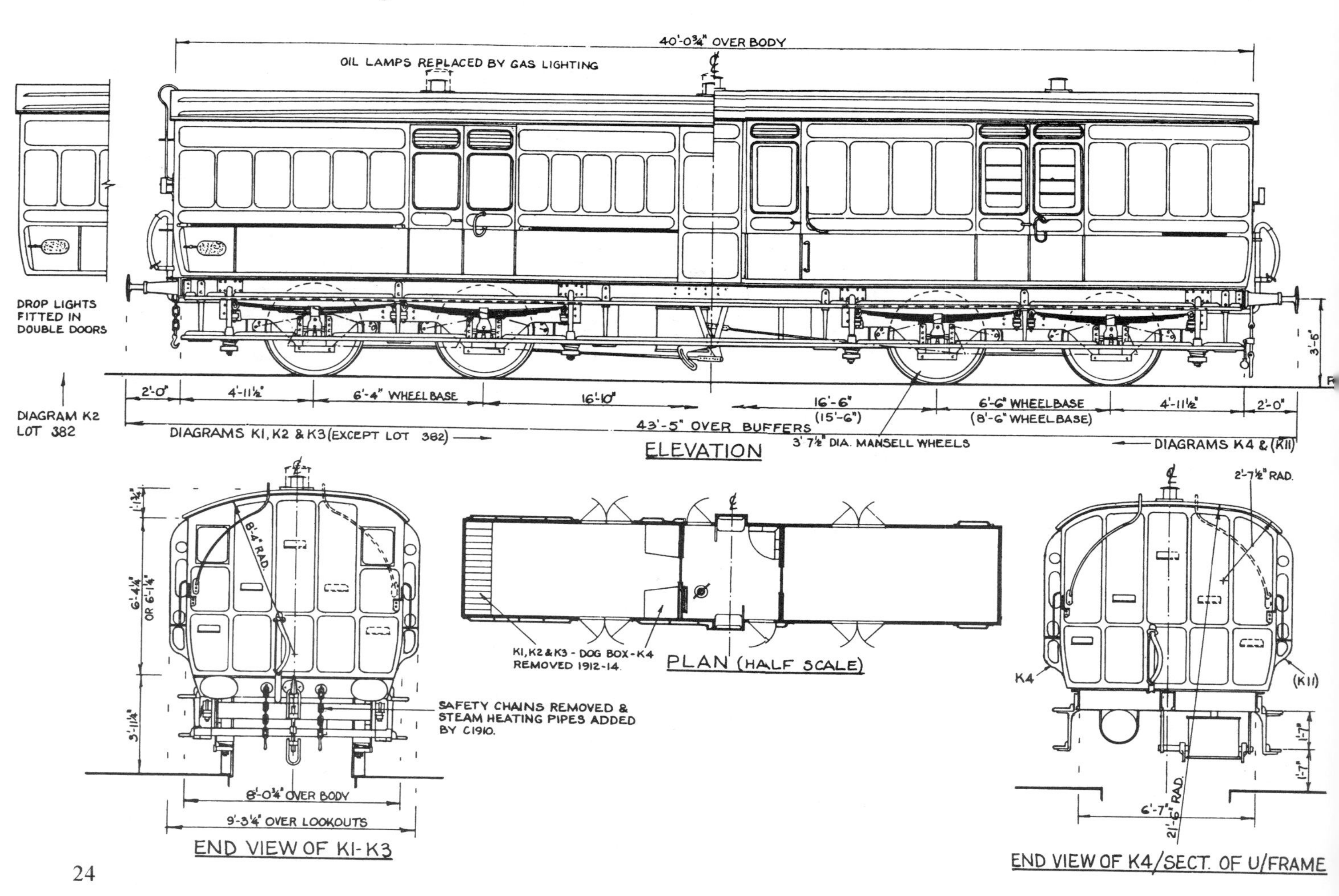

Great Western 40 Foot Passenger Brake vans

Great Western two door 40 foot passenger brake van, formerly to diagram K4, late in life in use as the Reading and Midland Stores Van No 4 to diagram Q18 on 28 February 1955 and numbered W58128. The destination board to the right of the guard's door reads 'Stores van to Wolverhampton via Banbury'. Note that many of the original panels have been suppressed as a result of repairs over the years and most of the lower foot boards removed and shell type roof ventilators added. (GR Driffield, courtesy G Warburton)

Great Western 40 foot passenger brake van No 246 to diagram K15 with four double doors in October 1934 lettered to work between Penzance and LMS, although the latter is obscured by a paper destination label. The side lookouts have been removed and plated over and its American bogies replaced by 8ft 6in Dean bogies. (Wild Swan Publications, HMRS collection P130)

No 238, also to diagram K15, at Snow Hill, Birmingham in 1947 looks tired in plain brown livery following the heavy traffic during World War 2. Nonetheless, most of the panelling and its gangway connections have survived. (PJ Garland, HMRS collection M20006)

Great Western 40 Foot Passenger Brake Vans

PROTOTYPE DETAILS

Diag	Lot	Built	Nos	Bogie (ft-in)	Extinct by
K14	865	2-3/98	1071-1090	8-6	6/48
	883	7-9/98	928-937		2/49
	895	9-10/98	631/2, 639-640, 936-943		1/47
K15	911	12/98-3/99	1091-1100	8-6	11/52
	1000	10/02	1111-1114		9/46
	1024	3-4/03	1115-1120		10/52
	1048	1-3/04	1121-1124		10/52
	1059	4/04	221-225		10/52
	1075	10-12/04	226-229, 231-236	8-0 volute	4/52
	1116	9-12/06	237-246	8-0 Amer.	3/48
K16	919	6-7/99	1101-1110	8-6 Amer.	7/51
	1017	1-2/03	201-210		9/49
	1033	5-7/03	211-220		12/50

Four Double Doors

All vehicle to diagrams K14, K15 and K16 had three centre roof profile. As built these vans had internal side lamps in the duckets and those to K15 had gangway connections. K14 and initial lots of K15 had 8ft 6in Dean bogies, while the last lot of K15 and all K16 had 8ft 6in American bogies.

Later in life many two and four door vans were repaired by plating over defective panelling, or removing vertical moulding. Many of both the two and four door types were in due course transferred to departmental service, including becoming stores vans, used by the Hotel Dept, mess vans for the Signals Dept, being equipped as tunnel vans, mess and tool vans for breakdown work. For further details, see *Model Railway Constructor* for June, August and September 1967, together with November 1979.

Great Western 40 foot passenger brake van No 216 to diagram K16 with four double doors at Birmingham Snow Hill in 1947. (PJ Garland, HMRS collection M20004)

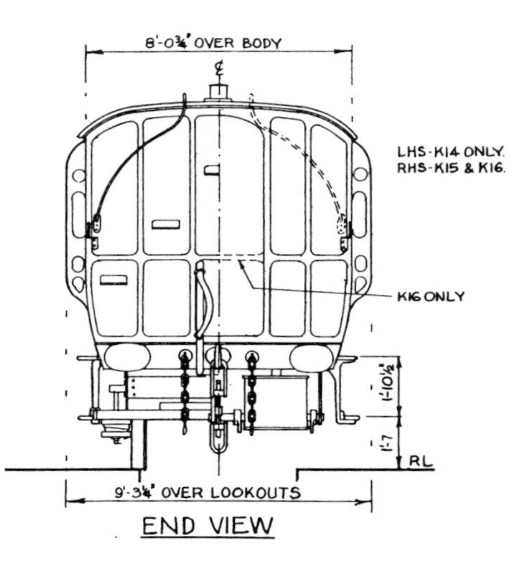

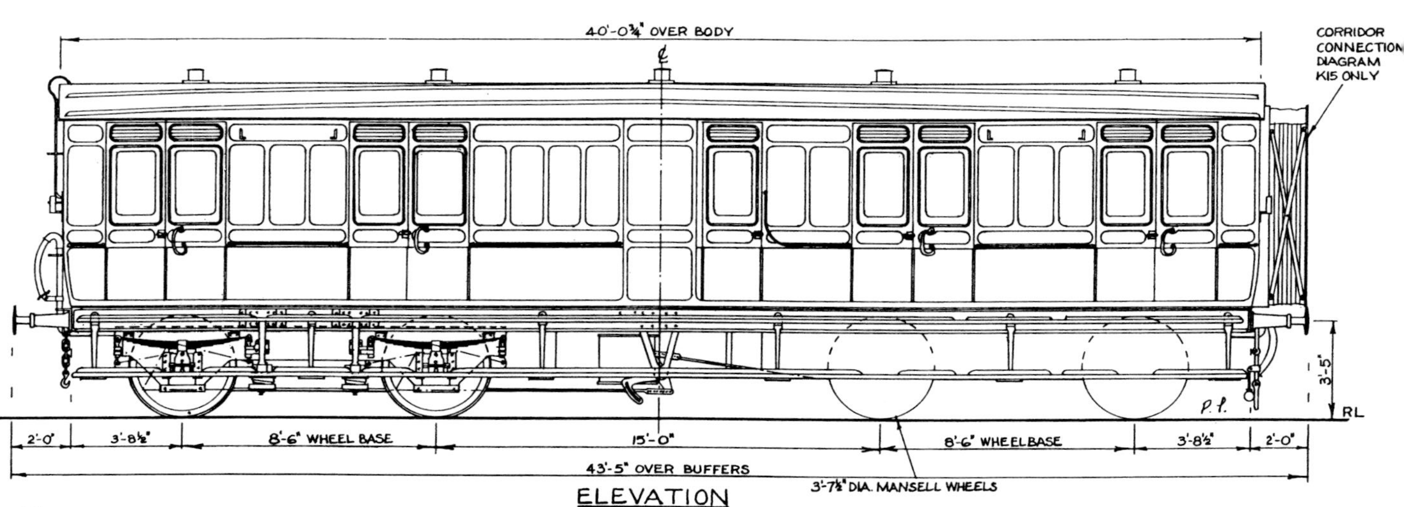

Rhymney Railway Six Wheel Passenger Brake Van

Rhymney Railway passenger brake van Nos 81-84 (GW 157-160) were built by Metropolitan C&W in 1894 with Westinghouse brake and open spoked wheels. These vans originally had oil lamps, but around 1900 were converted to electric lighting. The removal of the lamp tops permitted the installation of four torpedo roof ventilators.

Nos 85 & 86, built in 1900 and No 99 in 1901 by Gloucester Carriage & Wagon, were similar, but with rounded bottom corners to upper panels, electric lighting and Mansell wheels. These became GW Nos 161-163 and were extinct by 1930. No 86 was altered to 4 wheel at an unknown date.

Rhymney Railway six wheel passenger brake van No 85 is depicted as built by the Gloucester carriage and Wagon Co in 1900. (G Warburton collection)

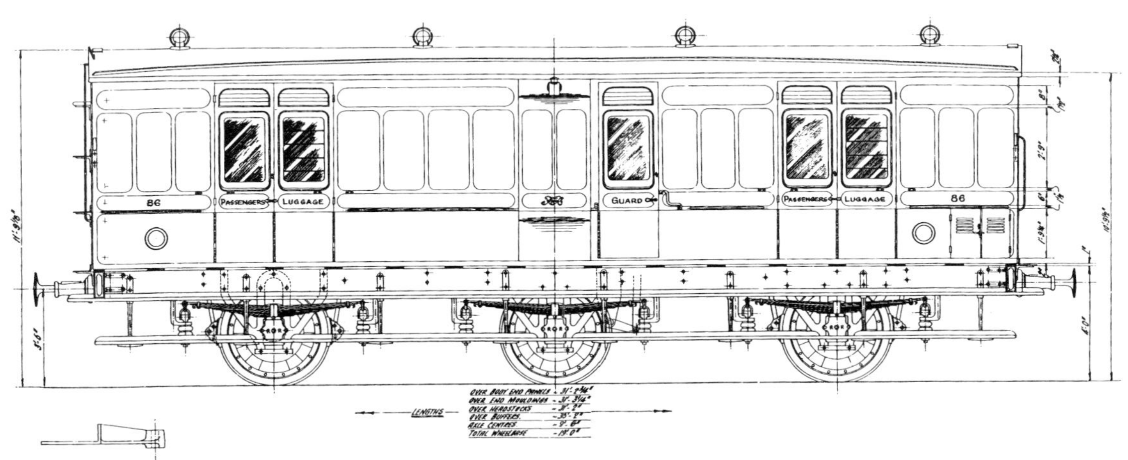

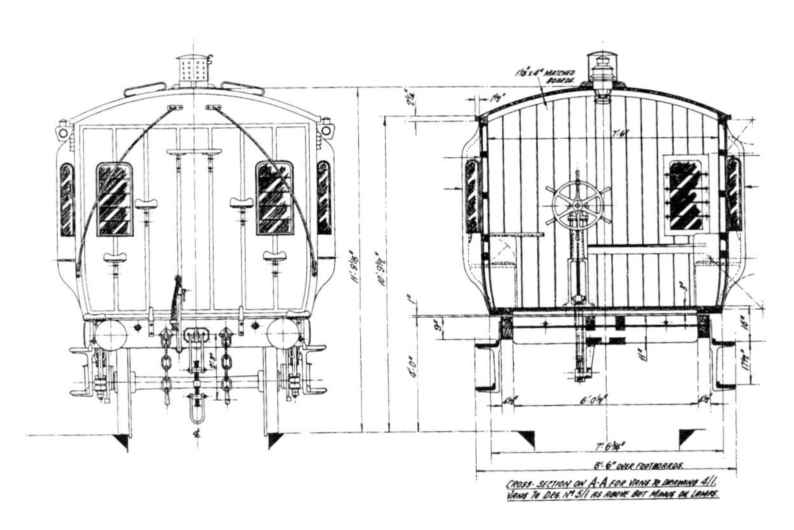

Taff Vale Railway Six Wheel Passenger Brake Van

Passenger brake vans Nos 239-241 & 243-245 were built by Bristol Wagon & Carriage Co in 1910 for the Taff Vale Railway. They were renumbered by the GW 173-178, becoming generally extinct by 1944. No 244, however, survived longer to be withdrawn in November 1956. These vans had vacuum brake and were gas lit. Both sides are identical with the guard's door to the right of the ducket and opening inwards.

Nos 267-270 built by Metro C&W in 1899, Nos 271-273 at Cathays in 1900 and Nos 274-277 by Ashbury in 1902 were similar but with low arc roof giving overall height of 11 feet 5¾ inches, together with taller lamp tops. These were renumbered 199/200/30/68-280 by GW, becoming generally extinct by December 1928 with No 277 lasting until August 1934.

Nos 280, 292-299 (GW Nos 281-289) were a development of the design built in 1921 by Cravens Ltd with smaller lookouts and recessed guard's doors. The lookouts were sometimes removed later in the vehicles' life and defective panelling repaired by plating over.

The 1921 version, with a simplified guard's lookout and recessed guard's door, is depicted as No 280 was one of nine built by Cravens in Cravens Ltd in 1921. Note that the eaves and lower body panels in the middle of the van now extend to the doorway and additional hand railing provided. (HMRS collection M1085)

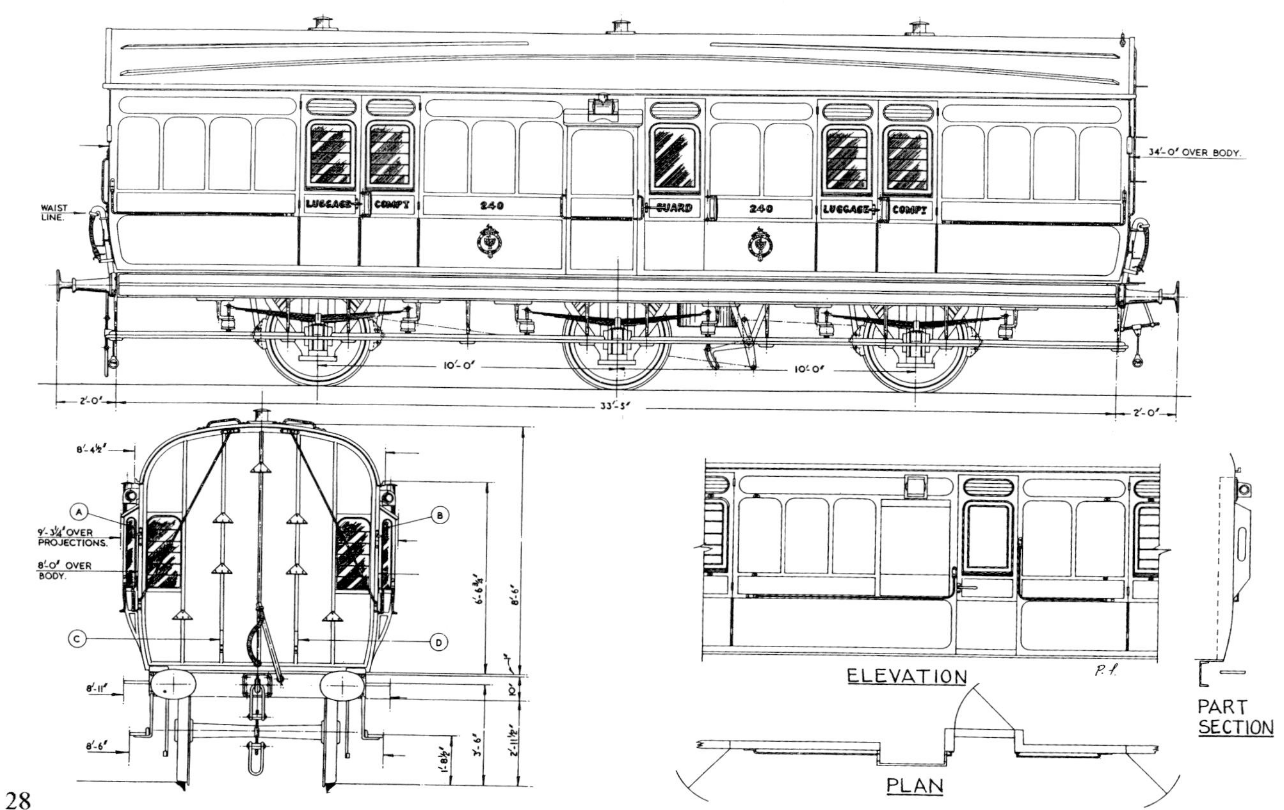

LB&SC Six Wheel Passenger Brake Van

These 26 foot long six wheel vans were built by W Stroudley in the 1880s and most rebuilt by RJ Billinton during his tenure of office from 1894 to 1905. No 53 was the only un-rebuilt one in ordinary service to survive into SR ownership, being allocated diagram 899 and number 738, but was withdrawn in September 1929 before the latter could be applied. All were oil lit and originally equipped with Westinghouse brake and allocated SR diagram 898. Typical LBSC Nos 9, 33, 117-142, 149-152, which were renumbered by the SR in the range Nos 707-737.

A former LBSC Stroudley six wheel passenger brake van which appears to have escaped rebuilding and is in use by SR for departmental purposes. Note that it is still fitted only with Westinghouse brake pipes. (G Warburton collection)

An ex-LBSC six wheel passenger brake van, as rebuilt by RJ Billinton, at Brighton on 3 June 1928. This van was numbered by the SR as No 719 and included in set No 914. Such vans were withdrawn between 1928 and 1933, probably without ever being fitted with vacuum brake. (LE Brailsford, courtesy of G Warburton).

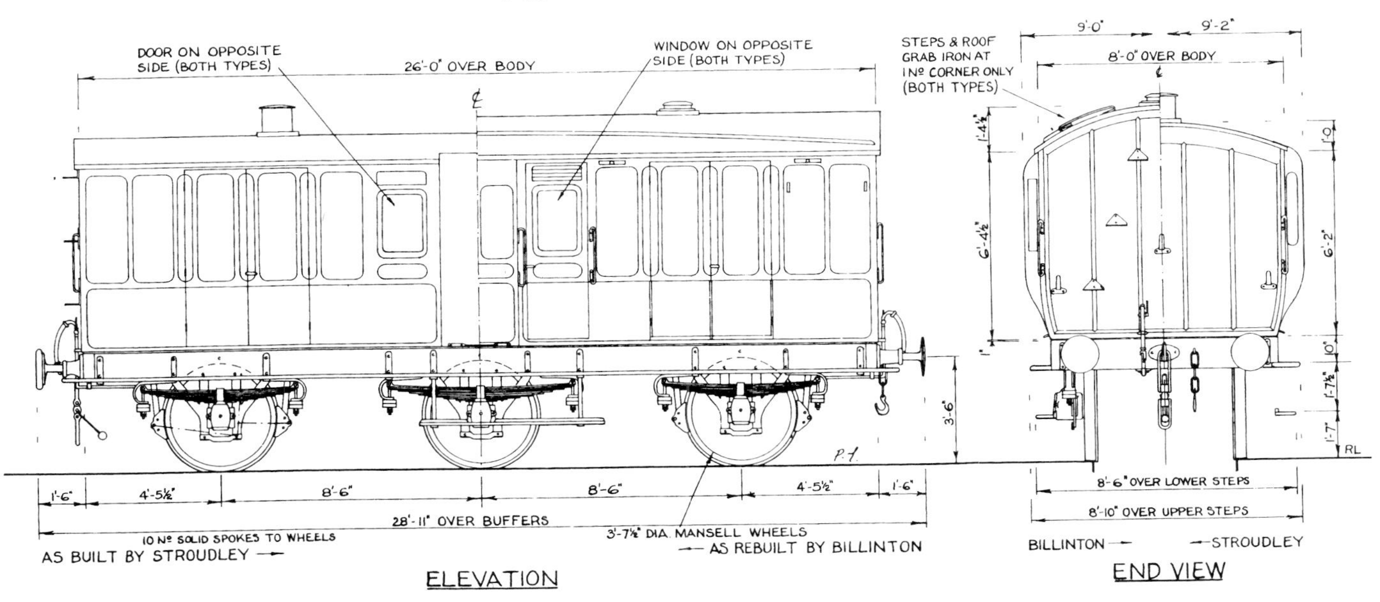

LC&DR Six Wheel 28 Foot Passenger Brake Van

These 28 foot long six wheel passenger brake vans were built by the London, Chatham and Dover Railway between 1887 and 1899. Initial batches were constructed with half round beading to the upper and waist panels, whilst later this was simplified to plain square corners and the drawing shows both types. As supplied they were equipped with oil lighting and the Westinghouse brake system, but the latter was altered to vacuum from 1899. Steam pipes will have been a later addition. The SR removed and plated over the duckets. Most were withdrawn by 1931 and many were transferred to service stock.

By the time this LCDR six wheel passenger brake van was photographed at London Bridge, following nationalisation in 1948, it had been, since 1934, allocated to the Engineer's Department, London East. It was built in 1887 and had originally been No 36 and later SR No 427. It shows the half round beading to the upper panels. Its duckets have been removed and plated over. The middle oil lamp has been replaced by the flue pipe to a stove and a hand brake lever fitted to the right hand end, perhaps on being transferred to departmental service. (G Warburton collection)

PROTOTYPE DETAILS

LC&DR Nos	SE&CR Nos	SR Nos
9-10/3-8, 27-30/6, 73-9, 81-97, 1060-8	470-1/4-9/88-91/7, 534-67	418 to 463

An unidentified example of the plain panelling is seen at Ramsgate in 1931 apparently still in revenue earning service. The side lookouts had by this time been suppressed. (JAG Coltas)

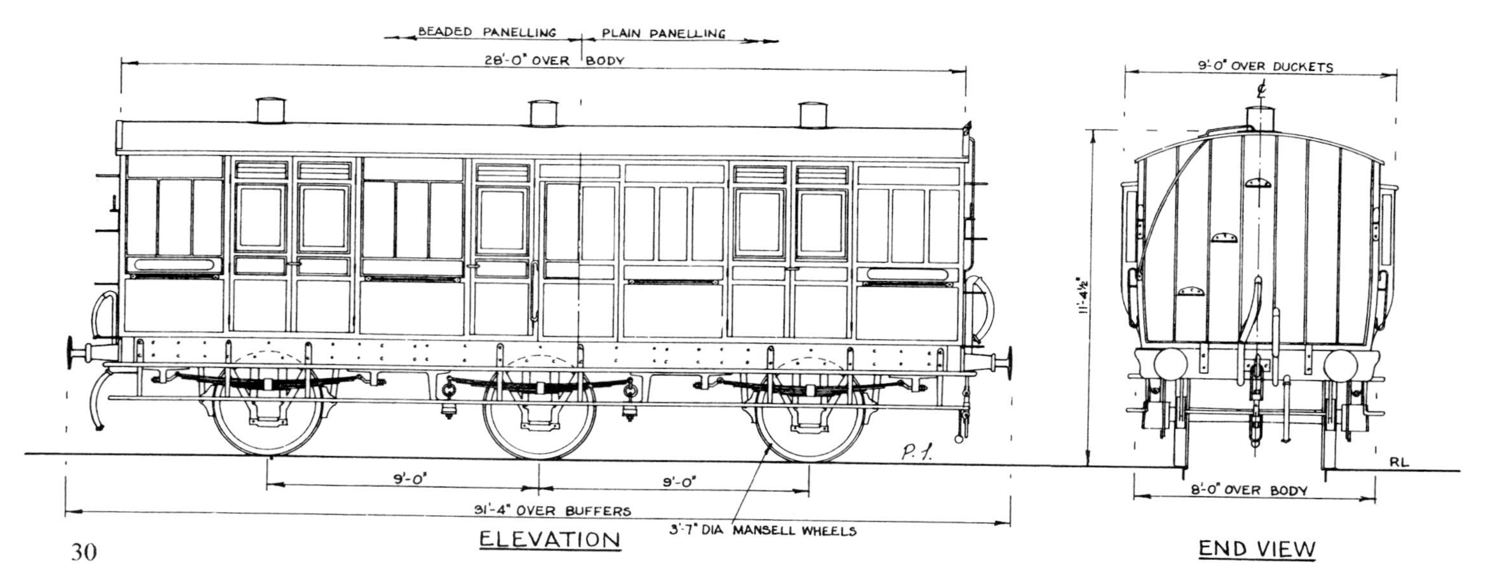

SE&CR Six Wheeled Passenger Brake Van

When the South Eastern & Chatham Railway commenced construction of these six wheel 6 ton passenger brake vans with central lookout and side duckets, one side was a mirror fashion of the other and these were covered by SR diagram 885 (Nos 564-591). The last batch, however, had identical sides and were to SR diagram 882 (Nos 468-485). It is not certain which the remainder were. All were dual braked and electrically lit. Nos 608-610 were equipped with a safe and allocated to diagram 886. They were withdrawn from revenue earning service between 1934 and 1941, but a few continued thereafter in departmental service thereby extending their lives by many years.

PROTOTYPE DETAILS

Builder	Year	SE&CR Nos	SR Nos
Cravens	1901/2	588-605	564-581
Hurst Nelson	1903	681-690	582-591
SE&CR	1903	5, 18, 43/4, 65/6, 72/5, 89, 95	549-558
Cravens	1905	694-713	592-610
Metro Amal	1905	714-733	611-630
SE&CR	1906	498,500/2/4/9	559-563
SE&CR	1907-9	3/4/8, 12/6/7, 21, 90/1/4/6-100, 501/6/8	468-485

SE&CR six ton passenger brake van No 682 as built by Hurst Nelson. Note the ventilated covers to the oil lamps. (Hurst Nelson/HMRS collection T13/28)

A similar van in SR days without any apparent form of identification and still with a set of full length step boards apart from the gap to accommodate the dynamo to the electric lighting set. (GY Hemingway)

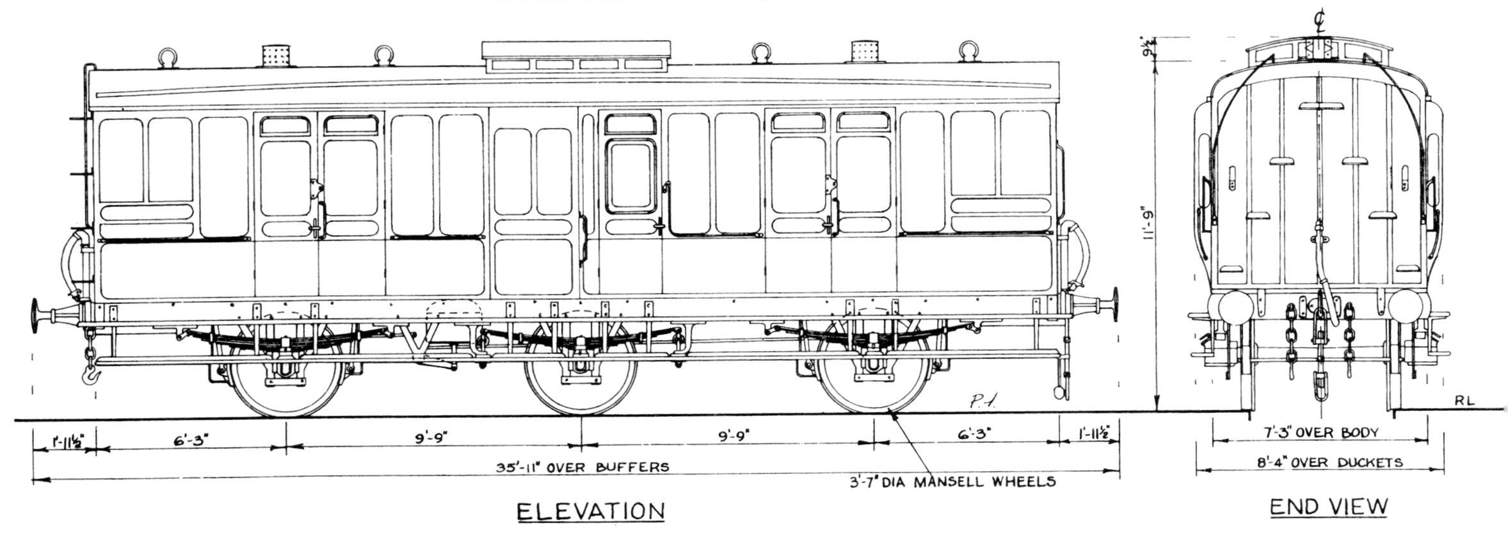

Southern Railway Four Wheeled 36 Foot Long Passenger Brake Van to Diagram 3092

In its last days the SECR had introduced 32 foot long four wheel luggage vans (p 40) and the Southern followed it with a covered carriage truck or utility van version in 1925 (p 60). Their appearance was more akin to goods than carriage stock and the Southern multiplied these two types. When by the mid 1930s the company required further passenger vans for use on parcels trains the design was developed into the 36 foot long four wheel vans with the guard's compartment in the middle and drop lights in the doors rather than lights in the sides, known as Van C. Cladding consisted of alternate pairs of horizontal boards of 6½ and 3½ inch width. Roof ventilators were fitted, but none in the sides or ends. Electric lighting and steam heating were provided. The underframes were made at Ashford or Lancing and the bodies fitted at Eastleigh.

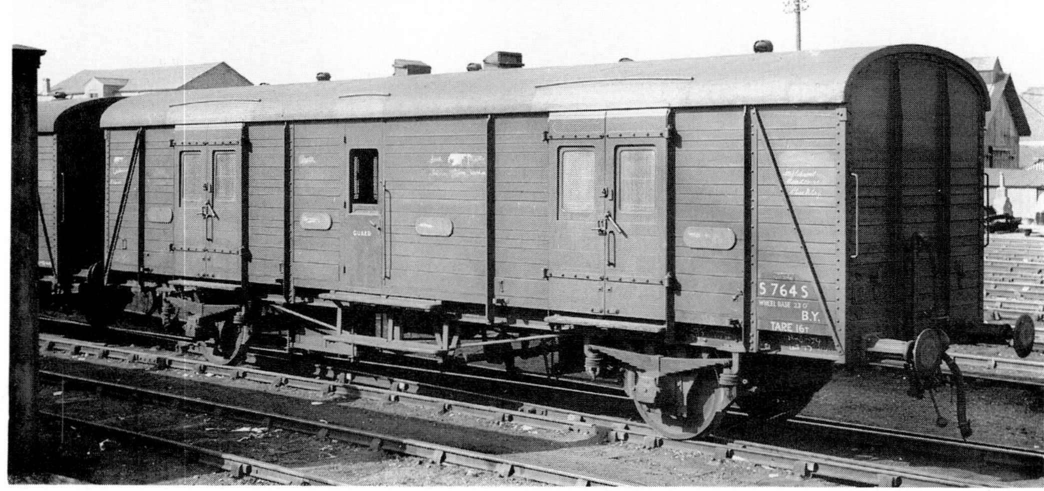

PROTOTYPE DETAILS

Built	Nos
1937	400-449
1938	651-750
1939	751-800
1940/1	931-980

Ex-SR 10 Ton four wheel passenger brake van No S764S seen on 22 April 1954 coded BY. The double doors appear not to be planked, but either sheeted over or made of fibre glass reinforced plastic. (PW Bartlett)

No S410, one of the initial batch of 1937, at London Bridge. The orange panels in the top corners indicate that it has been fitted with a stove. (Lens of Sutton)

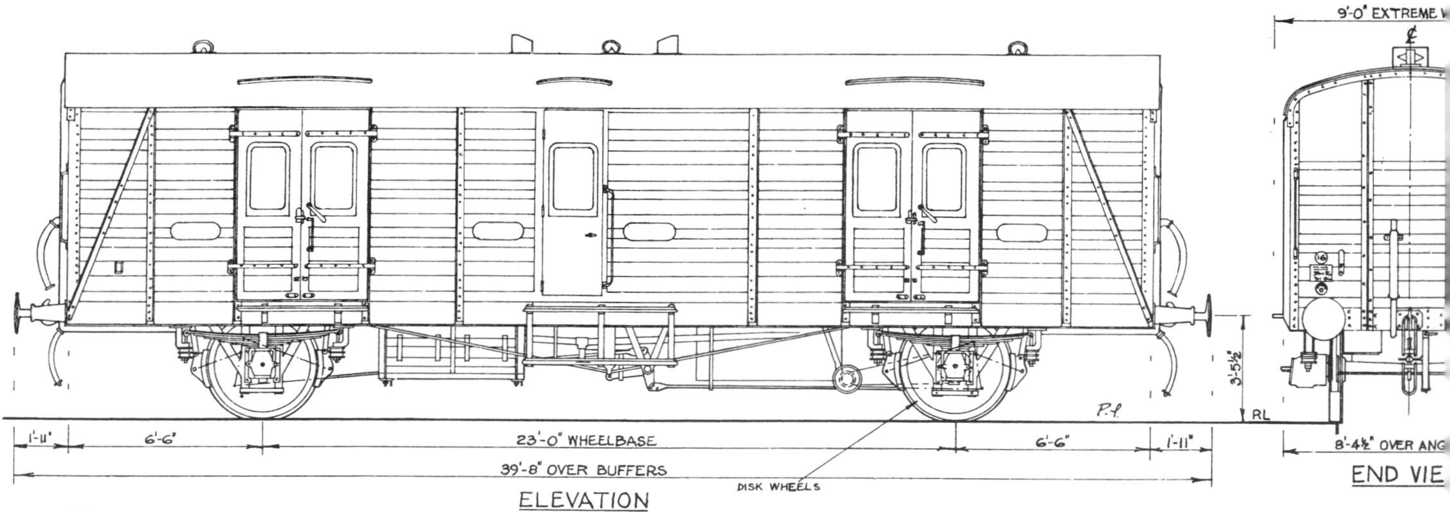

SR Non-corridor Bogie Passenger Brake Van B to Diagram 3093

These 50 foot long vehicles conformed to the normal Southern Railway method of van construction, which followed goods rather than passenger practice, and consisted of steel framing planked internally with alternate pairs of wide and narrow boards (6½ and 3½ inch). The roof had the deep elliptical shape which REL Maunsell used both on SECR and SR stock.

Known as "Van B" these were used for parcel, newspaper, and fast freight trains, but were not normally worked off the Southern system.
Altogether 130 were built. Between 1945 and 1950, Nos 368-399 were fitted with stoves in the guards compartment; these were known as "Van B stove" and distinguished by an orange coloured guards door panel.

Ex-Southern Railway bogie passenger luggage brake van No S381 at Eastleigh on 29 October 1949, having been recently out-shopped in green with yellow panels. (AE West, courtesy MS King)

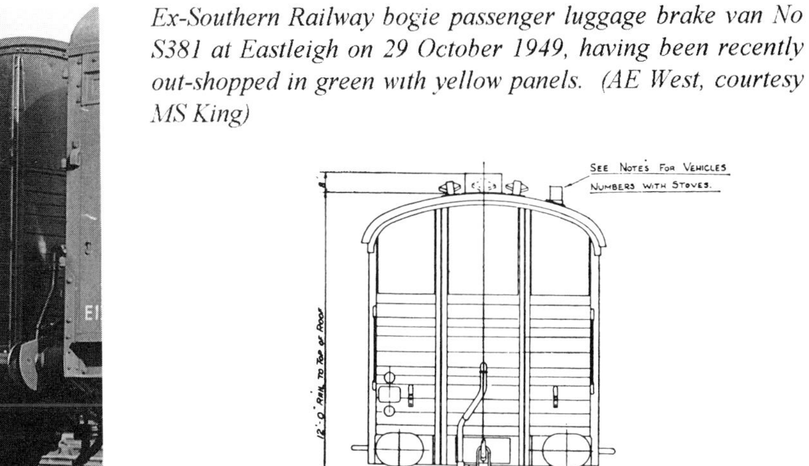

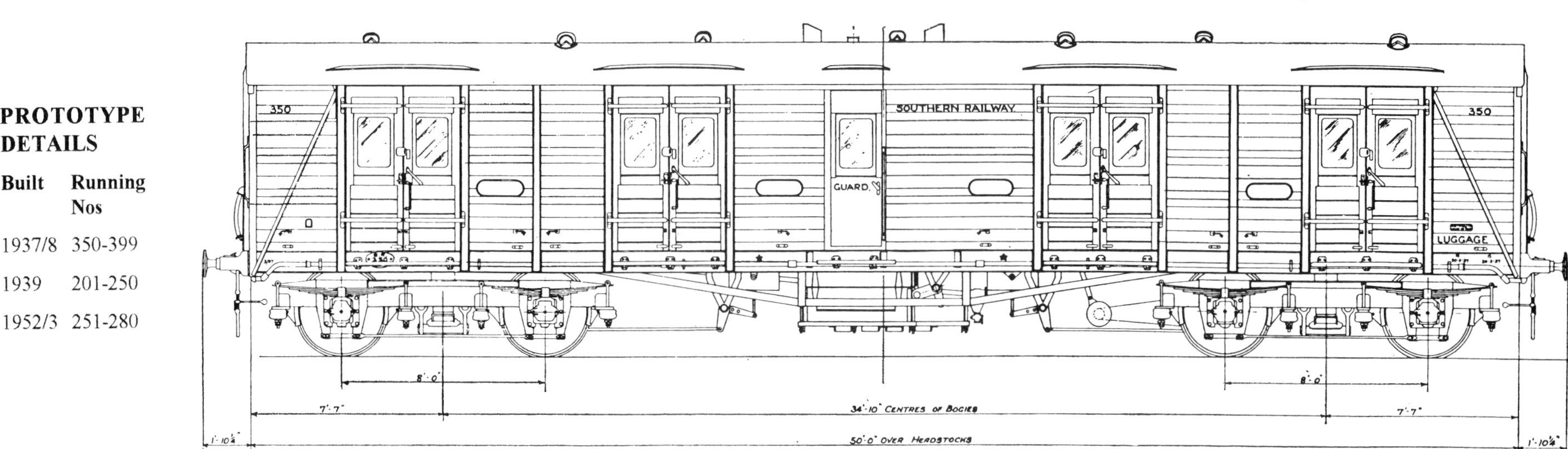

PROTOTYPE DETAILS

Built	Running Nos
1937/8	350-399
1939	201-250
1952/3	251-280

Metropolitan Railway Four Wheel Passenger Brake Van

Six four wheel passenger brake vans, numbered 1 to 6, were put into service on the Metropolitan Railway between 1899 and 1905 to diagram 123. They were fitted with Stone's electric lighting system and automatic vacuum brake with an 18 inch diameter cylinder. The underframe is almost the same as that under the Met milk vans described on page 121. The Mansell wheels may have been exchanged for steel disc type during the life of the vehicles.

Metropolitan Railway 27 foot long four wheel passenger brake van No 3. The varnished teak livery includes the company's coat of arms, lining round the panels, the lettering LUGGAGE and GUARD. Note the typical round topped Met door with drop light for the guard. The only other natural light was provided by the pair of roof lights (HMRS Cruickshank collection, courtesy L Bevis-Smith)

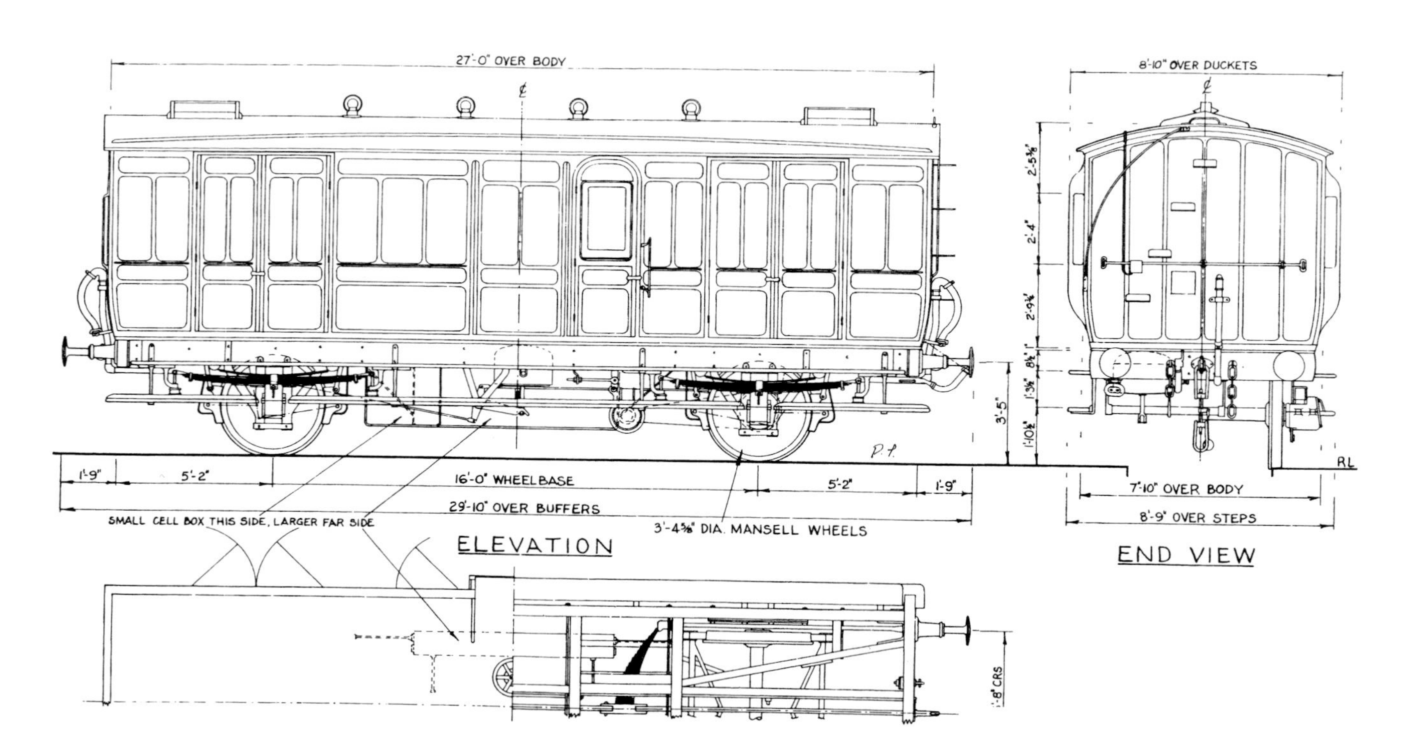

LMS 42 Ft Bogie Utility Van

These were multi-purpose luggage and parcels vans/covered carriage trucks to Diagram 1870. All were built at Wolverton, except Lot 848 which were constructed at Derby. General appearance was similar to contemporary flush-sided coaches, but with flat sides and longitudinal raised beading strips above and below the windows. The first lots were finished in fully lined livery. Withdrawals commenced in 1964.

PROTOTYPE DETAILS

Lot	Year	Nos
690	1933	37700-37749
750	1934	37750-37774
751	1934	37775-37799
848	1935	37800-37849
863	1935	37850-37874
864	1935	37875-37899
1050	1937	37900-37939

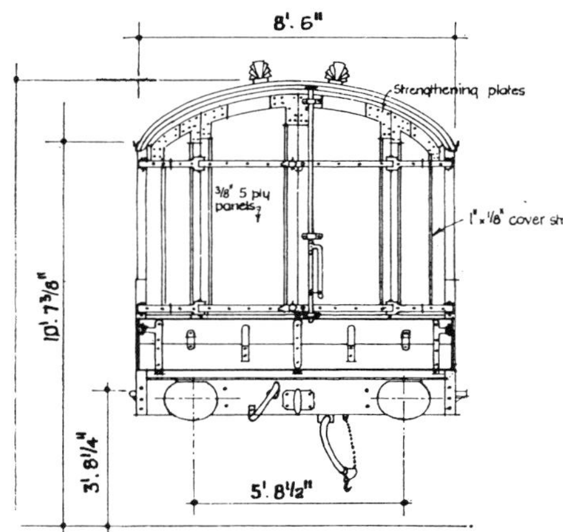

LMS 42 foot bogie utility van No 37759 built at Wolverton in 1934 is seen here in BR carmine livery at Old Oak Common on 8 April 1951. (AE West, courtesy of MS King)

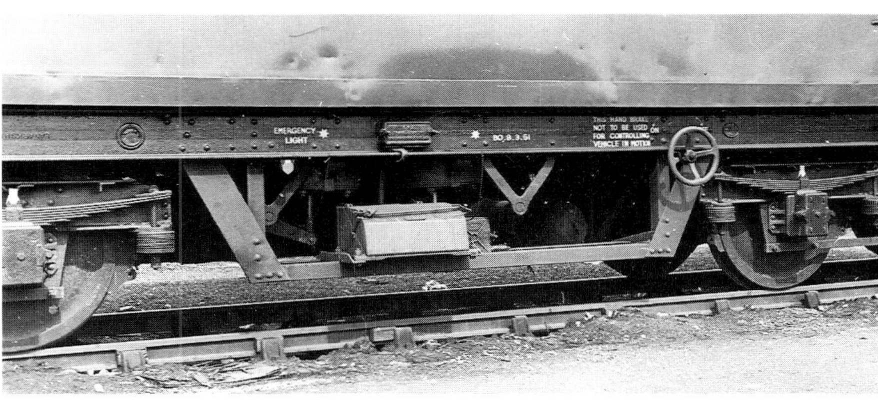

Detail of the regulator box, brake wheel and underframe trussing of the same vehicle. (AE West, courtesy of MS King)

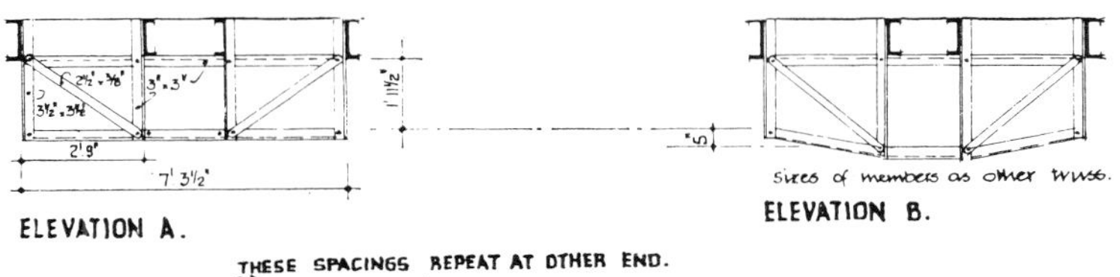

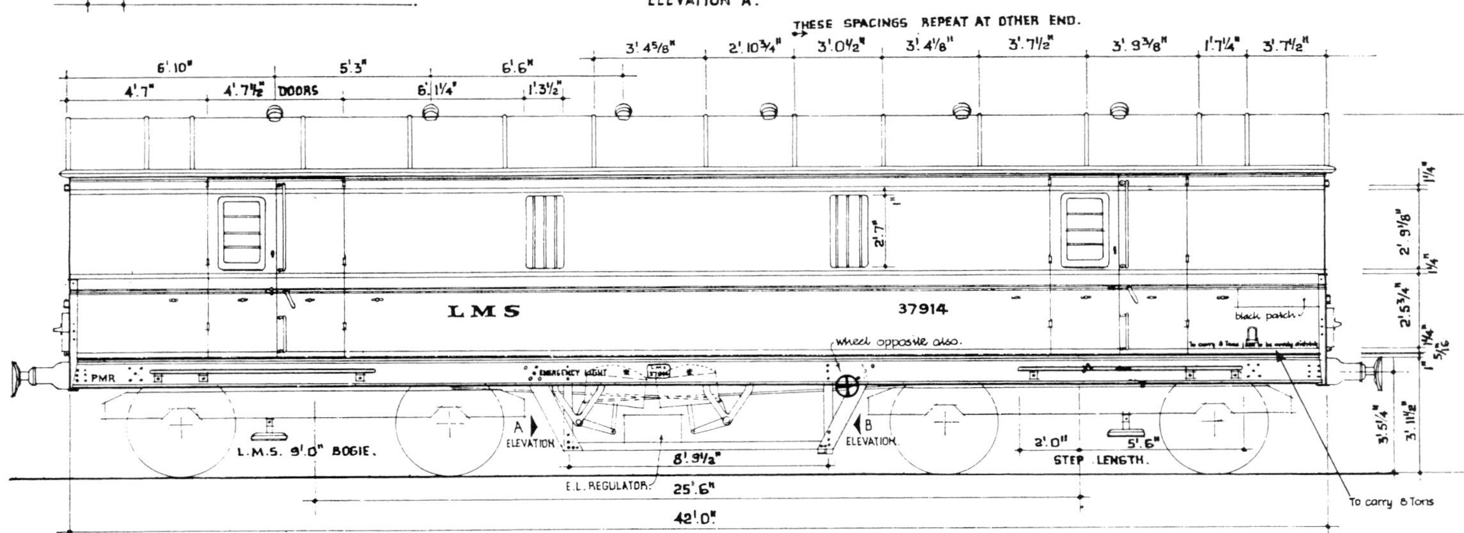

MR Six Wheel Parcels Van to Diagram D422

These vehicles were intended for use as part of passenger trains. Before a train departed from the terminus the compartments were chalked with the names of stations to be serviced *en route* and parcels loaded in appropriate compartments. Additional consignments could be loaded at intermediate stations without fear of confusion. On arrival at a designated station, the appropriate compartment was cleared out. No groping around in gloomy interiors trying to extract packages no hasty oversights due to trying to read, often in poor conditions, bad labelling, and no time wasted in the process. Just read the names chalked on the outside of compartments, add to or clear out completely the contents and the system becomes much more positive.
The Midland was not the only railway to operate this kind of vehicle; examples could be found on Cambrian Railways and the LNWR. Other Companies probably used them but, if so, they seem to have fallen out of fashion before grouping. The demise of the idea poses a question, of course. The Midland vehicles built in 1910 to Lot 730 seem to have been the last built to this general design. They became extinct in revenue earning service by 1951, but one still in departmental service in May 1967.
The drawing calls for little comment except to point out that there are steps, a long handrail and a short grab iron at both ends. As built the foot boards had a hinged flap in the upper board to allow access to the brake lever.

PROTOTYPE DETAILS

LMS 1st Nos	LMS 2nd Nos
34 , 379, 460, 482, 484, 489, 499, 508, 513, 514, 517, 522	34988 to 34999

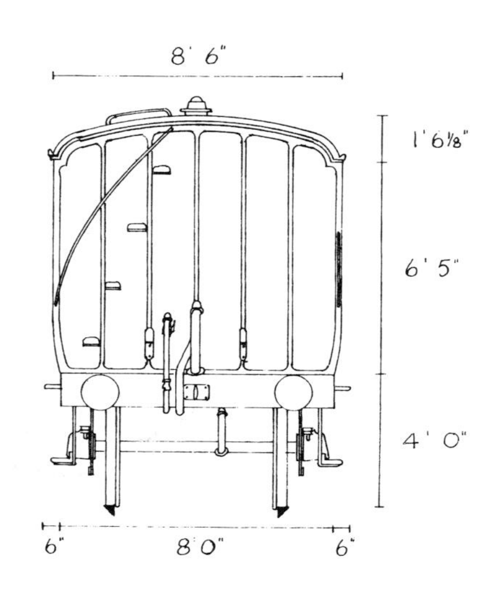

Following withdrawal from revenue earning service, one of these vehicles was included in the Chief Engineer's Weed Killer Train No 2 as No 198823, presumably for use as a mess van. The foot boards have been altered to leave gaps for the brake lever, drop lights and even curtains fitted to most windows and a ladder hung below the upper footboard. (G Warburton coll.)

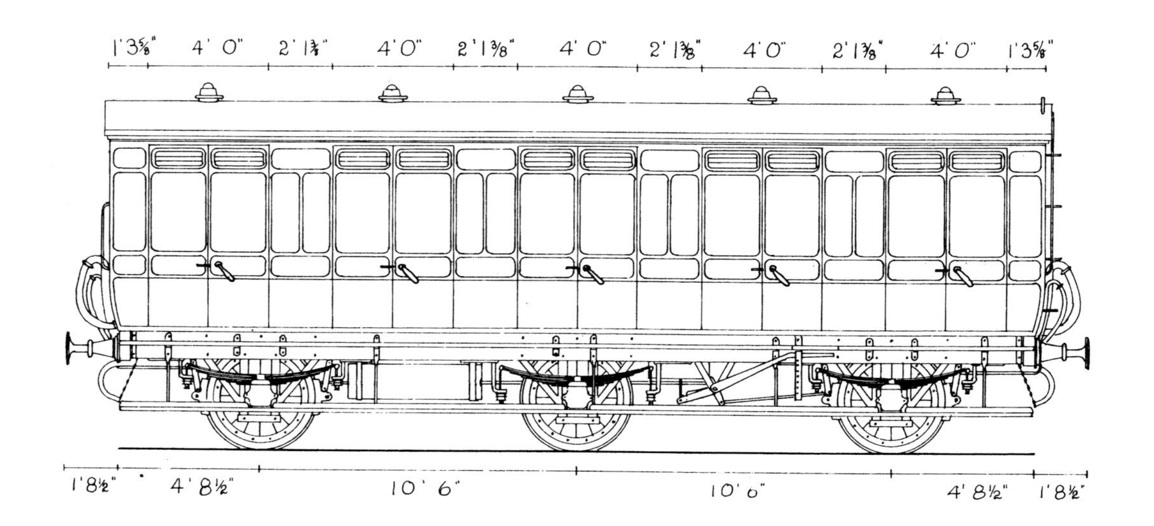

L&SWR Passenger Luggage Van

A batch of 50 of these four wheel vans was built in 1887 and, as built, had only one brake lever. Later, the South Western's own other-side lever was fitted. This took the form of a shorter lever connected to a stub lever on the cross bar by a single link. All the vans had vacuum brakes and at a later date some were fitted with through Westinghouse and steam heating pipes.

A number were withdrawn prior to the 1912 renumbering scheme. By the time the Southern allocated a block of numbers 1252-1290 more had gone or had been transferred to departmental service and only those vehicles listed below actually carried those numbers, the remainder went out of revenue service still carrying their 1912 numbers. These vans were withdrawn from the mainland revenue service between 1926 and 1933.

Three vans were transferred to the Isle of Wight in 1926, SR Nos 1254/75/83, the first having been renumbered only three months before being transferred to the island.

PROTOTYPE DETAILS

Pre-1912	Post-1912	SR	IoW
51-100	5051/3/60/2/5-9/71/4/7/ 9/81-6/8/93-96/8-5100	1253, (1254*), 1256/ 8/9/61/4/ 7-72/5*/6/ 8/80/2/3*/4-7/9/90	2232-4

L&SWR 24 foot four wheel passenger brake van No 40s built in July 1887 and transferred to departmental service in 1922 seen at Esher. It lasted in this condition until the 1960s. (DJ Wigley, courtesy MS King)

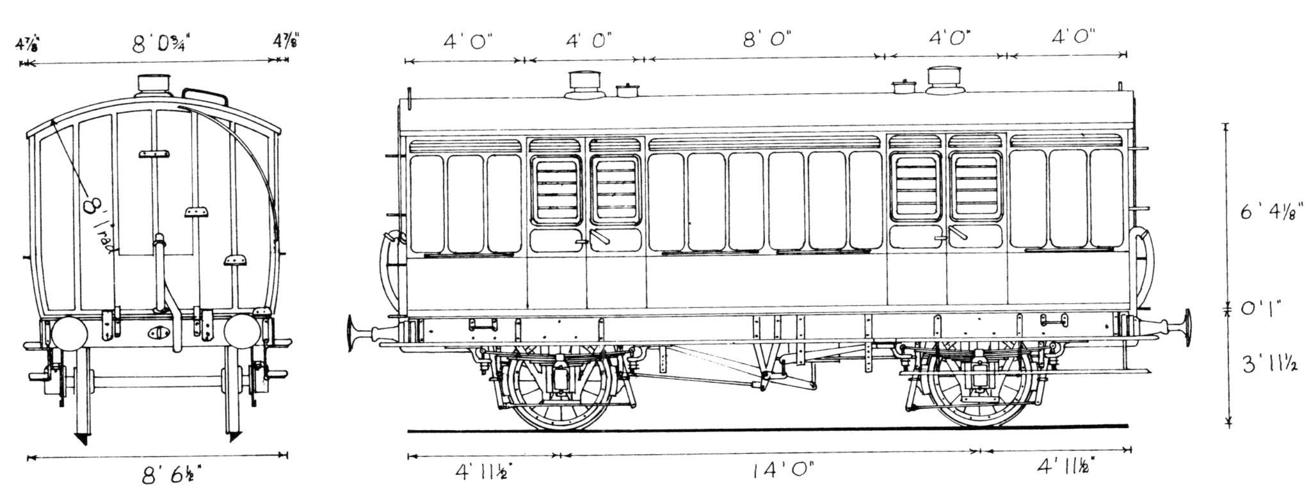

Sundry GER 22 Foot Vans

From 1888 a series of 22 feet long four wheeled vans were produced by the GER over a period of twelve years for a variety of purposes, such as passenger train, continental luggage and bullion vans and for the conveyance of yeast, meat, fruit and fish. Two main body styles were used, the first with one pair of doors and the second, five inches taller, with two double doors per side. A drawing for each is reproduced. The other diagrams largely represented internal differences, such as the provision of partitions or shelves. These vehicles were fitted with Westinghouse brake and some may have been dual fitted, or provided with through pipe for vacuum brakes. Steam heating pipes were added to many during the period 1913 and 1914.

PROTOTYPE DETAILS

Type	Built	Order	Quantity	GER Nos	GER Nos	LNER Nos	Diagram/	Withdrawn
Yeast/pass van	9-10/88	D22	20	13-32	1813-1832	-	32 / 1	6/22-6/31
	6/93	K32	25	33-57	1833-1857	6166-6180	32 / 1	6/23-5/31
Continental lug	c'05	conv.	4	-	1840-1843	-	38 / 1	Reverted '18
Meat & fruit	12/88	F22	20	1-20	2001-2020	wagon Nos	33 / 1	'27
Fish & fruit	3/97	P39	10	-	1858-1867	6188-6197	34 / 2	8/31-1/35
	10/97	B41	10	-	1868-1877	6198-6207	34 / 2	5/31-2/37
	6-10/99	R45	10	-	1878-1887	6208-6217	34 / 2	6/30-2/37
Continental lug	'05	conv.	1	-	1860	6190	37 / 2	Revt'd prior to '23
Parcels	9-12/96	F39	3	(729-731)	2030-2032	6185-6187	35 / 2	5/31-7/34
	'09	c'09	3	-	1861,62/64	6191,92/94	35 / 2	5/31-7/34
Bullion	7/93	P32	1	-	2029	-	36 / 3	6/31

Former GER No 1874 fruit van built in November 1897 with a pair of doors on each side seen at Stratford, probably following withdrawal on 20 February 1937, after which it was transferred to departmental stock as No 962353. (GY Hemingway, courtesy HMRS & J Watling)

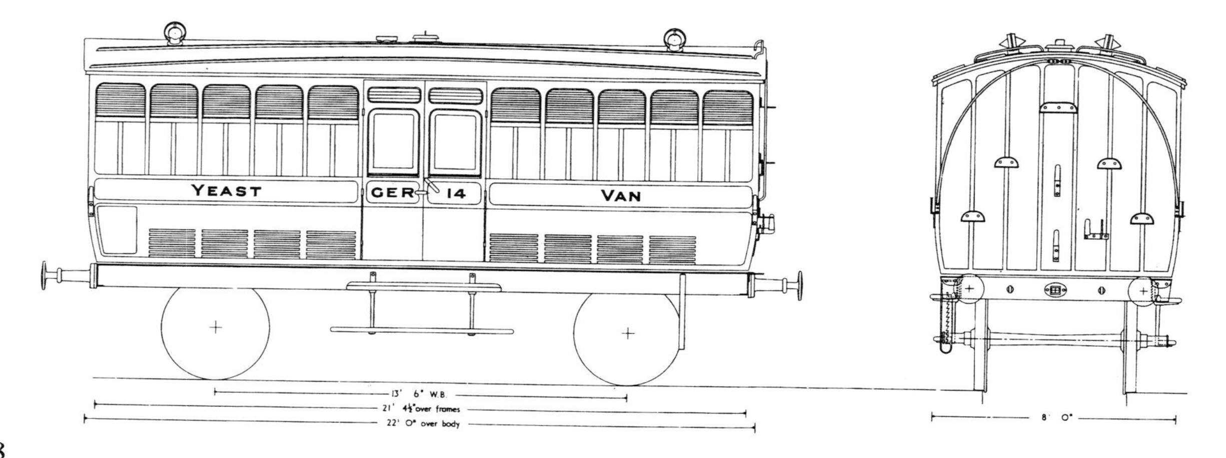

GER 22 Foot Sundry Vans

Until 1897 each type of vehicle had its own number series, after which the miscellaneous vehicles were renumbered into one series. In 1926 the LNER renumbered these again, Nos 1857 and 2015 failing to last this long. Four were allocated for the conveyance of luggage to and from the Continent, as listed in the table, and re-designated parcel vans in about 1909. Towards the end of their lives further vans were converted for other uses, such as laundry vans. The surviving meat and fruit vans to diagram 33 were transferred to wagon stock, sample numbers being 13210/12/15, 13280-81/85, and allocated diagram 53 in 1922 with Westinghouse brake and steam heating pipes, if present, removed, only to be withdrawn by 1927. Nos 6201/03-04 were converted for use as Fruit Traffic Office Vans in 1937 including the fitting of automatic vacuum brake, and renumbered the following year in the LNER's departmental list as Nos 962351-53. Nos 6199, 6209/14-15 were also transferred to departmental stock. Many vans ended up on the Wisbech and Upwell Tramway.

For further details see *Model Railway Constructor*, January 1986, pp 27-31.

The body of a Diagram 32 yeast or passenger train van with only a single set out doors per side put out to grass at Friday Bridge, near Wisbech. This shows the panelling arrangement for the early vans and also the guttering added after passing into the new owner's hands. (J Watling)

One of three Fruit Traffic Office vans to survive into the BR era is No E962353 at Stratford in BR livery of carmine with straw lettering, originally built as a fruit van in 1897. Note vacuum through pipe only and additional grab handles. (J Gardner, courtesy J Watling)

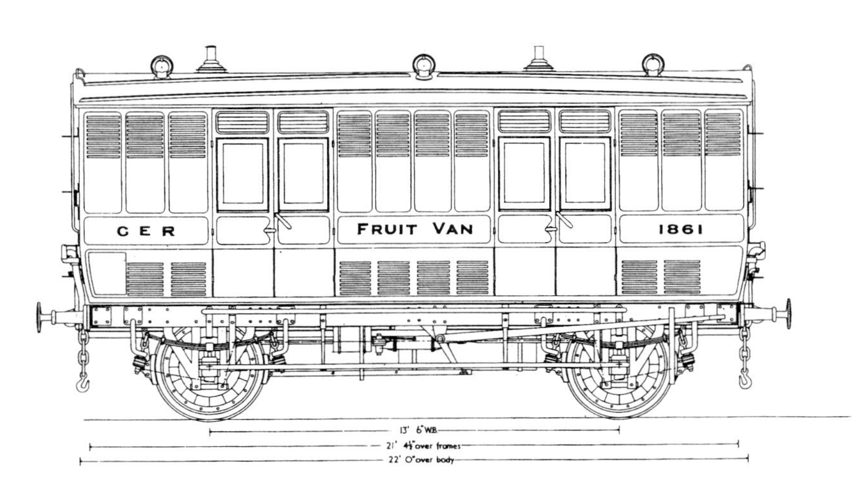

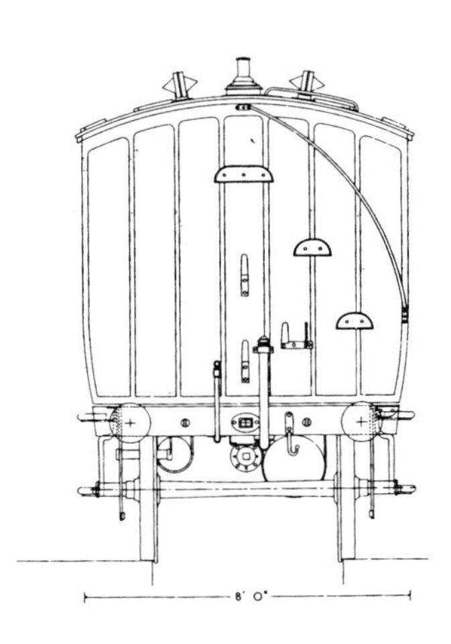

SE&CR and Southern Railway Four Wheel 32 Foot Long Passenger Luggage/Parcels Van

Although the requirement for a high standard of running equipment was obviously necessary for non-passenger coaching stock, for the most part this did not need to extend to the bodywork. Maunsell's arrival at Ashford brought many innovations on the SE&CR and this included passenger luggage/parcels vans with outside steel framing supporting timber planking more akin to then modern goods van construction. This was to set the style on the soon to be formed Southern Railway and on into the British Railways era for this type of vehicle, together with passenger brake vans, covered carriage trucks and scenery vans, some mounted on bogies as well as the usual four wheeled underframes.

Initially 6½ inch horizontal planking was used throughout, but from the late 1930s it was found more economic to alternate 6½ and 3½ inch wide planks, whilst finally from 1950 plywood cladding was employed. Five vans were equipped with air control pipes to enable them to run in push-pull sets on the Central and Western Sections of the Southern Region.

Southern Railway four wheel utility van No 1171 still in green livery at Old Oak Common on 4 April 1951. Built at Ashford (Kent) in 1935 with the body cladding of 6½ inch wide planks. (AE West, courtesy of MS King)

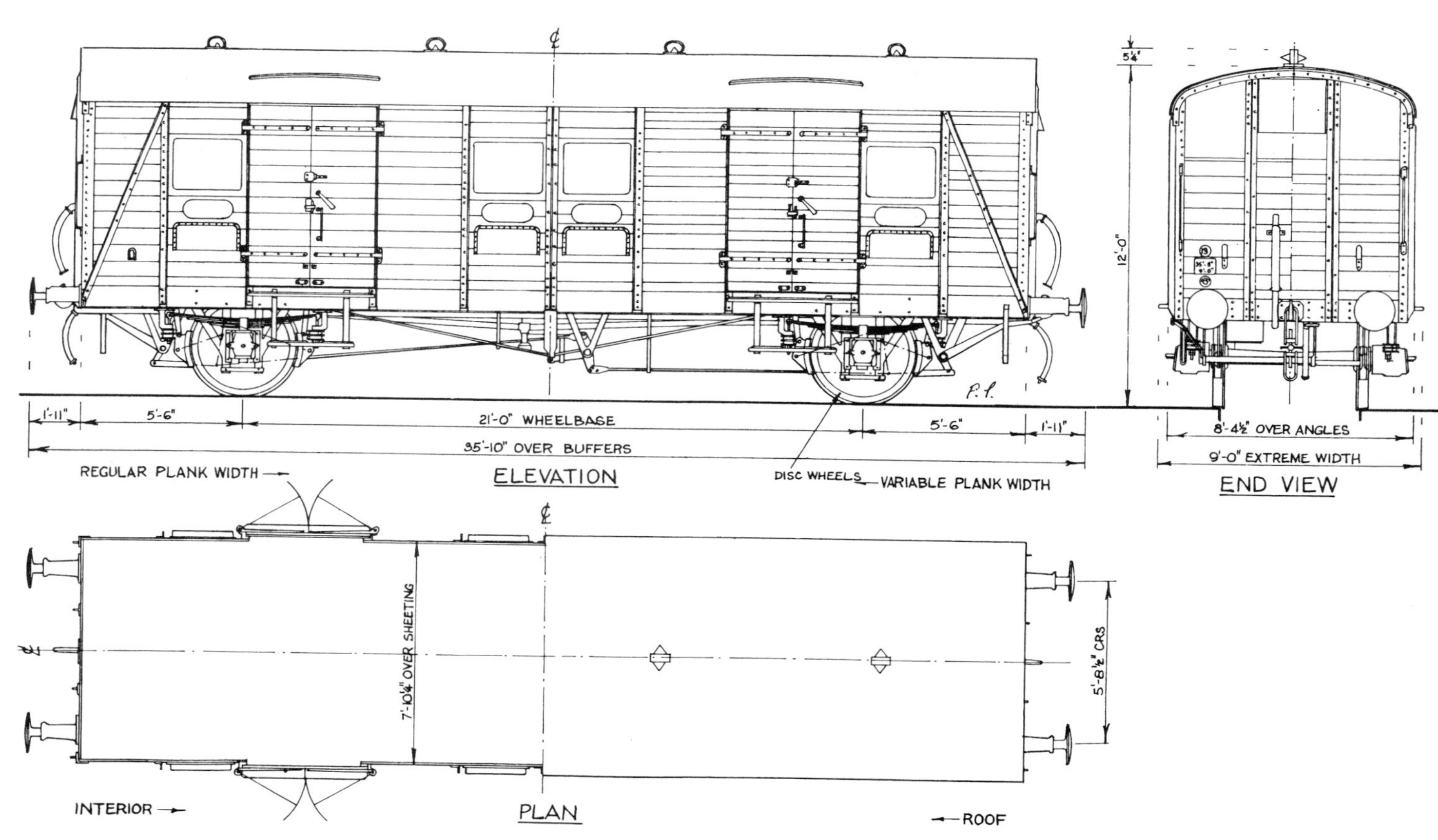

SE&CR and Southern Railway Four Wheeled 32 Foot Long Passenger Luggage/Parcels Van

Presumably due to difficulties in the supply of steel during the war a number of vans were built using some channel section stanchions instead of angle iron section. This is demonstrated by No S1813 built in 1942 at Lancing, seen here in green at Stewarts Lane on 21 July 1951. *(AE West, courtesy of MS King)*

PROTOTYPE DETAILS

Running Nos		Built by	Built
SECR	SR		
132	1972	Ashford	1919
121-5, 136-50	1973-1992	Bristol C&W	1921
152-5-7/8/60-3/6-70/2-5/7/9-82	1993-2016	Ashford	1922

Built	Built by	Running Nos	No off	Planking (in)	Ext't
10/34-5/35	Ashford	2181-2240	50	6.5	8/64
4-12/35	Ashford	1154-1250	97	6.5	1/81
3/36-4/37	Ashford	1054-1153	100	6.5	12/85
10-12/38	Ashford	1921-1970	50	6.5	6/83
2-12/39	Ashford	1251-1358	108	6.5	9/83
		1359-1398	40	Alternate 3.5/6.5	2/83
2-8/40	Lancing & Eastleigh	1821-1920	100	Pairs of 3.5/6.5	7/86
1942	Lancing	1781-1820, 2091-2170	120	6.5*	10/84
1943	Lancing	1053, 1692-1730, 2083-2090	48	Pairs of 3.5/6.5	12/82
6-8/47	Ashford	1501-1560	60	Pairs of 3.5/6.5	12/82
1-8/51	Wolverton	1451-1500	50	Pairs of 3.5/6.5	12/83
1950/1	Ashford, Lancing & Eastleigh	1561-1671	111	Ply	11/85

Notes: * U section vertical stanchions.

The final production utilised plywood cladding a shown here of No S1574 built at Ashford in 1950/1, although the bodies of some this batch were constructed at Lancing and Eastleigh. (JH Lewis)

Southern Railway Bogie Corridor Luggage Vans

These vehicles were designed by REL Maunsell in 1929 and altogether 120 were built between 1930 and 1937. They were used on a variety of services, including express passenger and the Waterloo-Southampton Docks boat trains. The majority were withdrawn in 1958-60; a few survivors were used for pigeon traffic from 1959-61. The bodies of 6½ inch wide planks were built on old LSWR carriage underframes which were lengthened to suit; however, the bogie centres remained unaltered and this produced three varieties of vehicle as listed below. The original bogies were re-used with certain modifications; the elliptical bolster springs were replaced by coil springs, but the wooden-centred Mansell wheels were retained at the outset, although by BR days they had been replaced by steel disc wheels. One of the last surviving vehicles of this type was used to convey Sir Winston Churchill's coffin to its place of burial on 30 January 1965.

PROTOTYPE DETAILS

Length (ft-in)	Bogie centres	Diagram	Built	Nos
51-3	34-3	3096/3098	1930/1	2331-2354
			1931	2482-2490
51-3	36-3	3100	1930	2281-2330
53-3	36-3	3097/3099	1931	2355-2370
			1931	2461-2481

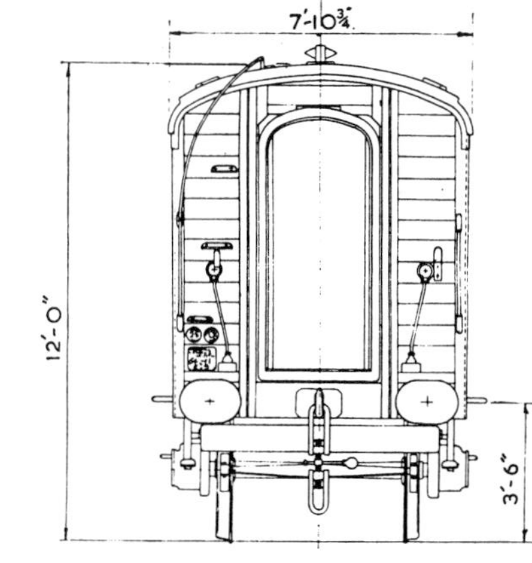

Southern Railway gangwayed bogie utility van used for the conveyance of passengers' luggage, parcels and newspapers seen here at Waterloo on 245 October 1950 in green livery. (AE West, courtesy of MS King)

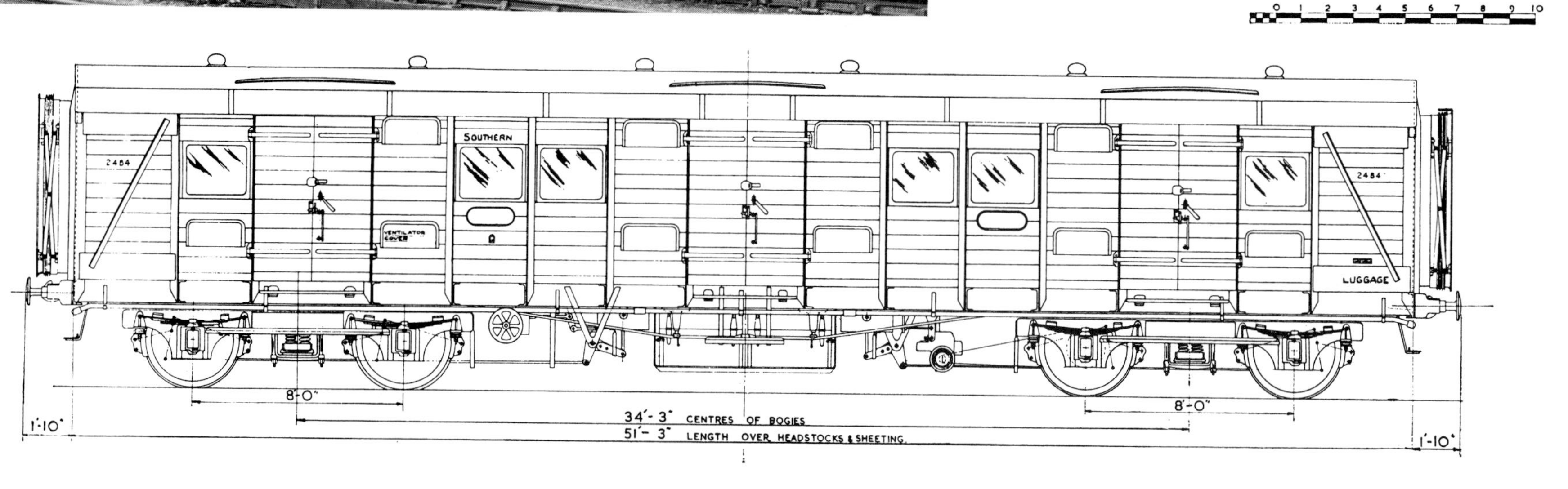

Caledonian Covered Carriage Truck

These covered carriage trucks were built to both passenger diagram 87A and the identical goods diagram 101. They were dual braked with an 18 inch vacuum and 8 inch Westinghouse cylinders. Lots G324 and H300 had 3'-9" diameter wheels, while the rest were 3'-6" diameter. Lot G324 had Iracier patent axleboxes. Those vehicles numbered in the goods series were reclassified as motor car vans and renumbered by the LMS in the non-passenger coaching stock series between 1927 and 1930.

In Caledonian days those in the passenger series vans were painted dark purple lake with yellow lining edged in a fine vermilion line and medium chrome yellow lettering, the initials CR being shaded lower left in vermilion. The goods vehicles were brick red with black ironwork and white lettering. Until re-classified goods rated stock was painted in LMS freight stock grey and white lettering.

PROTOTYPE DETAILS

Diag	Lot	Built	CR No	LMS No 1923	LMS No 1933	Extinct	Remarks
87A	H300	7/12	125/34, 180-7	6636/91-8	37167-75	11/57	
	H322	6/14	123/33/191-4	6634/44, 6702-5	37176-81	10/60	No 194 as elephant van
	H350	6/20	11/4, 89, 152/70/95	6524/7, 6601/63/81, 6706	37182-7	6/59	
101	G324	1913	73283-92	308250/35291/3	37455-63	2/58	LMS No 1930: 8305-8/13/4/6/7/19/20
	G346	1913	73537-42	304748/5313/943/9318	37167/464-9	2/58	LMS No 1930: 8309-11/5/8

Ex-CR covered carriage truck built as No 73541 in 1914 as goods stock is seen in BR days as M37468 on 9 February 1955 having already been condemned. (GR Driffield)

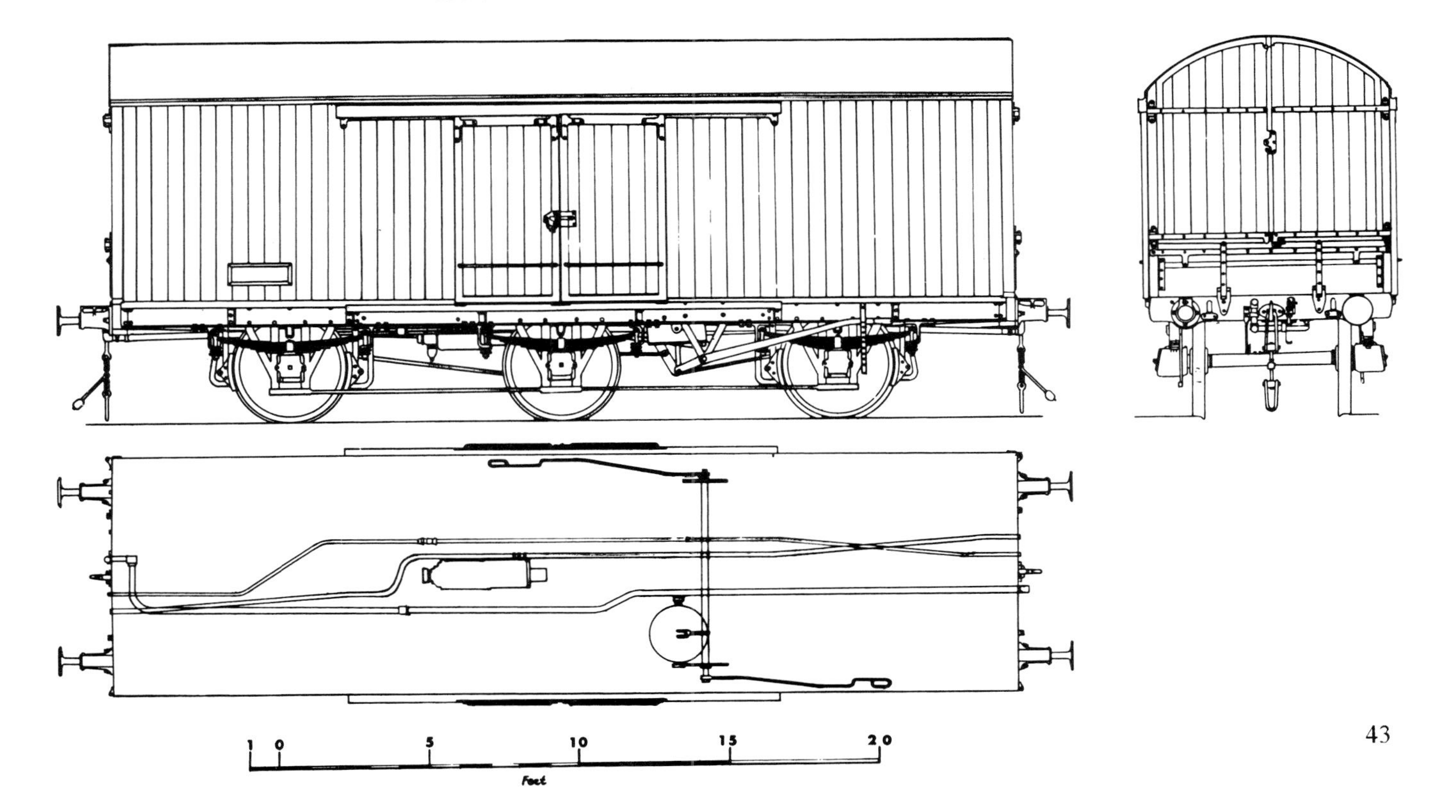

G&SW Milk and Motor Car Van

Due to the deep louvres, this 25 foot long dual braked Glasgow & South Western Railway van was capable of use for either a milk traffic or the conveyance of motor cars. The 15 foot wheelbase meant that long after Nationalisation the vehicle could run without speed restrictions. The louvres were removed from these vehicles towards the end, of their working life in a piecemeal fashion. One photograph shows an example with one louvre missing. In each case of removal the resulting holes were boarded up neatly to the full length – not just spliced to cover the hole.

Ex-G&SW milk and motorcar van No M37477 with all but one panel of lourves remaining. (BP Hoper)

PROTOTYPE DETAILS

G&SW Nos.	148-163 (1914), 164-167 (1915)
LMS 1st Nos	7326/7/9-7343/5, 8297/9, 8300/4
LMS 2nd Nos	37474-34791

Plate – Ex G&SW covered carriage truck No M37474 at St Rollox Works on 17 September 1956 with only one out of the original two louvred panel left. (FW Shuttleworth)

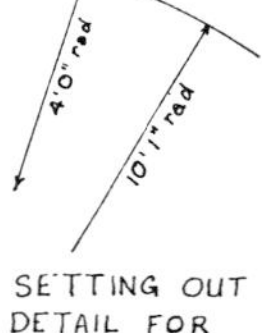

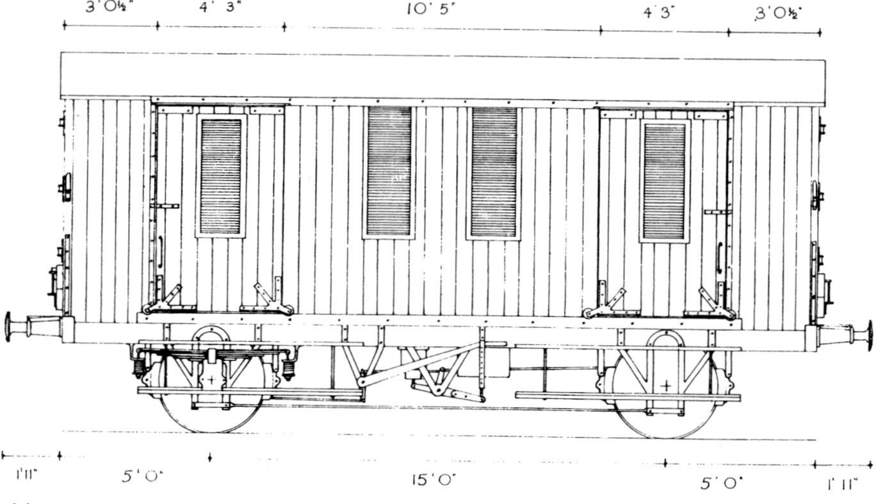

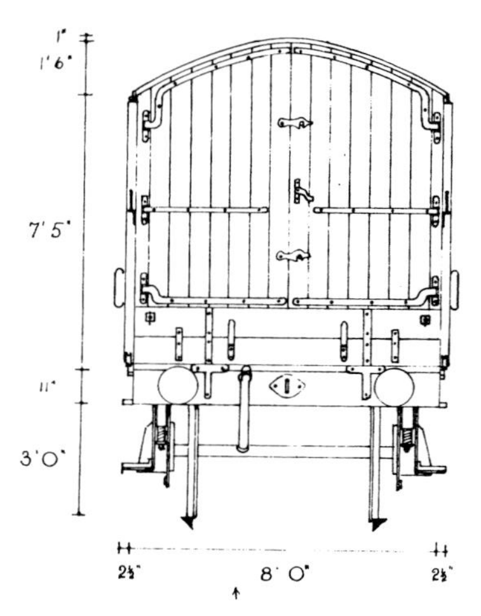

LMS Six Wheel Combination Carriage Truck

Early LMS covered combination trucks were built on six wheel underframes recovered from redundant Midland Railway coaches. These were not all quite the same and therefore led to two diagrams being issued, viz: D1871 for a 30 foot long vehicle with a 21ft 6in wheelbase and D1872 30 ft 5in long and 21 foot wheelbase, as per the drawing. Later lots of D1872 were reduced by 4 inch in length, the wheelbase remaining the same.

The two diagrams appear, apart from dimensional differences, to have the same style of body, but some D1872's were built upon a more old-fashioned underframe. They had longer leaf springs and round-section tie rods connecting the lower part of the axle-box. In addition, diagonal tie rods were taken from the outer axle-box to the ends of the underframe.

In 1959 they were prohibited from passenger trains and a considerable number were transferred to departmental stock. Steps were removed and ends boarded up, etc.

When built, full livery of crimson lake body, lined in yellow was employed. The lines were both sides of the main outside frame members, but only on the top of the diagonal framing, between the side and end doors. The ends were initially crimson lake, the roof dark grey and the underframe black. "To carry 6 tons" was stencilled at the bottom extreme left-hand side, with "LMS" on the left-hand door and the number on the right-hand door, both just above the rail. These would be serif-style passenger lettering. Later the ends were black and the lining was omitted, after 1934 or thereabouts, but unfortunately no photograph has been located to confirm the lettering position. Prior to 1934 random numbers were used, including D1871 - 7288, 7322; D1872 – 658, 1688, 1823 and 4739.

PROTOTYPE DETAILS

Diagram	Length (ft-in)	Wheel base (ft-in)	Date Built	LMS 2nd Nos	Extinct by
1871	30-0	21-6	1926	35030-128	4/64
1872	30-5	21-0	1925-32	35025-9, 35129-473	6/68
1872	30-1	21-0	1934	35374-473	6/66

LMS six wheel covered combination truck No M35399M built at Wolverton in 1934 to diagram 1872 on a recovered 30 foot 5 inch long carriage underframe. Note the tie rods between the axle-guards and inclined rods at each end. (The Coutanche collection)

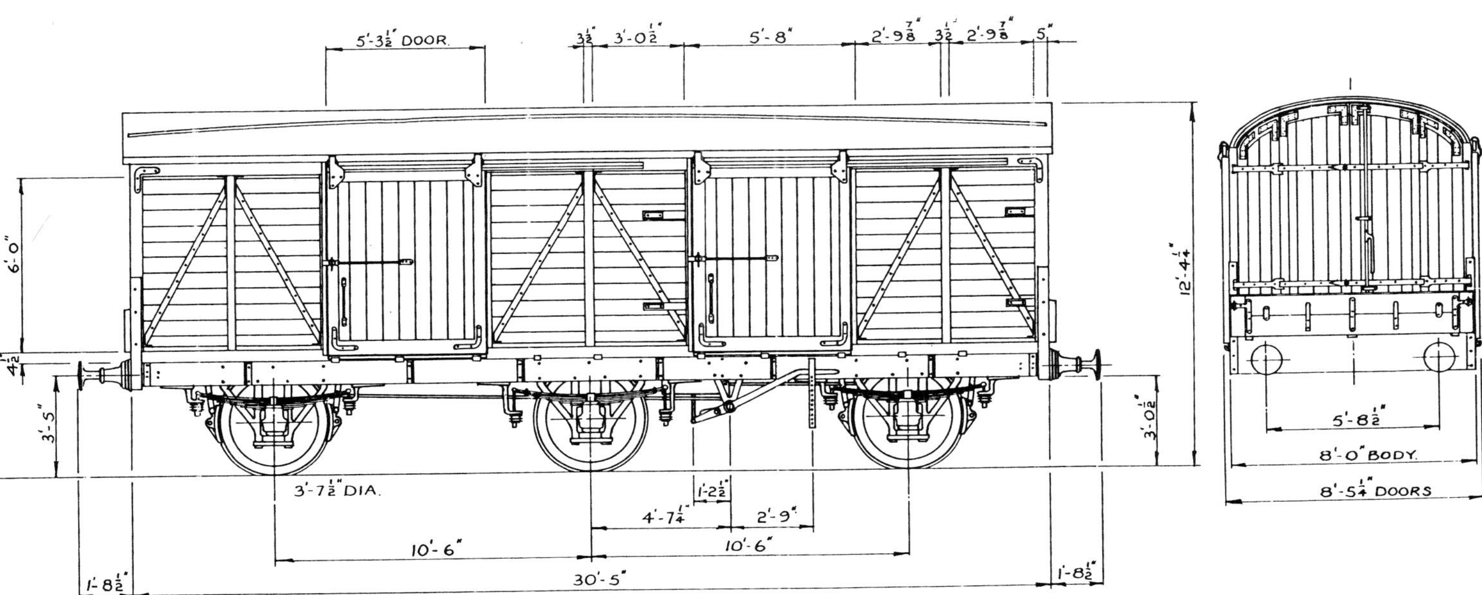

LNWR Six Wheel Combination Trucks to Diagrams 444 and 444A

To the Nor' Western a combination truck was the same as a Utility to the Southern and a General Utility Van to the more verbose British Rail. The combination trucks under consideration were provided with side doors for the convenience of parcels and general merchandise traffic, end doors - much favoured for loading vehicles and milk churns, and louvred sides - for the ventilation of perishable loads such as fish, fruit and vegetables. Top lights were provided to let in light to aid loading and unloading. The initial 30 vehicles built in 1910 were given low numbers in a separate list for carriage trucks, but had 11000 added to them under the LNWR's renumbering scheme of 1910, to avoid duplication with other npc stock.

Some of these vehicles were dual fitted with vacuum and Westinghouse brakes. All had handbrakes as shown on the chassis drawing, of course. The heavy black lines around the top lights on the drawing represent the glazing beads, or bolections, to the top lights which project fractionally in front of the surrounding, surface. The Westinghouse train pipes do not appear to have been fitted to any of these vehicles.

PROTOTYPE DETAILS

Diagram	Built	LNWR Nos (sample)	LMS 1st Nos	LMS 2nd Nos	Ext't
444 Sliding doors	1910–15	11003/10/228-30/308-10/64-74/402-6/10-4, 12214	4040-4116, 4118-4150	36833-36941	1957
444A Hinged doors	1915-22	11089/260/367-9/71-4/407/15/543, 12193-223/50	4151-4211, 4718-4720	36942-36999	1960

Ex-LNWR six wheel combination truck No 36892, previously LMS No 4109, in about 1946. (R Carpenter collection)

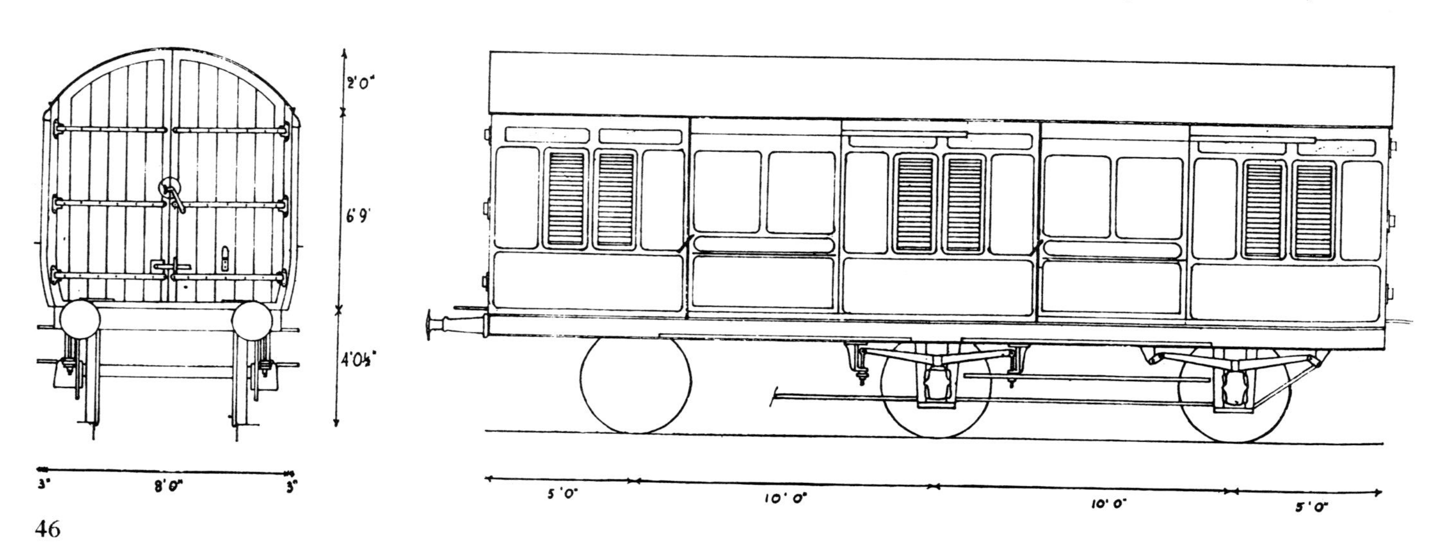

LNWR Six Wheel Combination Trucks to Diagrams 444 and 444A

Vehicles to diagram 444A date from 1915 and had they have hinged rather than sliding doors. This permitted some extra six inches width to be made available for the load, of course, and they might have been built with some military load in mind.
Many examples of both types were taken into departmental service during the early 1950s, particularly as cell trucks and weighing machine vans, when they last into the '70s.

Former LNWR six wheel covered combination truck LMS 2nd No 36887 (LMS 1st No 4101) to diagram 444 near the end of its life. Note board repairs to the left hand sliding door and lower body panels. (SNJ White, courtesy R Anderson)

An ex-LNWR six wheeled covered combination truck to diagram 444A, with pairs of cupboard instead of sliding, doors, is illustrated at Wolverton in early BR days, together with an early LMS and ex-LNWR diagram 444 CCTs. (PB Whitehouse, Millbrook House collection)

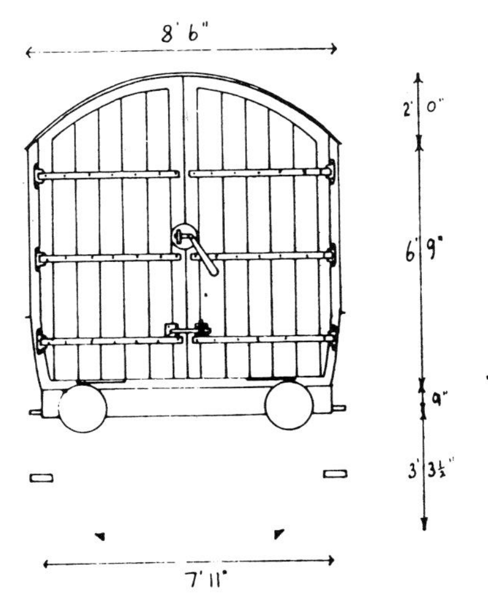

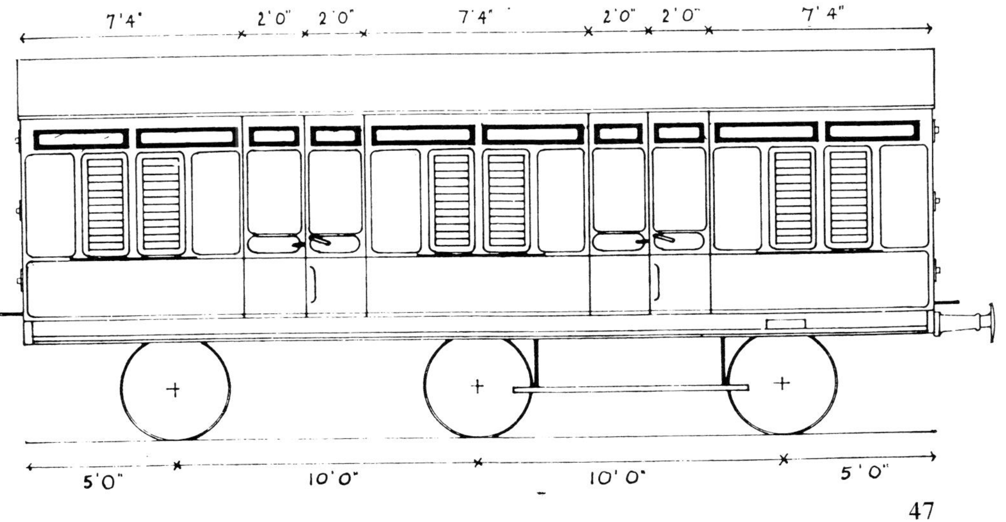

LNWR Four Wheel Covered Combination Truck to Diagrams 445 and 445A

Vehicles to diagram 445 date from the early 1890s and pre-date the toplight style. 15 years later diagram 445A was introduced. This was 9 inches lower in height, 8 inches of which was achieved by a reduction in the depth of the eaves. As built, they were painted chocolate brown all over the body and the body lined in full passenger style but without white panels. The louvres were finished in varnished wood.

They were substantially constructed and, after years of revenue duty, many were transferred to department stock. Some of these vehicles were mounted on chassis where the axlebox slides were outside, not inside, the main frames.

LNWR numbers 11763, 11915, 11918, 11943 and 11950 are noted as being elephant trucks. It is not known whether the LMS continued the practice but if they did, the equivalent LMS numbers are (1st) 4396, 4442, 4445, 4470 and (2nd) 36735, 36737, 36740.

Top right. *Ex-LNWR covered carriage truck to diagram 445A, seen here in crimson lake livery as LMS No 36831, earlier LMS No 4598, at Cardington on 2 December 1939. (AE West, courtesy MS King)*

Middle right. *LNWR covered carriage truck to diagram 445, in use as a cell truck No DM279974. (R Anderson collection)*

PROTOTYPE DETAILS

Diag	Built	LNWR Numbers (Sample, add 11000 after 1910)	LMS 1st Nos	LMS 2nd Nos	Ext't
445	1892-98	23, 76, 96, 357, 400/53-5, 505/8, 657-78, 759-93, 885-98, 914-78	4352-4505	36725-49	4/40
445A	1907-09	24, 75, 198, 292, 307, 456, 604-10, 613-8, 628-32, 640-7, 1127-46	4506-4576, 4578-4599	36750-36832	12/56

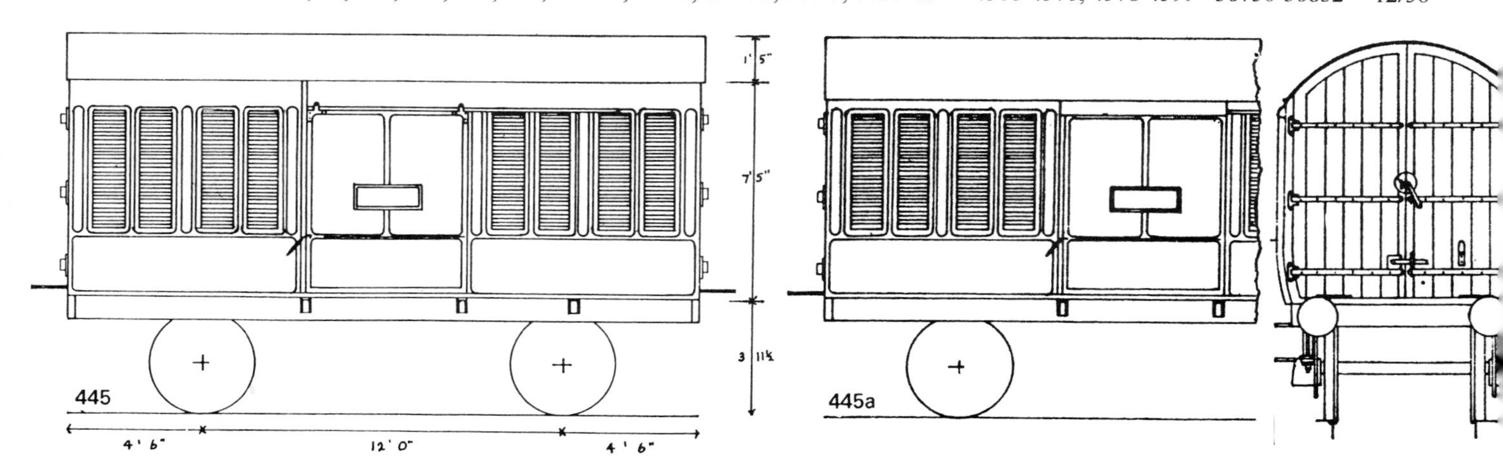

Lancashire and Yorkshire 21 Foot Covered Carriage Trucks

Fifteen covered carriage trucks were added to LYR stock between 1895 and 1908 as featured in the drawing. Previous building had provided similar vehicles in shorter body lengths and three others were built to 24 foot and 25 foot lengths for lease to horse carriage makers in the Manchester area at the turn of the century. All were included in Diagram 113, although of differing sizes. They were painted in the LYR carriage livery of tan and lake with dark brown ends. The colours and straight sides set them apart from the similar LNWR carriage trucks.

PROTOTYPE DETAILS

LYR Nos Sample	**LMS 1st Nos** Sample	**LMS 2nd Nos**
1	5654	-
135-140,	5695/6/7,5684/5/6/8	37102-37107
164, 165	5698, 5699	-

Nos. 126, built in 1895, and 163 were withdrawn without carrying first LMS numbers

Official photograph of No. 135 built in 1897. It has been finished in 'photographic' greys to show the detail and the livery differences, as the carriage livery did not register on the old film emulsions. Like all the other LYR covered carriages, it has dual Westinghouse/vacuum braking. (BC Lane collection)

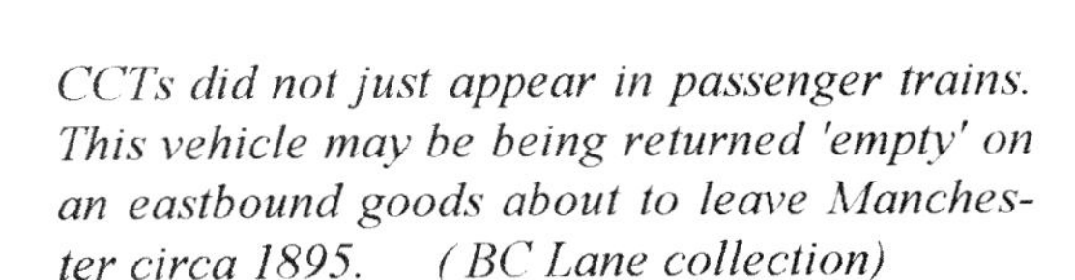

CCTs did not just appear in passenger trains. This vehicle may be being returned 'empty' on an eastbound goods about to leave Manchester circa 1895. (BC Lane collection)

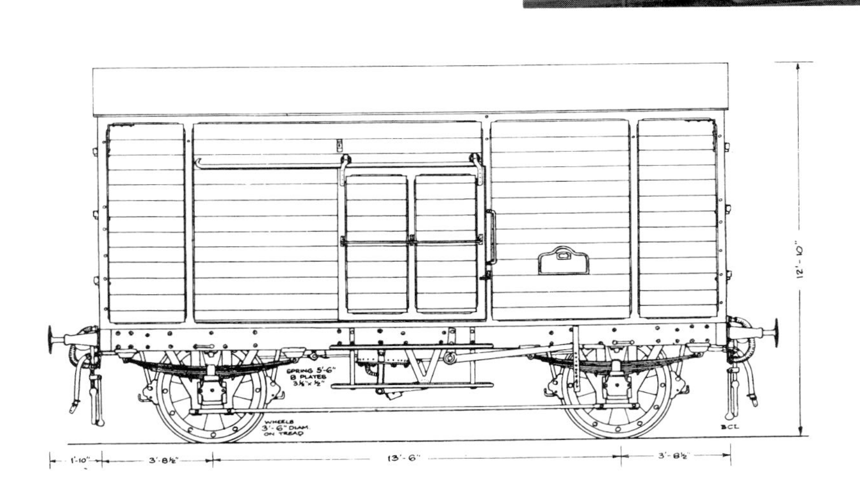

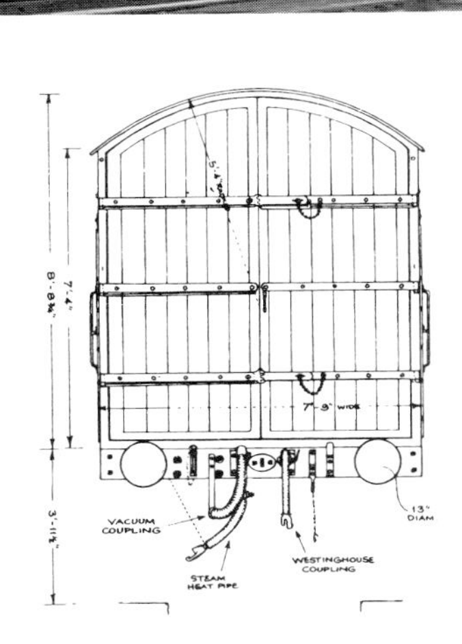

Lancashire & Yorkshire Covered Carriage Truck for Aeroplanes

During and immediately after the first World War the military authorities found it desirable to ship aeroplanes about the country by train. Several makers had their factories in the north of England. In true LYR practice and even more necessary due to war time restrictions, old carriage stock was converted for the purpose. Like the 'Fruit Vans' (page 104), the interior was gutted and certain doors fixed with the centre compartment being altered to double doors of the 2ft 2in size, while the other doors remained the usual 2ft measurement. End doors were provided as fitted to CCTs and the roof was raised by several inches to allow an internal height of 8ft 2in on the first 12, but later conversions had this increased to 8ft 7in.

Many varieties of six wheel carriage were converted from two compartment luggage/brakes to make a total of 79 (Diag118) before 26 were again altered to 'Combination trucks' (Diag 118A) leaving 53 with the full bodies. They were finished in the standard carriage livery of tan and lake with all windows painted white on the inside. Large numbers were centred on Southport and marked to be returned there. After the grouping they found general use within the LMS system and all received first LMS numbers. 40 remained in 1933 to be renumbered but all appear to have been withdrawn within the next decade.

PROTOTYPE DETAILS

Diag	L&Y Nos (with gaps)	LMS 1st Nos	LMS 2nd Nos
118	170-248	5732/6/51/7/60-2/73/8/ 82-4, 5801/7 (sample)	37110-37149
118 A	110-132, 163-165	5632-5639, 5694, 5698, 5699	Ext'n by 1933

In LMS days the vans found employment all over the LMS, not necessarily carrying aeroplanes. (BC Lane collection)

LYR official photograph of No. 174 converted from an 1888 third class brake. This is the only photograph to show one window unpainted. All the conversions were dual brake fitted plus the statutory hand brake. (NG Coates collection)

IMPORTANT
TO BE RETURNED TO
SOUTHPORT
WHEN EMPTY
BY FIRST MEANS
REQUIRED FOR
MILITARY PURPOSES

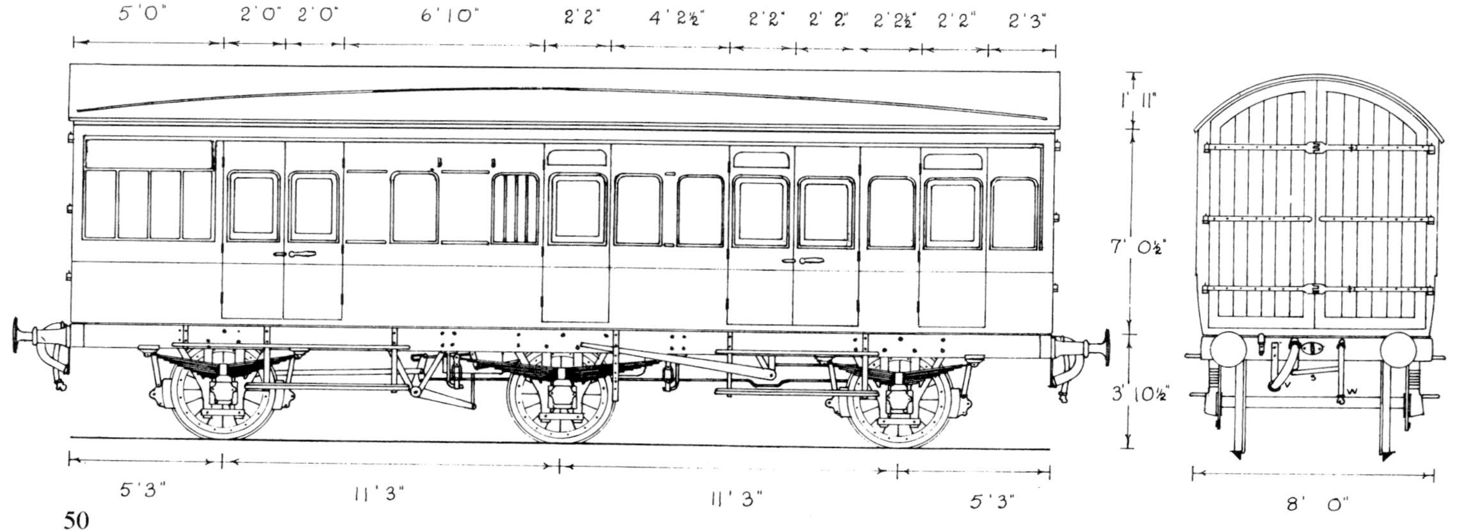

MR Six Wheel 4½ Ton Motor Car Van to Diagrams 414 and 414A

With the emergence of the 20th century, a large number of motor car manufacturers set up in the Midlands. There were, therefore, enough motor car manufacturers on the Midland Railway's territory to account for a substantial traffic and to convey their products the company built six wheel 31 foot long motor car vans. The first Lot 609 to Diagram 414, as shown on the drawing, had square corners to the side panelling, whereas subsequent lots were produced with rounded corners to Diagram 414A.

The ends are panelled, but it is probable that the louvres in the end doors were filled in fairly quickly after grouping, for this feature of MR end doors is rarely found still in existence in LMS days.

The Midland could have called these vehicles combination trucks, utilities, etc but, although they were provided with ventilation for perishable traffic, they were labelled Motor Car Vans. It is possible that in the days of this company these vehicles were used exclusively for motor car traffic because it seems to have had a very literal turn of mind with regard to classification.

PROTOTYPE DETAILS

Lot	Built	MR Nos	LMS 1st Nos	LMS 2nd Nos	Ext't
609	1906	601-625	955-979	37384-37407	10/47
699	1908	M&SW 226	1961	37408	7/45
705	1909	47	954	37409	8/51
735	1911	643-654	980-991	37410-37421	1/52
806	1913	656-667	992-1003	37422-37433	4/55

Midland Railway six wheel motor car van No 607 from the first Lot 609 as built in 1906 with square cornered panels. (R Anderson collection)

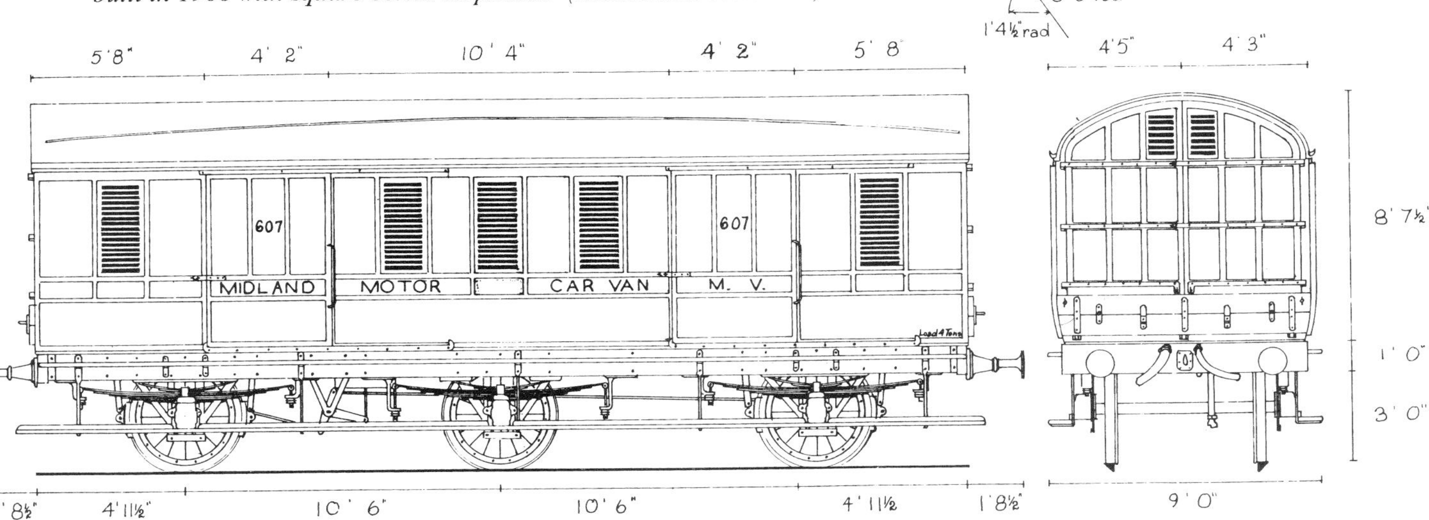

MR 20 and 25 Foot Covered Carriage Trucks

To maximise internal capacity, initial construction of MR covered carriage trucks in the early 1880s of 20 and 25 foot lengths, represented by diagrams D402 and D403 respectively, had a high arched roof profile. This unfortunately led to restrictions on the routes in Scotland and on the GER, Metropolitan, Taff Vale and Tilbury lines, etc. The Midland Railway therefore decided to produce some vehicles with a greater route availability, generally the same as before, but seven inches lower to diagrams D406 and D407. The sides and ends are identical to the previous vehicles, but with seven inches taken off the top edge. In turn this led to a slight adjustment of the position of the end door hinges, but that is all. The roof profile is the same, although there was now no logical reason for it being so.

A 20 foot long Midland Railway covered carriage truck No 382 built in 1889 to diagram D406 with lowered roof specifically for use on the Metropolitan lines. The 25 foot long version to diagram D407 was similar. Note the provision of safety chains. The hand brake lever is probably on the other side. (AG Ellis collection)

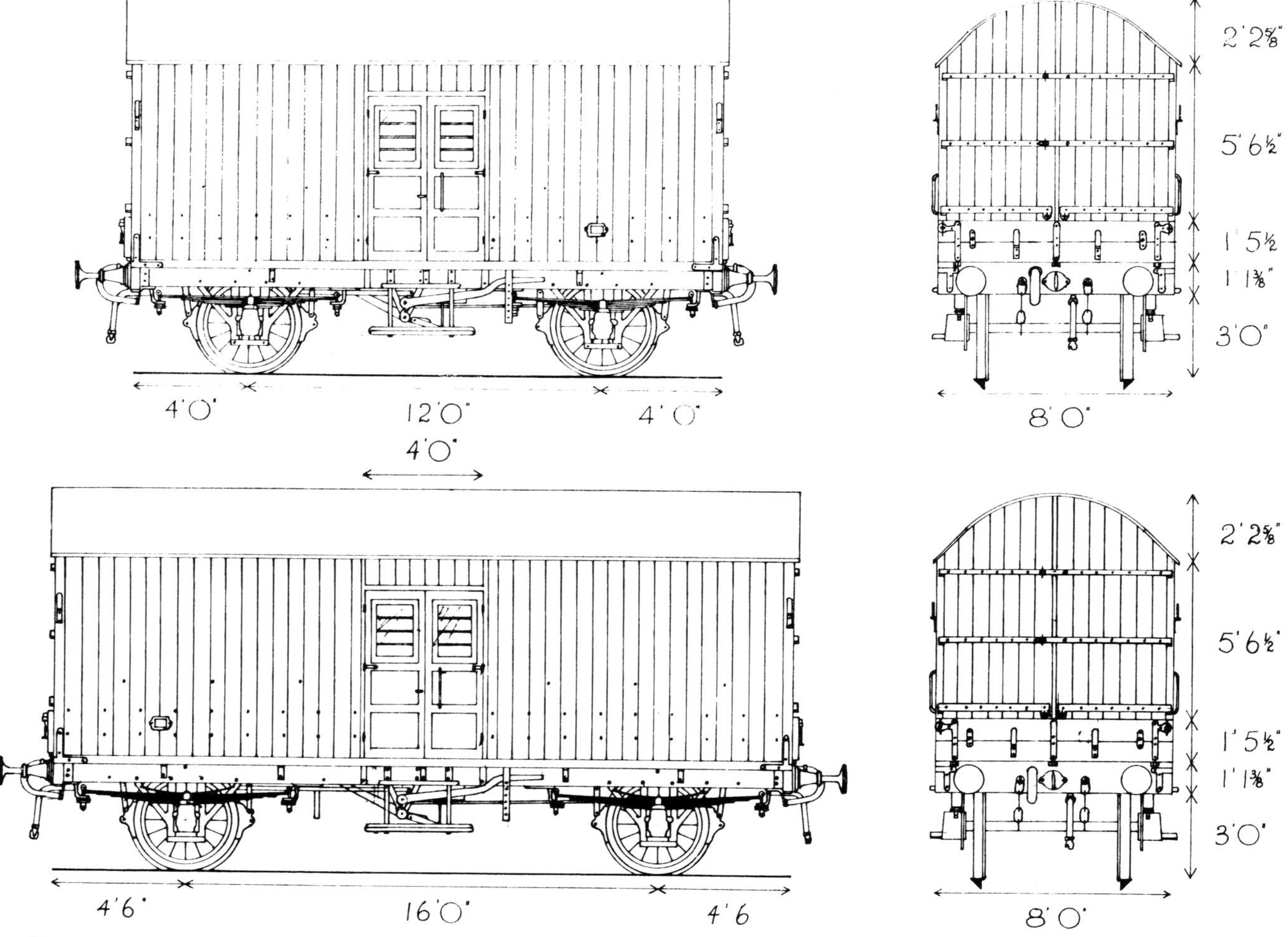

MR 20 and 25 Foot Covered Carriage Trucks

PROTOTYPE DETAILS

Diag	Length (ft-in)	Height (ft-in)	Lot	Built	MR Nos	LMS 1st Nos	LMS 2nd Nos	Extinct by:
D402	20-0	13-3	59	1884	90, 97	-	-	Pre '23
			187 (Part)	1888	4, 18, 24, 37, 53/5, 63/8, 88, 94, 103/6/22	653/7/60/3/5/6/8/9/73/80/3/4	37077-8	'35
D403	25-0	13-3	121	C'85	22/3, 44, 101	659/64/78	-	Pre '32
			148	C'86	74, 96	670/4	-	Pre '32
			277	1891	206/15/22, 491	691/8	-	Pre '32
			351	C'95	544-5	720/1	35084	3/35
			373	1896	213/6/8, 546	689/92/4, 722	37085	10/34
D406	20-0	12-8	187 (part)	1888	21, 56, 77, 98, 100/2/5/23-5 +	658/67/71/6/7/9/82/5-7	37076	6/34
			228	1889	370-389	699-718	37079-83	3/36
D407	25-0	12-8	516	1901	1/3/5/6, 104, 214/7/9-21	651/2/4/5/81/90/3/5-7	37086-95	11/46

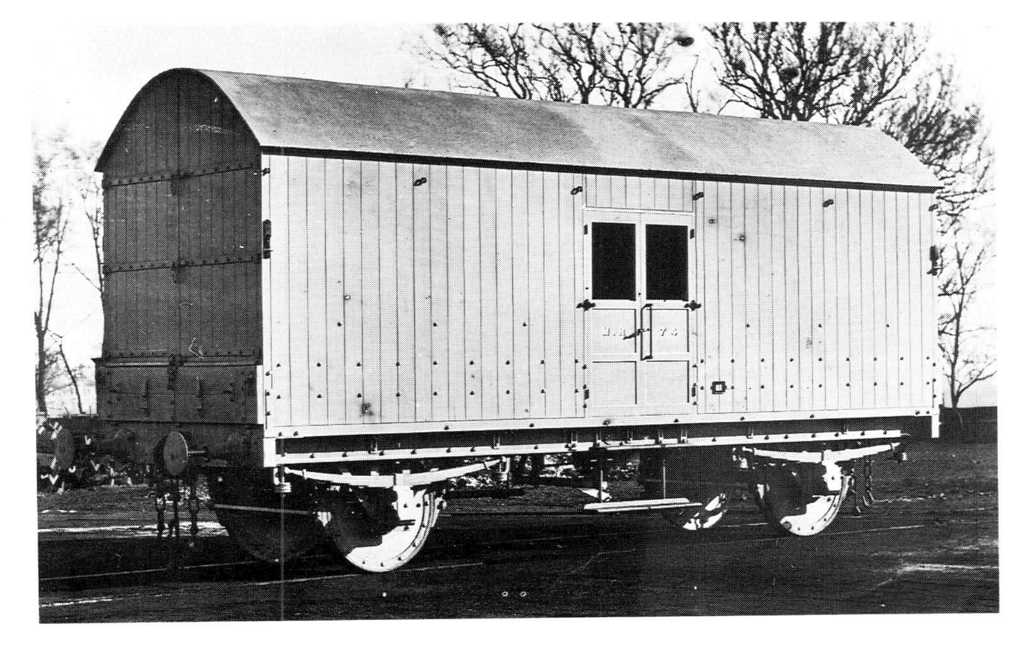

A high roofed 25 foot long Midland Railway covered carriage truck No 74 to diagram D403 generally similar in construction to the shorter version to diagram 402. It appears to have been built without a hand brake lever. (G Warburton collection)

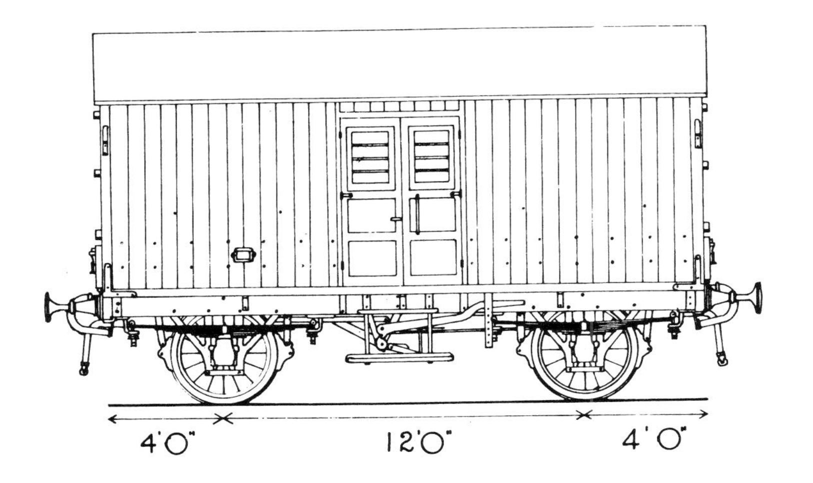

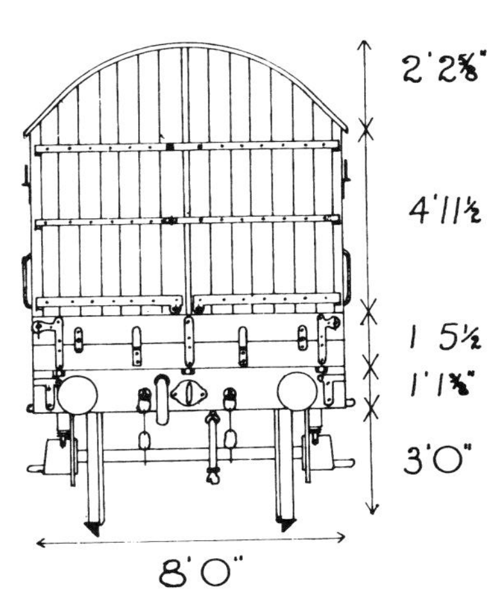

North Staffs Six Wheel Aeroplane Van

At some time during the Great War, the NSR converted eleven 35ft 6in long six wheel third class coaches into an ambulance train. Ten of these were later converted into what NSR diagram 10 describes as aeroplane or milk Vans. It is presumed that the compartments were removed during the first conversion, and the second involved fitting two large outside-sliding doors to each side, and three-part doors to each end. The torpedo vents on the roof seem not to have been removed at any time and were located in (presumably two) rows of six, centred over the original doors on either side.

An Up NSR milk train on L&NWR metals near Shilton in 1921. Behind LNWR No 1978 Merlin *4-4-0 of the Renown class, the first vehicle is an aeroplane van converted from a six wheel third class coach, followed by two six wheel NSR milk vans (see page 109) and a LNWR/WCJS 45 foot passenger brake van. (LGRP, courtesy LT George)*

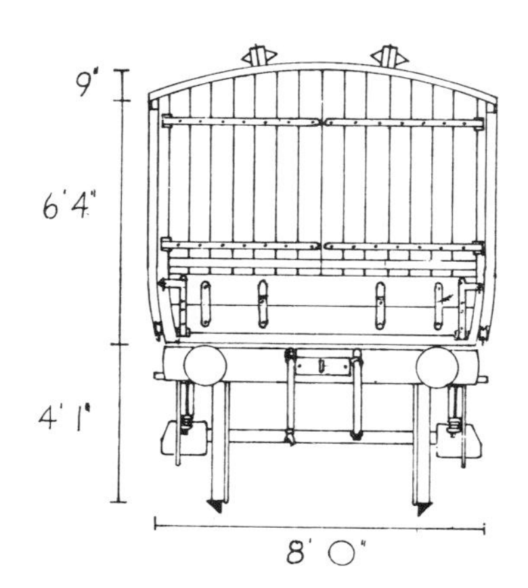

PROTOTYPE DETAILS

NSR Nos	LMS 1st Nos	LMS 2nd Nos
060/92, 0262/5/6/70, 0326/65/6/72	06002/3/11/52/3/5	38688-38693

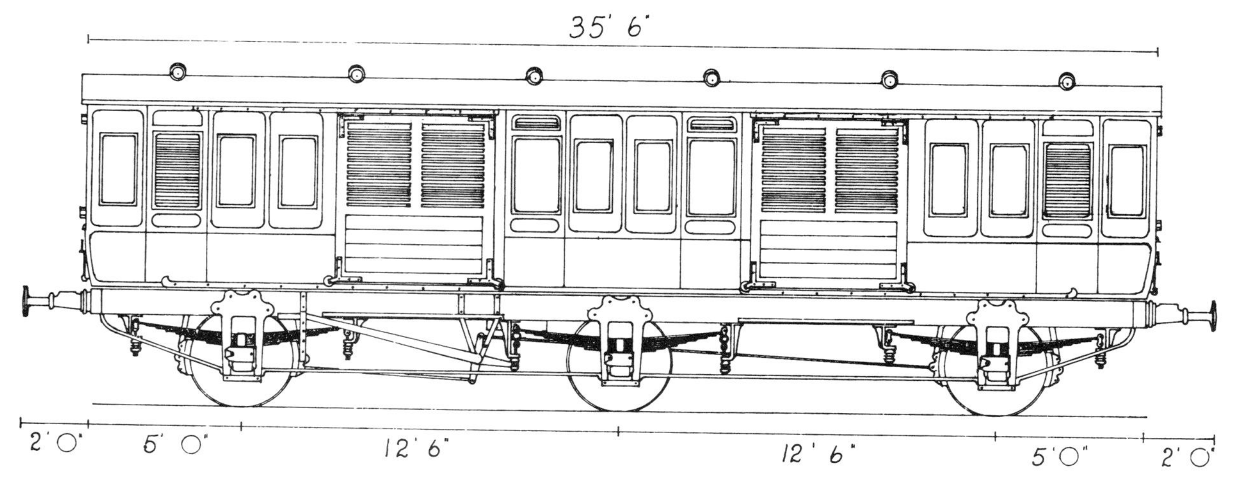

N.B. ALL WINDOWS ARE EITHER SHEETED IN OR PAINTED OVER.

Great Central Covered Carriage Truck

Similar four wheeled covered carriage trucks were built to two diagrams for the Great Central Railway, the only significant difference being ten of 5 ton and six of 8 ton load capacity. During the GC period their bodies were varnished teak with black underframe and, when freshly outshopped, white roofs. Lettering was in gold or yellow around 4½ inches high. Under LNER ownership they were painted brown with white lettering including the letter code LCK.

Further vehicles of the 5 ton design were built for the CLC and those taken over by the LNER coded 1265/7. Originally piped for Westinghouse brake, this was subsequently removed. Through steam pipe was added during the early life of the vehicles.

PROTOTYPE DETAILS

GC Nos	LNER Nos	GC Diag/ LNER code	Built	Year	Load (tons)
975-980	629-634	1U5/5203	Brown Marshall	1905	8
1513-1522	637-646	1U4/5202	Gorton	1899	5

CLC Nos	Built	Year
436-441	Brown Marshall	1897
58	Gorton	1901
66	Gorton	1902
63, 64, 67	Gorton	1903

Great Central 5 ton covered carriage truck as LNER No 646 post 1936 lettering style and probably photographed after World War 2. Note the double steps below the sliding side doors. (AG Ellis, courtesy B Ellis)

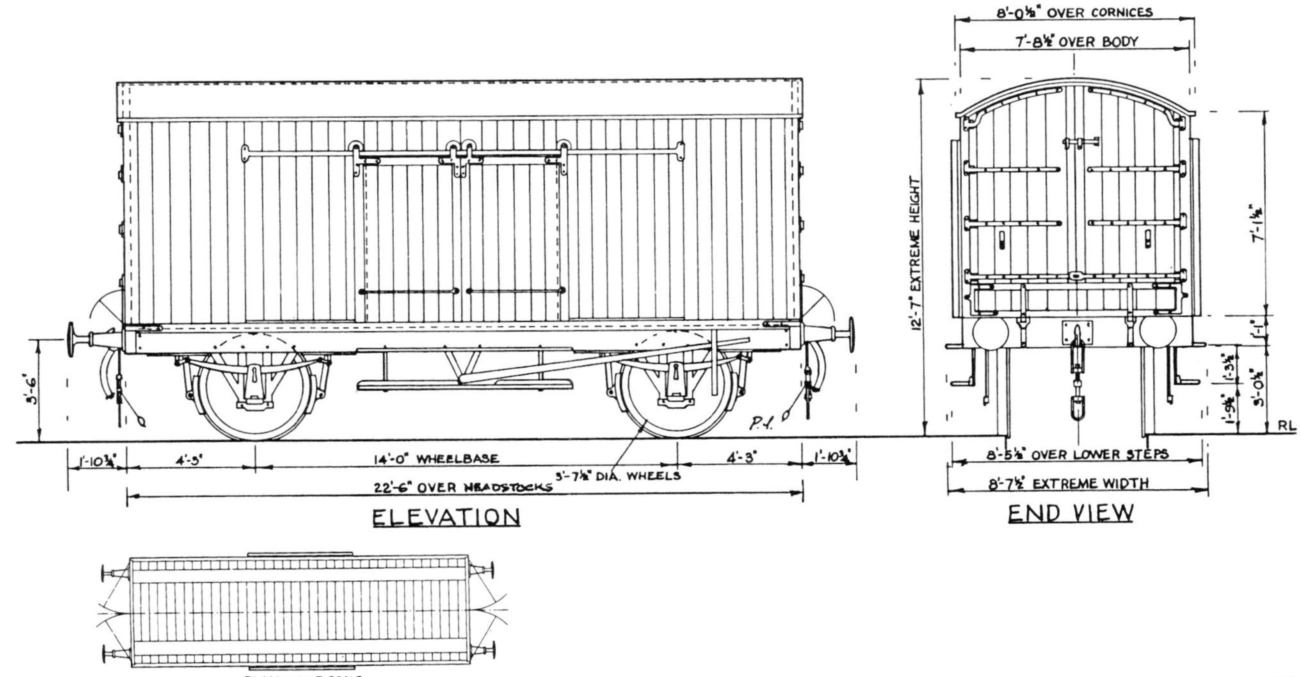

Great Eastern Railway Six Wheel Covered Carriage Truck

The Great Eastern Railway introduced a six-wheel design of covered carriage truck in 1910, when five were built to diagram 39E. In 1912 thirty more were added and all were later coded 6186 by the LNER. As well as being able to convey carriages and motor cars, loaded through the end doors, the inclusion of roof and louvred side ventilators and the provision of side doors, together with natural and artificial lighting enabled them to be commandeered for the transport of fruit and flowers, important seasonal trades in East Anglia and Lincolnshire.

Originally gas lit, towards the end of their lives this was removed. To give access to the roof to attend to the lamps, steps and handrails were fitted at one end only. At the opposite end there was a hand brake lever on only one side.

Ex-Great Eastern Railway six wheel covered carriage truck as LNER No XCK 853 at Essendine (GN) in the late 1930s with vertical bars in the windows. The LH and RH inscriptions read:

NOT TO BE LOADED TO MERSEY DOCK ESTATE
NOT TO BE WORK OVER THE S.E&C. SECTION OF THE SOUTHERN RAILWAY, EXCEPT BETWEEN HOLBORN LOW LEVEL AND CLAPHAM JUNCTION OR VICTORIA.

LENGTH INSIDE – 31FT 01IN
WIDTH OVER BODY – 8FT 8½IN
EXTREME WIDTH – 9FT 0IN
WHEELBASE – 22FT 6IN
LOAD - 8 - TONS
TARE – 13 – 11 – 2

(GY Hemingway)

PROTOTYPE DETAILS

GER Nos	LNER Nos	Extinct
1888-1922	853-887	1956

An unidentified former GER six wheel covered carriage truck towards the end of its days, the bodywork showing signs of having been patched up. Note foreshortened foot boards to give access to the hand brake lever at far end and the absence of the gas tank. (P. Tatlow collection)

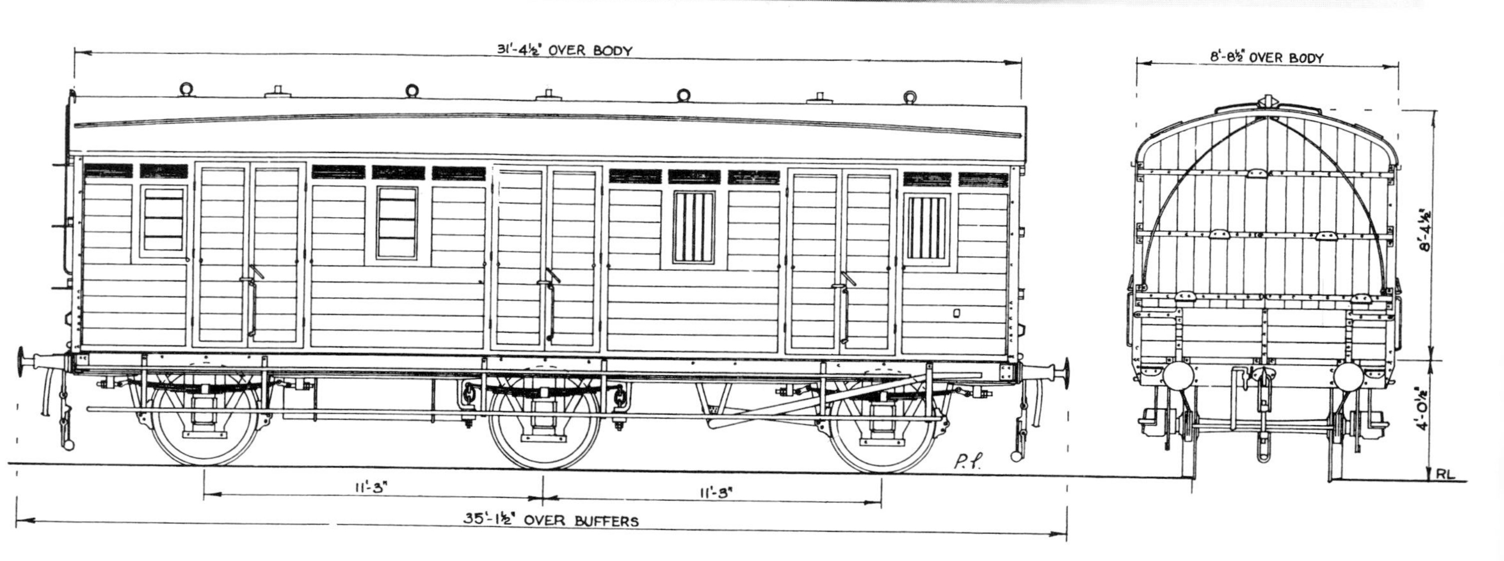

North British Bogie Covered Carriage Truck

Two 49 foot 6 inch long bogie covered carriage trucks, Nos 124 and 125 were built by the North British at its Carriage and Wagon Works at Cowlairs in Glasgow in 1914. Typical of their type, they were fitted with both vacuum and Westinghouse automatic brake systems, together with through steam pipe, but no lighting. The only unusual feature was a steel plate floor, provided perhaps to afford an increased headroom of two inches inside the van body. According to LNER diagram 102B (code 3048), the load capacity was 10 tons and tare weight 23 tons 10 cwt 2 qtrs. They may have been used for the conveyance of theatrical scenery, as much a road carriages. Over the years the half round beading covering the joint between the framing and horizontal planking will have been discarded.

Following take over by the LNER in 1923, these vehicles were letter coded BCK and renumbered 1007 and 1008

Left *Ex-NB bogie covered carriage truck as British Railways No E1008 taken at Bridlington 23 May 1953. (GR Driffield)*

BCK
1007
LENGTH INSIDE 49ft 2ins
WIDTH OVER BODY 7ft 6ins
EXT. WIDTH 8ft 6ins
LOAD 10 TONS
TARE 23-10-2

Roof radius 5'8" to outside

N.E
BCK
1007

6' 11¼"
1' 9¾"
4' 1"
8' 6"

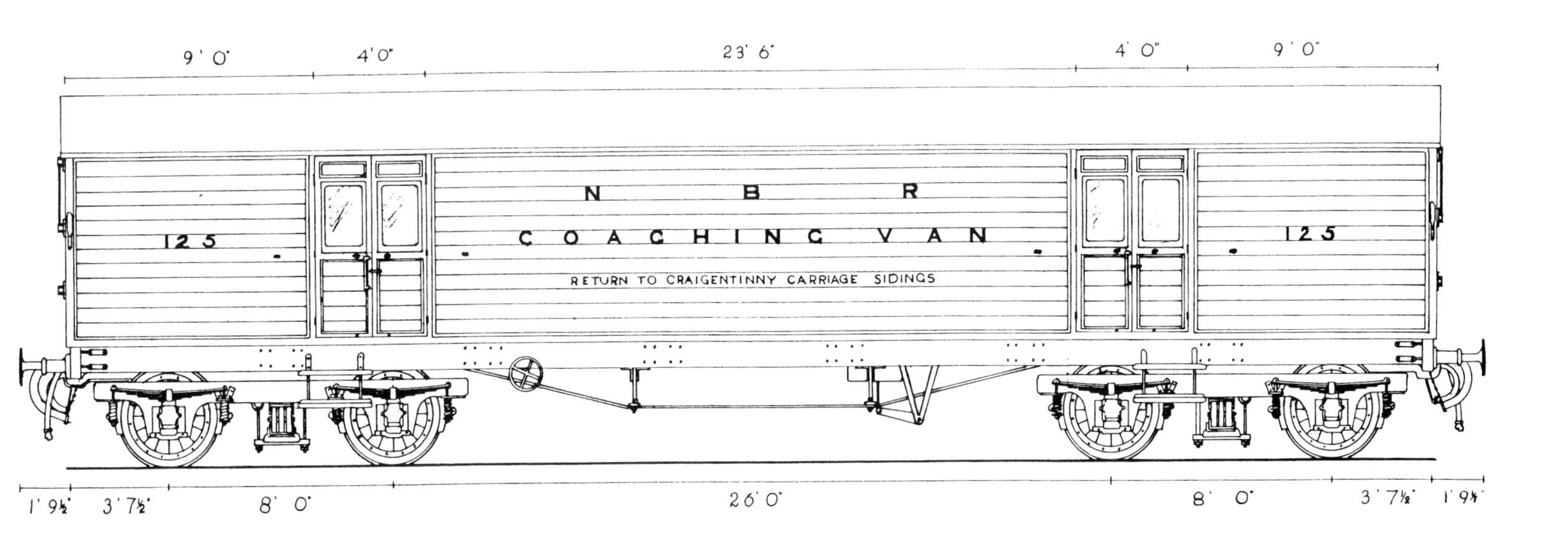

LNER Extra Long Covered Carriage Truck

The move away from Mansell wheel centres for non-passenger coaching stock led to an increase in permitted axle load and hence the adoption of longer wheel base vehicles, with typically former six wheeled types now being achieved on only two axles. Such was the extra long covered carriage truck introduced by the LNER in 1939 to diagram 6, sixty of which were built at York that year, Nos 1242 to 1301, and letter coded LLCK and telegraph coded 8006. After the war 57 more were also produced there in 1950 under the auspices of BR, as Nos E1306 to E1362. The body was 37ft 6in long by 8 foot wide and provided with three sets of sliding doors per side. It was carried on a 23ft 6in wheel base underframe.

An LNER design of extra long covered carriage truck built by BR at York in 1950. Although to a pre-nationalisation design, it appears to have been given the prefix B to its number 1312. (PW Bartlett collection)

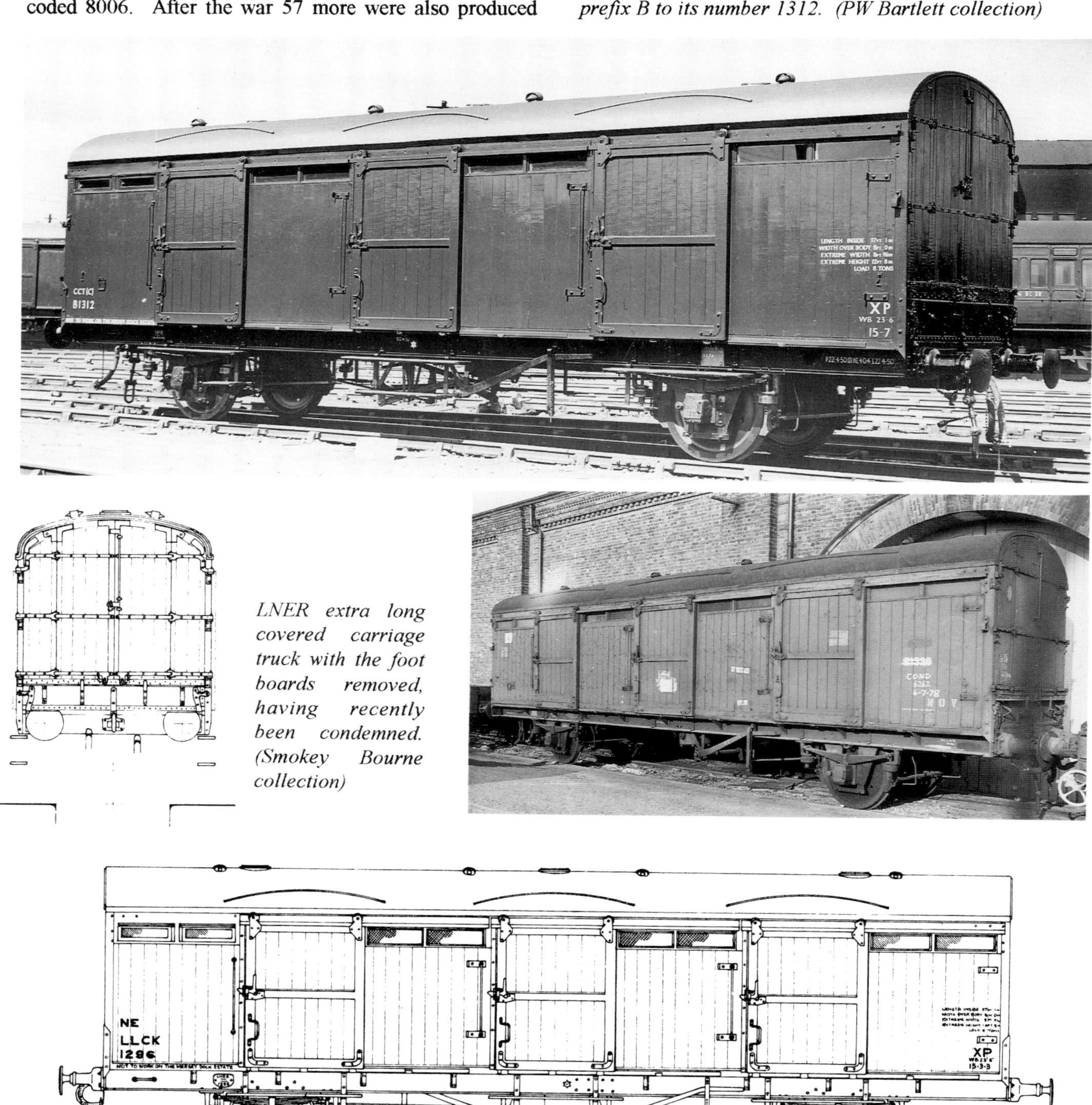

LNER extra long covered carriage truck with the foot boards removed, having recently been condemned. (Smokey Bourne collection)

Great Western 3 Ton Covered Carriage Truck Python

In 1906 the Great Western introduced two series of 27ft 4½in long covered carriage trucks, coded Python. Those to diagram P13 had a 19 foot wheel base, whereas the wheel base of the second batch to diagram P14 was one foot less. Eight years later a further batch was constructed to diagram P19 with an eighteen foot wheelbase, but now 28ft 6in long over headstocks. Diagram P20 covers a single vehicle, No 580, with a strengthened floor for the conveyance of circus elephants. All bore a similarity in style and the composite drawing shows the various features.

PROTOTYPE DETAILS

Diagram	P13	P14	P19/P20
Introduced	1906	1906	1914
Length over headstocks	27'-4½"	27'-4½"	28'-6"
Wheelbase	19'-0"	18'-0"	18'-0"
Nos	521-530	531-560	561-579/580

Ex-GW covered carriage truck Python No W556 to Lot 1197 diagram P14 with 18 foot wheel-base, seen here in BR ownership. (PW Bartlett collection)

Great Western Python A No 580 to diagram P20 at Kingswear on 22 August 1947. This vehicle was specially strengthened to enable it to carry elephants. Note the deep window lights and the shirt button monogram on the side. (G Warburton collection)

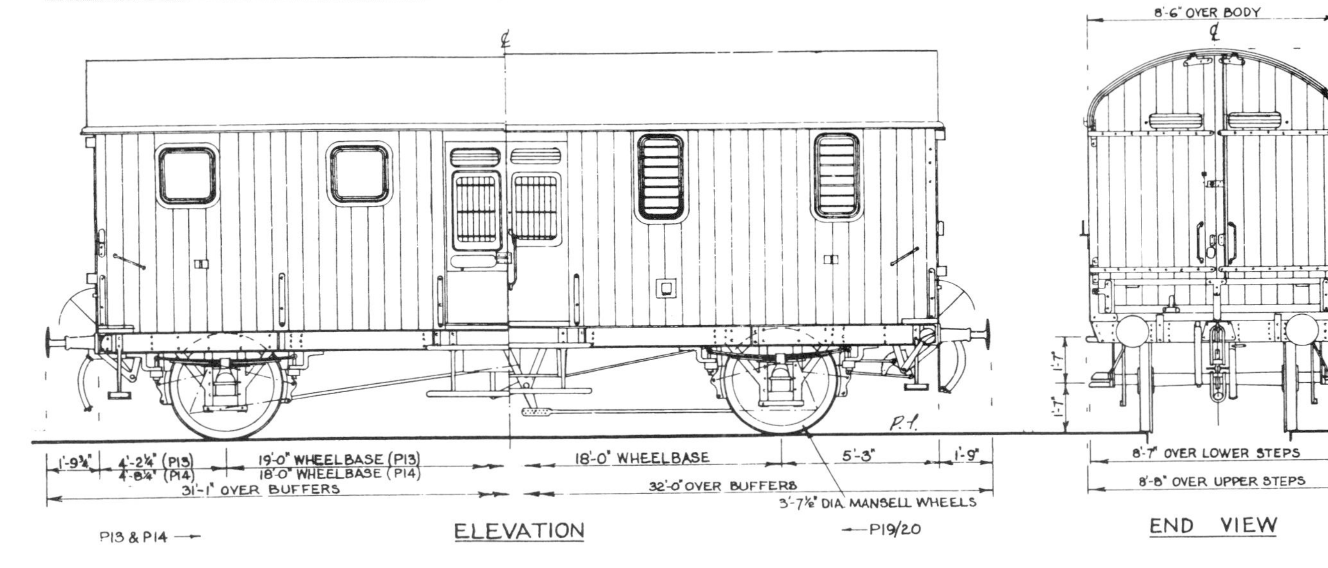

Southern Railway Four Wheel 32 Foot Long Covered Carriage Truck

The covered carriage truck version of the SE&CR passenger luggage/parcels van was developed by the Southern Railway and introduced in 1928 as utility vans to Diagram 3101. From then on 390 were built over the years up to 1955 with similar variations to the body cladding, although most were either the original 6½ inch wide planks, or during the BR period plywood. Apart from the initial batch of 50 built by the Midland Railway Carriage & Wagon Co, Ashford built most of the remainder, Eastleigh assisting with the bodywork of some and Lancing undertaking the last order for 50. As they were withdrawn from revenue earning service, many were converted for departmental use as mess vans and barrier wagons etc.

Recently repainted SR utility van No S2372, built in 1931, in green livery still and coded COVCAR and in smaller letters CCT on 29 October 1949 at Eastleigh. Note the full width and height end doors to enable a motor vehicle or other large object to be loaded. (AE West, courtesy MS King)

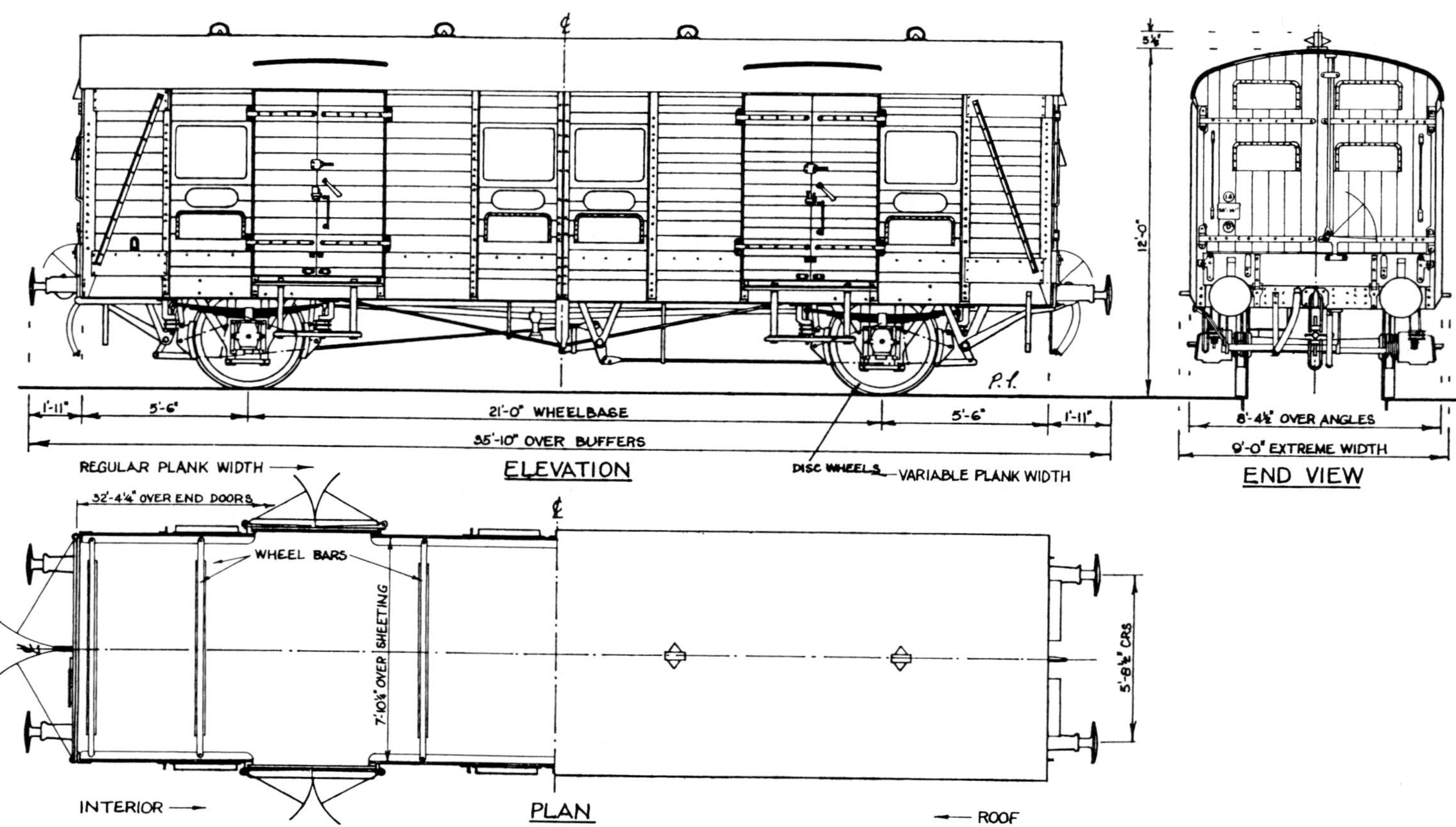

Southern Railway Four Wheel 32 Foot Long Covered Carriage Truck

PROTOTYPE DETAILS

Built	Running Nos	Cladd'g (in)	Ext't by
1928	2023-2072	6½	7/64
1929	2251-2280	6½	12/62
1931	2371-2410	6½	3/70
1931/2	2411-2460	6½	3/70
1933	2241-2250	6½	7/69
1933	2491-2500	6½	3/70
1938	1731-1780	3½/6½ + 6½ doors	11/82
1951	1411-1450	Ply	1/86
1951	1977-1991	Ply	12/82
1951	2006-2020	Ply	2/86
1951	2073-2082	Ply	6/82
1951	2171-2180	Ply	10/82
1951	2231-2240	Ply	2/86
1955	2501-2550	Ply	2/86

Plywood bodied utility van No S2178S was built in 1951 and shows the revised lettering panel with the number divided by the diagonal framing. Note that the doors continue to be planked. (G Warburton collection)

One of the first batch of vans to be built following World War 2 in 1951 and with the fixed elements of the sides clad in plywood. Note oval the chalk boards under the windows painted black. (BR, SR)

Rhymney and Taff Vale Covered Carriage Trucks

Rhymney Railway Six Wheel Covered Carriage Truck

This single example of the Rhymney Railway's six wheel covered carriage truck was built in 1911 and given the No 36. The hand brake operates on the centre wheels only, the Westinghouse brake is applied the outer wheels and through vacuum pipe is provided. The height of the vehicle was reduced by 8 inches in December 1922 by altering the dimensions indicated by * on the drawing. It was renumbered by the GW as 40 and withdrawn December 1935.

Taff Vale Railway 5 Ton Covered Carriage Truck

The Taff Vale's 5 ton covered carriage trucks Nos 412 &413 were built in 1897 and 414-417 in 1905, all at Cathays. These were renumbered by the GW as Nos 63-5/7/9/70 and were extinct by July 1948. Vacuum and hand brake with Westinghouse and steam through pipes were fitted. An illustration of an ex Taff Vale covered carriage truck as GW No 70 will be found on page 71 of *A pictorial record of GWR coaches, Part 1* by JH Russell, OPC, 1972.

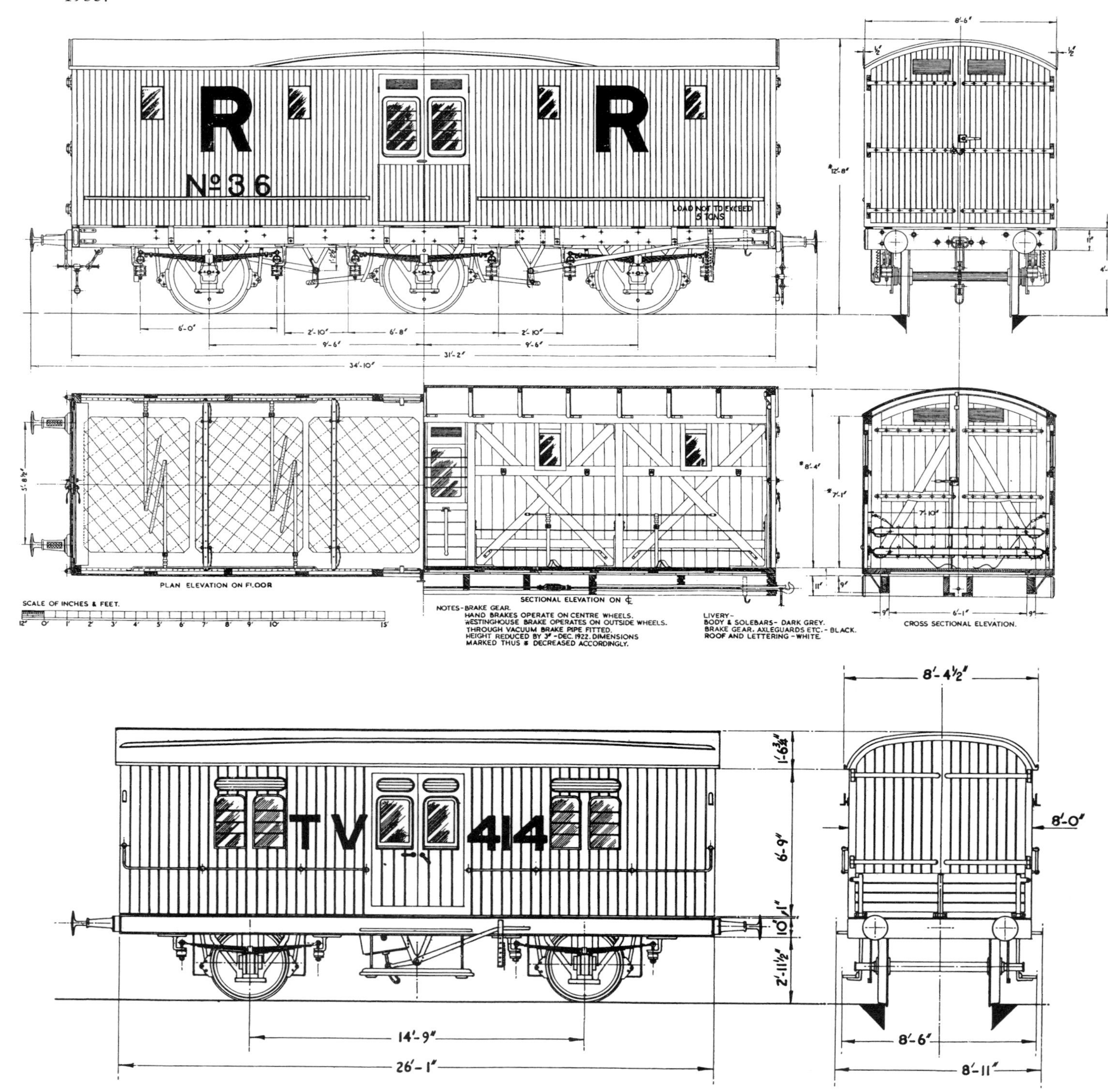

Caledonian Railway Carriage Truck and Fish and Game Van

The original drawing for this vehicle by J. Wright and Sons is dated 16 February 1871, and it is reasonable to expect the vehicle(s) to have entered service later that year, or early the next year.
Most open carriage trucks had similar features. First, there are two transverse wooden beams which can be fixed in a variety of positions, to suit the length of carriage being transported, by means of holes and pins in a plate on the top of the sides and a clip and ratchet on the outside of the sides. There is a single, open ended bracket on each beam which located the carriage wheels laterally. Only one bracket was provided so that a variety of track widths could be accommodated, simply by slewing the carriage. The carriage wheels were lashed to the beams with leather straps to provide additional stability. Normally the carriage shafts were removed and carried underneath the carriage. A runway was provided on this vehicle for carriage wheels, made of 1 inch thick wooden slats. There are also ribs covering the joints between the end six floor planks, at either end of the vehicle. It is presumed that these ribs were footholds for the men manhandling the loads.
The framing to sides and ends is flush with the slatted boarding on the back and 2 inches proud of it on the outside face. The ends are hinged to the floor and drop down when released. When in the down position they are carried by the brackets mounted over the buffer casings.
This type of vehicle was also suitable for carrying fish, and therefore game traffic, when not in use as a carriage truck. It is a mystery why it was designated a van in this service, particularly as the previous Fish & Game van was called a truck. It is suspected that these vehicles would have been painted in a semi-passenger livery of chocolate and yellow lettering.

CR 3 ton open carriage truck No 1618. Note the alarm cord attached to the side and the vacuum brake pipe standard, presumably capable of being folded down to allow vehicle to be loaded over the end. (British Railways)

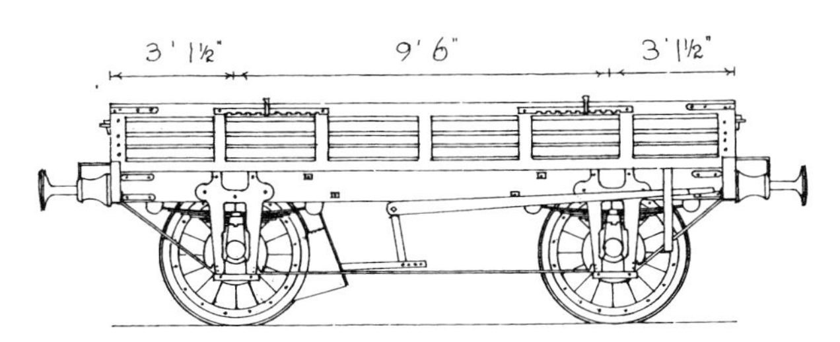

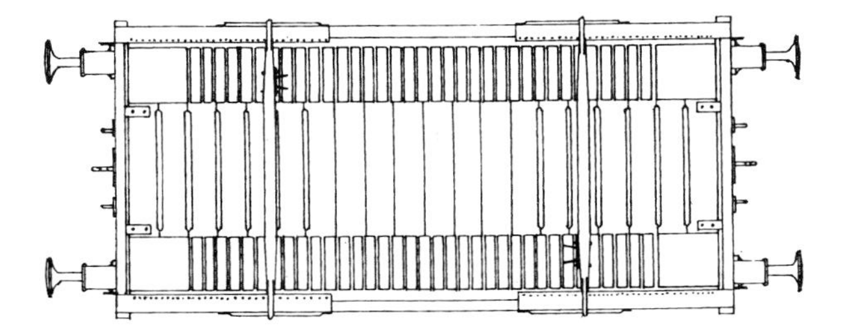

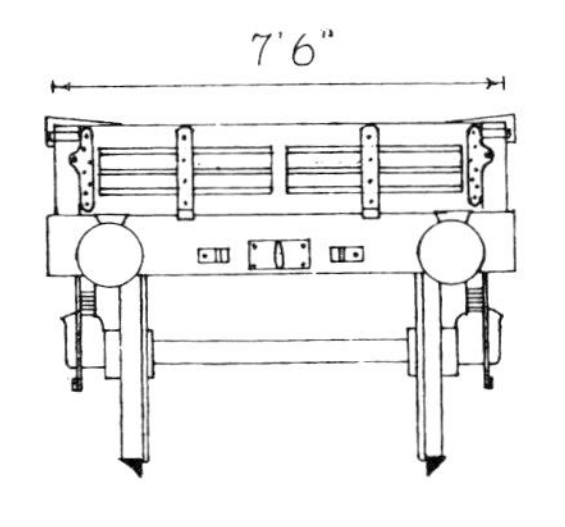

This photograph shows an open carriage truck behind a very early rail bus on the Connel Ferry rail motor service. It has a slightly lower end door but this may have been a modification for the Connel Ferry Service. (AG Ellis)

LMS Open Carriage Truck

Already having inherited many pre-grouping open carriage trucks, it was rare for the grouping companies to build this type, covered ones being preferred, but the LMS built some, at Derby, with a 20 foot wheelbase in 1939 and 1940. A thoroughly modern all steel design to diagram D2027 at 28 feet over headstocks, it was longer than most previous examples. It has been suggested that the impending military traffic for the war with Germany was the cause, if so, however, one would expect the other companies to do likewise, but they did not.

PROTOTYPE DETAILS

Lot	1185	1263
Built	1939	1940
Nos	41200-24	41225-39

Three views of LMS open carriage truck No 41211 at Cardington on 18 October 1939 when very new, having been built at Derby that year. Note the clean lines and use of welded construction. (AE West, courtesy of MS King)

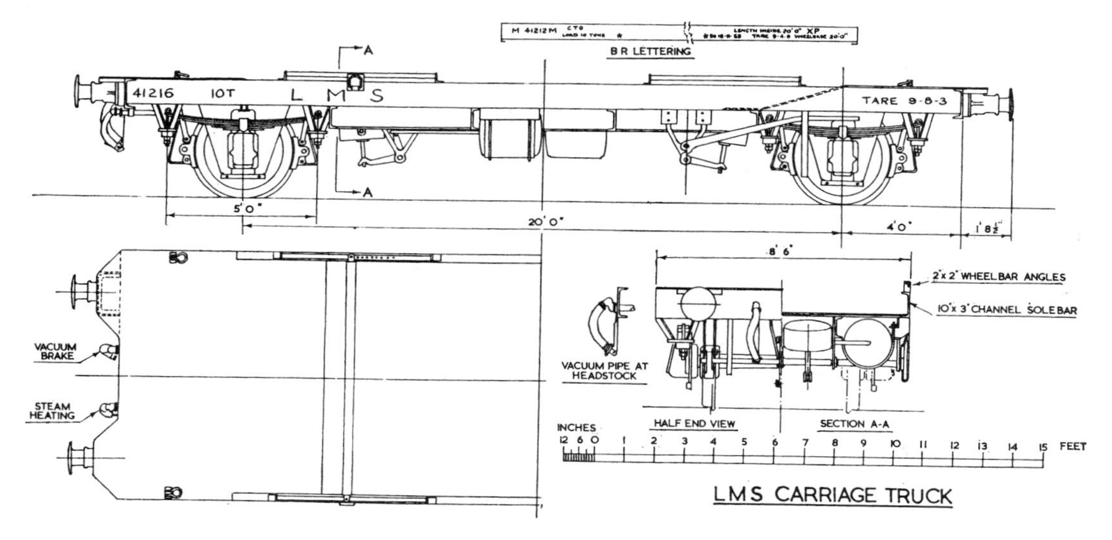

Lancashire and Yorkshire Bogie Open Carriage Truck

Ten bogie carriage trucks were ordered (V16) in 1900 with timber frames while a further four with steel frames were added in 1913. The latter were 8ft wide rather than the original 7ft 9in. With their 6ft 6in wheelbase bogies, the underframes were almost identical to contemporary carriage stock apart from the addition of the statutory hand brake. They were employed mainly by theatrical parties for the movement of scenery, suitably sheeted over. The diagram book shows the 1913 vehicles to be numbered (confusingly) 129-132 but they certainly carried 166-169, the lower numbers being carried by 4 wheel carriage trucks. After the grouping they all received crimson livery and 'first' LMS numbers and half of them lasted to the outbreak of war with one of the original batch lasting to 1947.

PROTOTYPE DETAILS

Built	1900	1913
Frame/Width (ft-in)	Timber/7-9	Steel/8-0
L&Y Nos	153-162	166-169
LMS 1st Nos	5713-5721	5700, 5726-8
LMS 2nd Nos	41989-96	41997-9
Extinct by	1947	1949

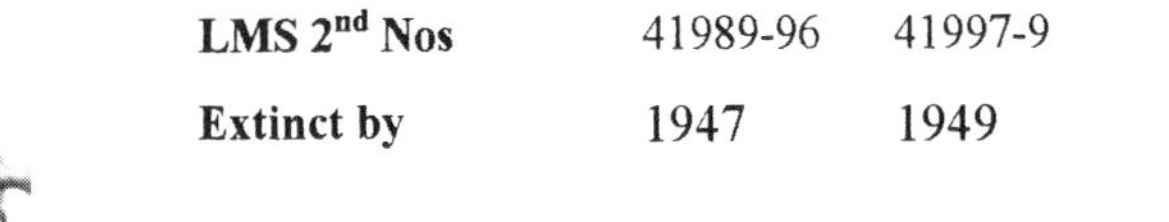

Above – *LYR official view of No. 157 painted in carmine lake with gilt transfers (BC Lane coll)*

Below – *End view of ex-L&Y bogie open scenery truck No 41999. (AE West, courtesy MS King)*

Below – *Ex-L&Y 16 ton 45 foot bogie open scenery truck No 41999 at Cardington on 8 March 1940. (AE West, courtesy MS King)*

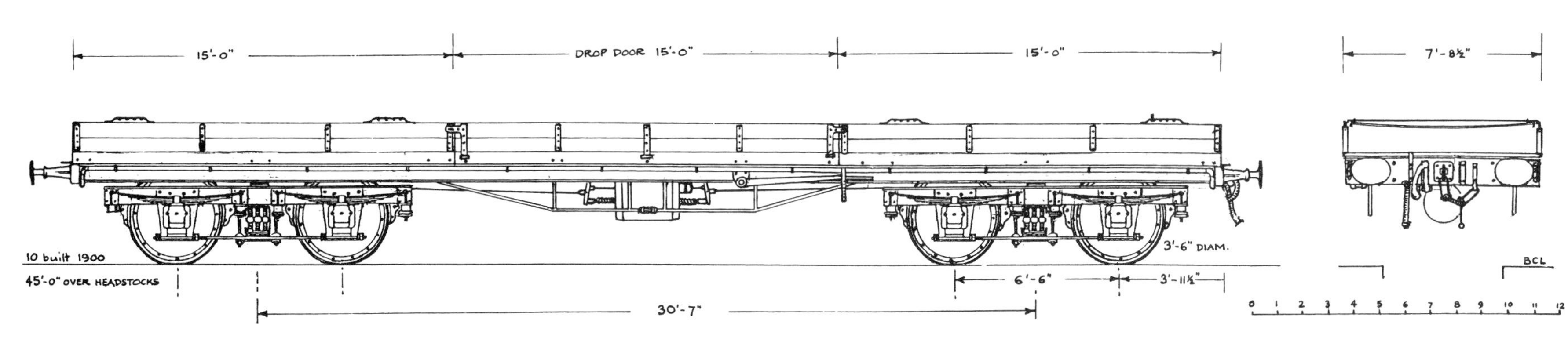

LNWR 21 Foot Open Carriage Truck to Diagram 466

Between 1899 and 1909 the LNWR built 312 open carriage trucks on a standard 21 foot underframe. A further 28 appeared in 1913 and a solitary example in 1920. They had wheel plates over the buffers to enable vehicles to loaded from end docks and some had folding down sides. Most were withdrawn by 1954, but one survived, on paper at least, until 1963.

PROTOTYPE DETAILS

LNWR (Sample, add 11000 after 1910)	LMS 1st Nos	LMS 2nd Nos
1, 8, 95, 150/85, 222/70/80, 332/9, 457, 583, 625, 1016-1048	4842-5177	40941, 41375, 41381-41517, 41538-41674

LNWR open carriage truck No 280 with its hand brake lever painted white to demonstrate the action of applying the brake. As the lever is lowered at the right hand end, rotation around the fulcrum below the letter A, painted on the solebar, forces up the short left hand lever, in a 'break back' action. This is attached to a cross shaft the rotation of which applies the brake shoe on the far side. Note this vehicle has fixed sides. Its number was increased to 11280 by the LNWR in 1910 and renumbered 4987 by the LMS and in 1932 41601. (D Jenkinson collection)

Another open carriage truck No 11442 still in LNWR livery in 1927, this time with dropsides and apparently fitted with three hole disc wheels. It shows the opposite side of the vehicle with the simple brake lever. (JP Richards, HMRS collection AAJ228)

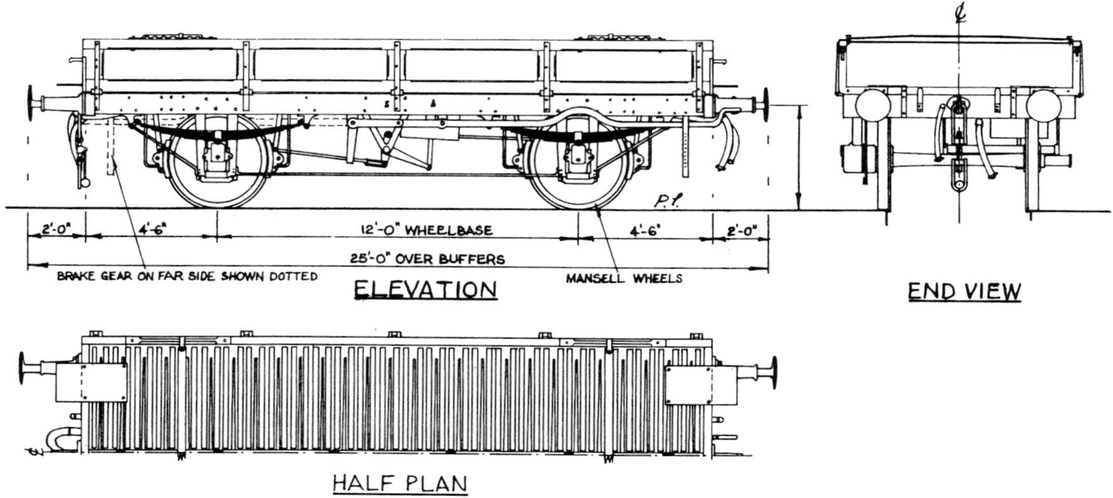

Midland Open Carriage Trucks

The Midland Railway's 5 ton 20 foot long open carriage trucks to diagram D409 were introduced in 1903 and construction continued until 1920, by which time 125 had been built. The last 52 built after 1915 had steel underframes, omitted the secondary springs and were rated at 6 tons. Apart from the possibility of Nos 273-322 of 1903, MR numbers are unknown. Three post 1932 LMS numbers, however, were 41759, 41788 and 41796 (1st LMS Nos u/k, 740 and 775), but may have included 41706-825.

Furness Railway Carriage Trucks

In 1870, six carriage trucks, similar to the drawing were added to the existing stock of four . They were built by the Metropolitan Carriage & Wagon Co, Birmingham, at a cost of £92 each. A further six similar vehicles were ordered in 1872 at the same cost, so it is assumed it was a repeat order. It is unlikely that any of these vehicles became part of the LMS stock at grouping, those examples noted in the diagram book prepared at the time of grouping are of later vintage.

Midland Railway 5 Ton open carriage truck built at Derby in 1904 photographed at Cardington on 30 March 1940 as LMS No 41759. Note secondary springs and bars along the top rail to which to attach the vehicle securing straps, also that the Mansell wheels have been replaced by steel disc wheels. (AE West courtesy MS King)

End of the same vehicle on the same occasion, from which the vacuum, Westinghouse and steam pipes can be seen. . (AE West courtesy MS King)

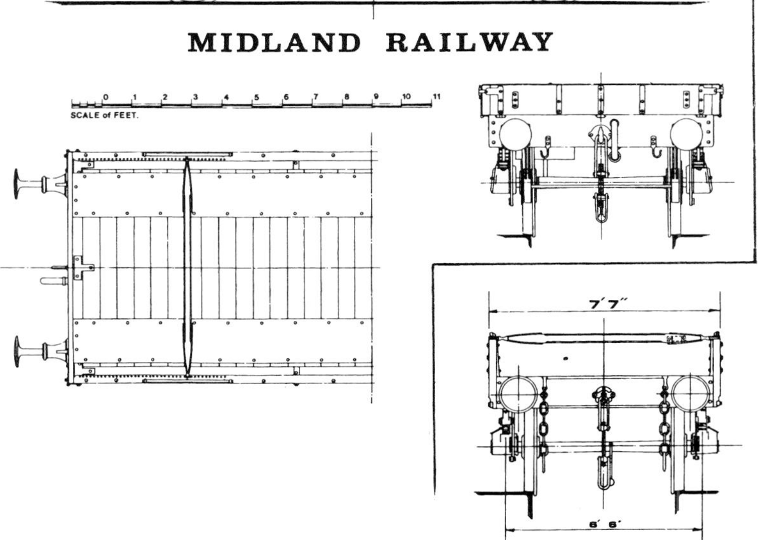

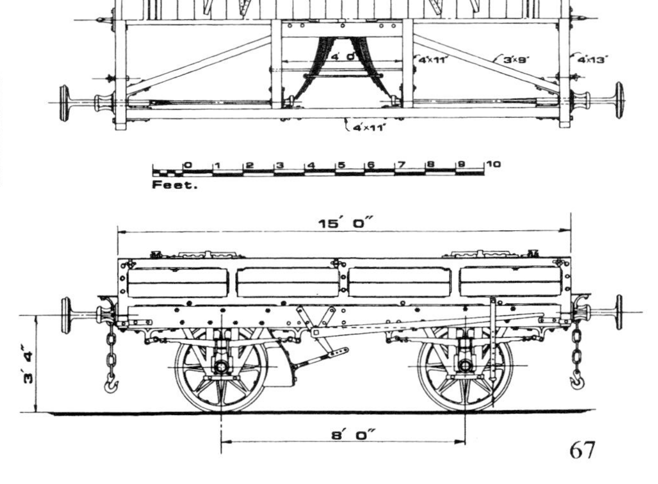

North Eastern Open Carriage Trucks

The development of open carriage trucks on the NER was mainly a progression of designs of increasing size from 15ft 6in in 1881 to a 45 foot long bogie version in 1907, although the 21 foot long four wheel version of 1901 continued to be built until 1922. Most were dual brake fitted with through steam pipes added from the early 1900s. The six wheel trucks were altered in 1917 by the removal of the drop sides and addition of four bolsters and allocated diagram for the conveyance of parts of aeroplanes in crates.

The most numerous of NER open carriage truck was the 21 foot long type to diagram 70, of which No 20 is an example built in June 1914. Note that the hand brake lever is pointed to the left had side and this will have been altered during the life of the vehicle. (IG Sadler collection)

PROTOTYPE DETAILS

Diag	Length (ft-in)	Wheel-base (ft-in)	Load (Tons)	Built	No off	Sample Nos
24	17-0	10-8	3¼	1891-99	99	65-70, 104-182
62	34-0	2 x 11-6	7	1901	5	200-4
70	21-0	12-0	5	1901-22	165	20-36, 55-62, 76-85, 128-134, 180-199
71	15-6	9-6		1881-84	19	14, 26, 32, 63/4, 83-86
120	45-0	7-0 + 21-0 + 7-0	10	1907-10	11	5, 32, 38, 65, 107, 115

DIAG 70 21'0"

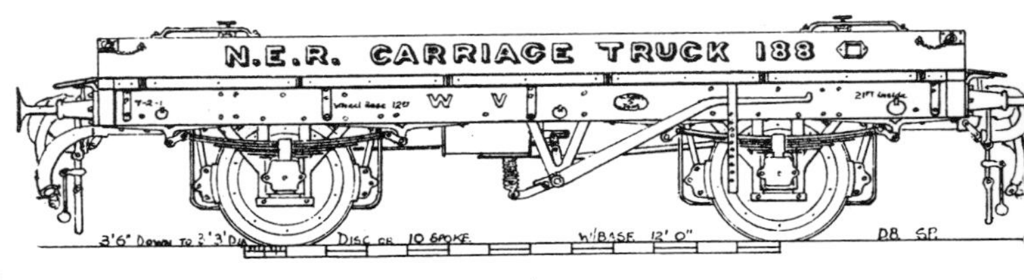

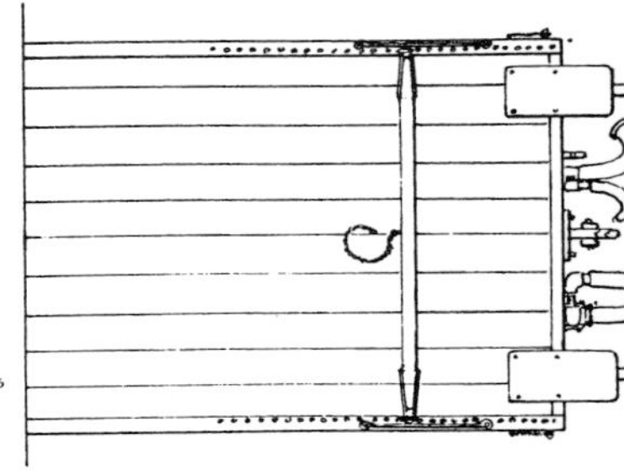

DIAG 24 17'0"

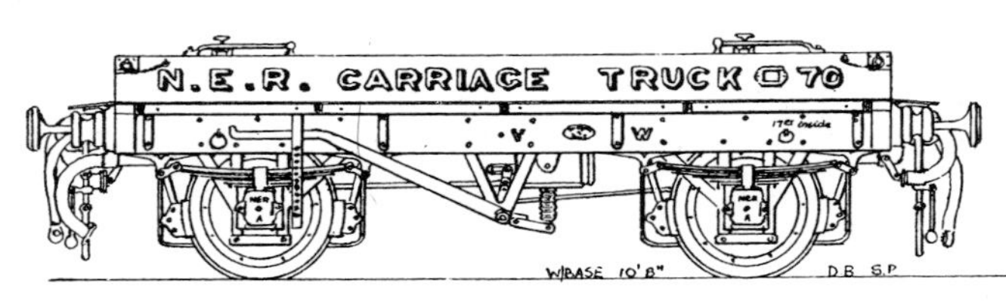

DIAG 71 15'6"

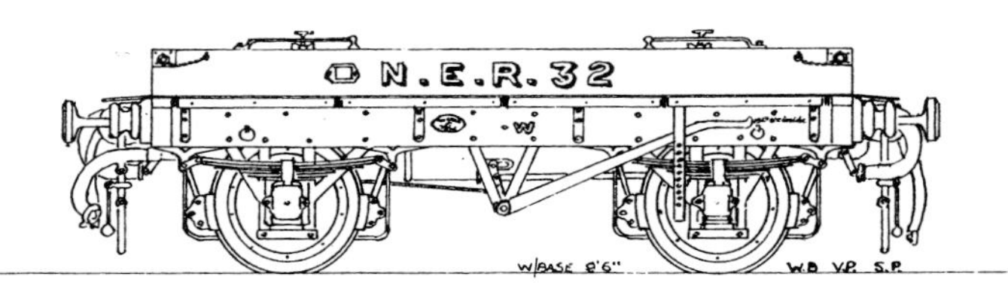

DIAG 62 34'8" JUN 1901

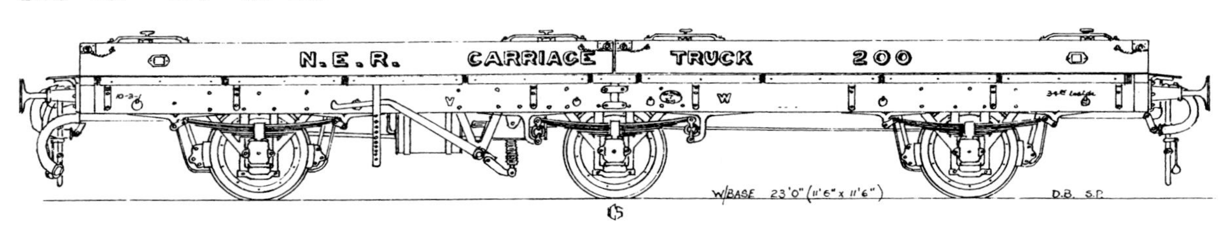

DIAG 120 45'0" JUN 1907

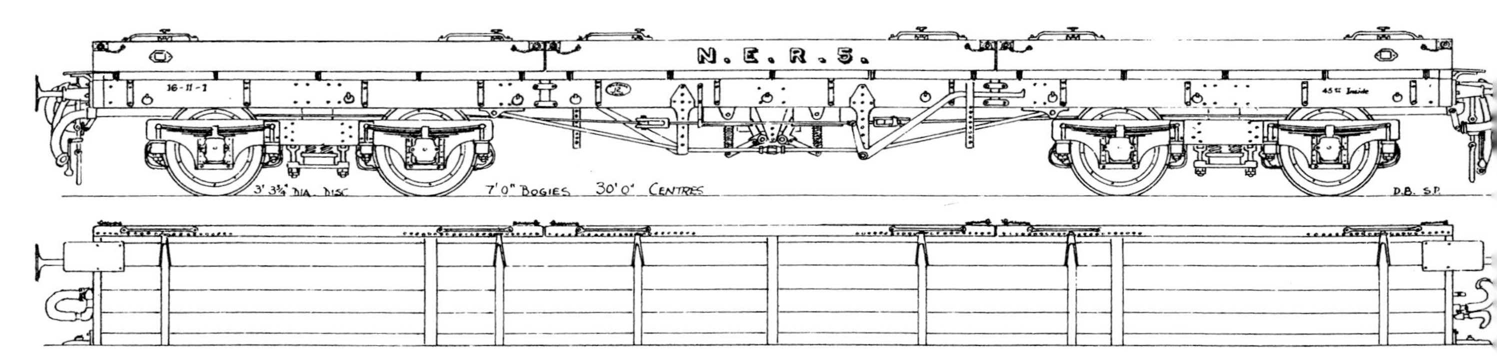

Great Western Open Carriage Truck Scorpion

Open carriage trucks to diagram P15 were 8 ton 21 foot long for the conveyance of road vehicles by passenger train. All were provided with automatic vacuum brake system and the Dean/Churchward each side hand brake. The Westinghouse brake was also fitted to those coded Scorpion B, thus enabling them to be worked to lines operating that system. This was probably removed during the 1930s. The others were known as Scorpion D. The sides are mounted on hinges, so that they can be folded down, and run-on ramps provided over the buffers to assist in end loading. The four transverse wheel bars are capable of adjustment so that they can be positioned closely each side of the road vehicle's wheels. Straps or chains are provided to secure the vehicle.

PROTOTYPE DETAILS

Lot	Type	Built	Nos
1158	B	1908	443-452
1206	B	1912	110/1/3-6/9/22-5/8-31
1206	D	1912	134-7/42
1216	D	1913	145/9-52/5/7/8/ 61/3/5/8/9/71/5
1217	B	1913	453-467
1244	D	1915	121/39-41/6/7/ 53/64/6/78-81/3/6
1245	B	1914	468-482
1255	D	1916	187-91/3-5/8/ 200/2/4/5/8/9

Top right – *Great Western open carriage truck Scorpion No W113 at Wadebridge on 15 March 1950 shows the extremely open simple nature of this type of vehicle. Nonetheless, they were originally equipped with vacuum and some also with Westinghouse brake gear to permit through running to all lines. This one was built to lot 1244 in 1915. Note the Mansell wheels centres. (AE West, courtesy MS King)*

Right – *The wheel bars are apparent in this view of the top of a P15 open carriage truck. (P Tatlow collection)*

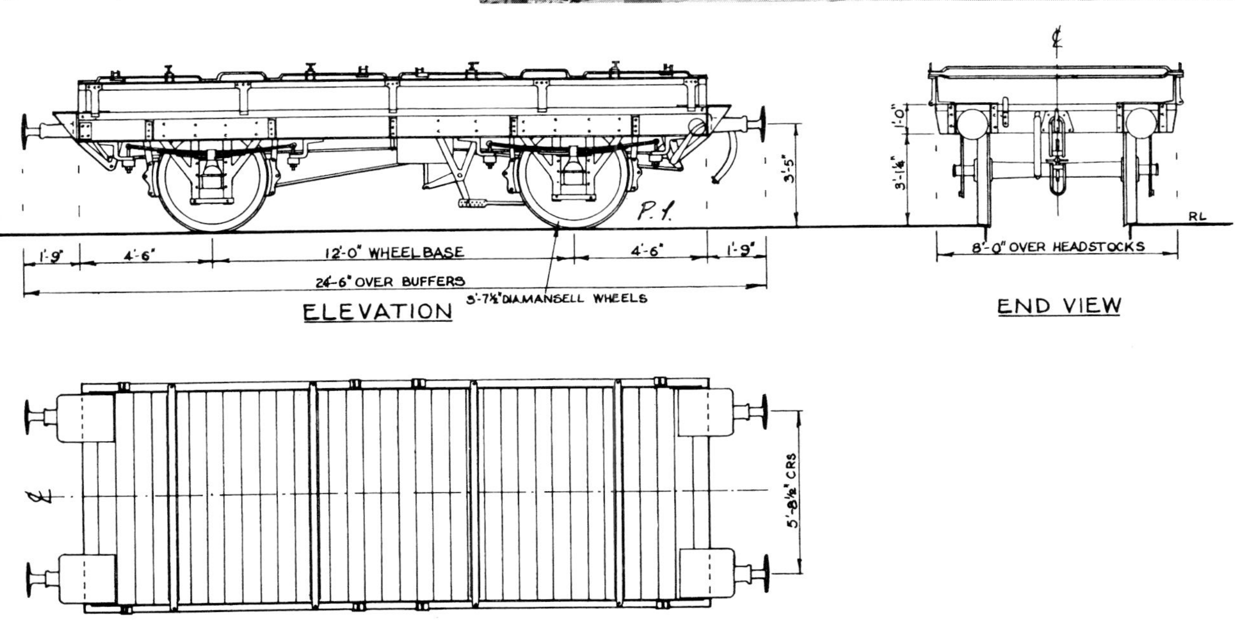

Caledonian Six Wheel Double Horsebox

These interesting horseboxes were built by the Caledonian Company's works at St Rollox, Glasgow between July 1907 and January 1908. Horseboxes, like some other types of npc vehicle, were often to be found behind the locomotive of both express and local passenger trains. The two horseboxes with groom's compartment between was mounted on a 6 wheel steel underframe, subsequently used for other 6 wheel non-passenger coaching stock designs. Although a Westinghouse line, the Caley fitted dual brakes.

PROTOTYPE DETAILS

CR Nos	LMS 1st Nos	LMS 2nd Nos	Extinct
118-141	6823-6846	43739-43761	1959

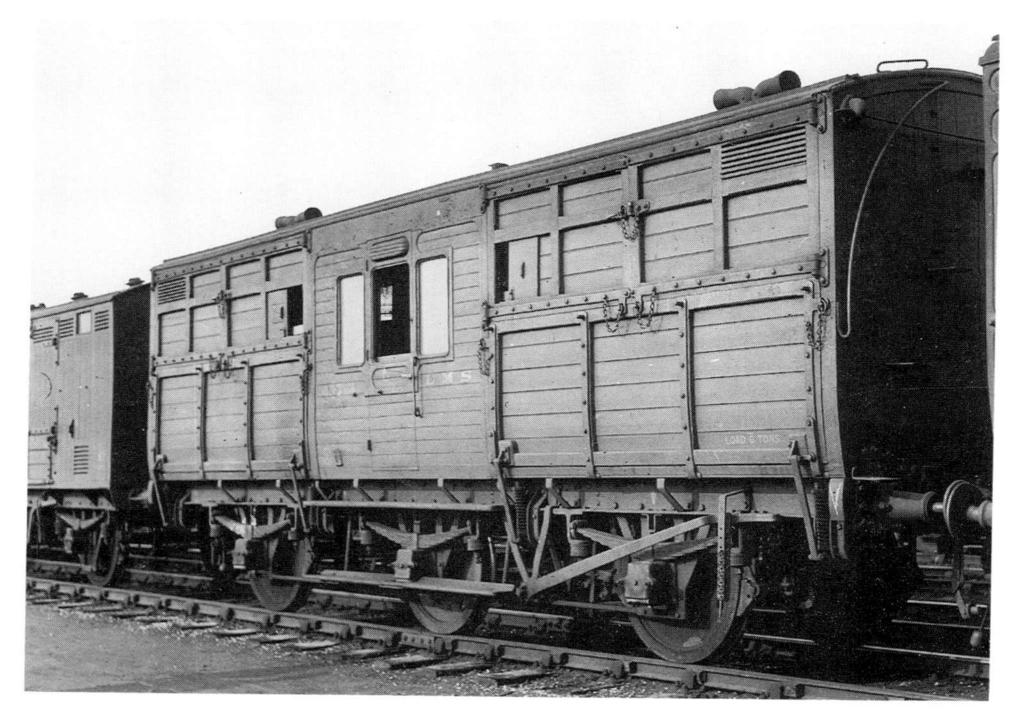

The form of construction of the CR six wheel double horsebox with a box each side of a central compartment is clearly depicted in this view of No 43751 in later LMS days. Note the disc wheels, together with the unusual roof ventilators adopted by the Caley. (LGRP, courtesy A Tortorella)

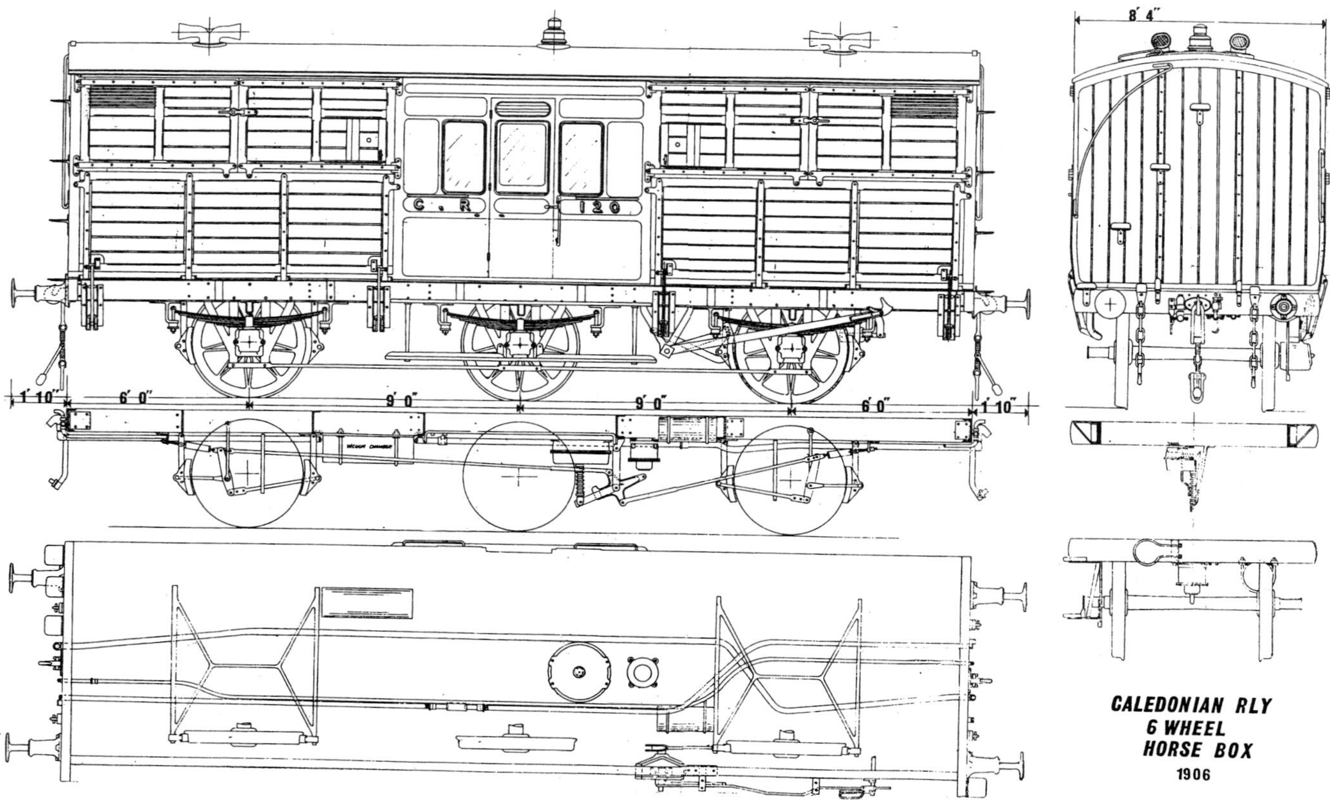

Furness Railway Horse Box and South Eastern Railway Six Wheel Double Horsebox

Furness Railway Horsebox

The drawing represents a group of three horse boxes built by the Metropolitan Carriage and Wagon Co. in 1871 at a cost of £192 10s 0d each, with a further and similar 16 being built in 1880. The latter vehicles lasted until grouping, appearing in the diagram book as Diagram 38, though they had all disappeared by the time of the LMS' renumbering scheme of 1933. Space was provided for three horses as well as a travelling groom. As with a lot of such vehicles, they would have been seen outside their immediate operating area of the Furness, being attached to trains used by horse owners when they wished to venture further abroad than could be expected on four legs.

SER Six Wheel Double Horsebox

These six wheel double ended horseboxes with groom's compartment were built for the SER by the Metropolitan Carriage and Wagon Co. in 1898/9 at a cost of £450 each. Their SER/SE&CR numbers were 89-94, later becoming SR Nos 3005-3010 to SR diagram 1010. When new they were finished in crimson lake lined in gold with vermilion edging and ironwork picked out in black. The running gear below the solebar was also black. They were withdrawn around 1934/5.
Regrettably no photograph of either of these types suitable for reproduction has been found.

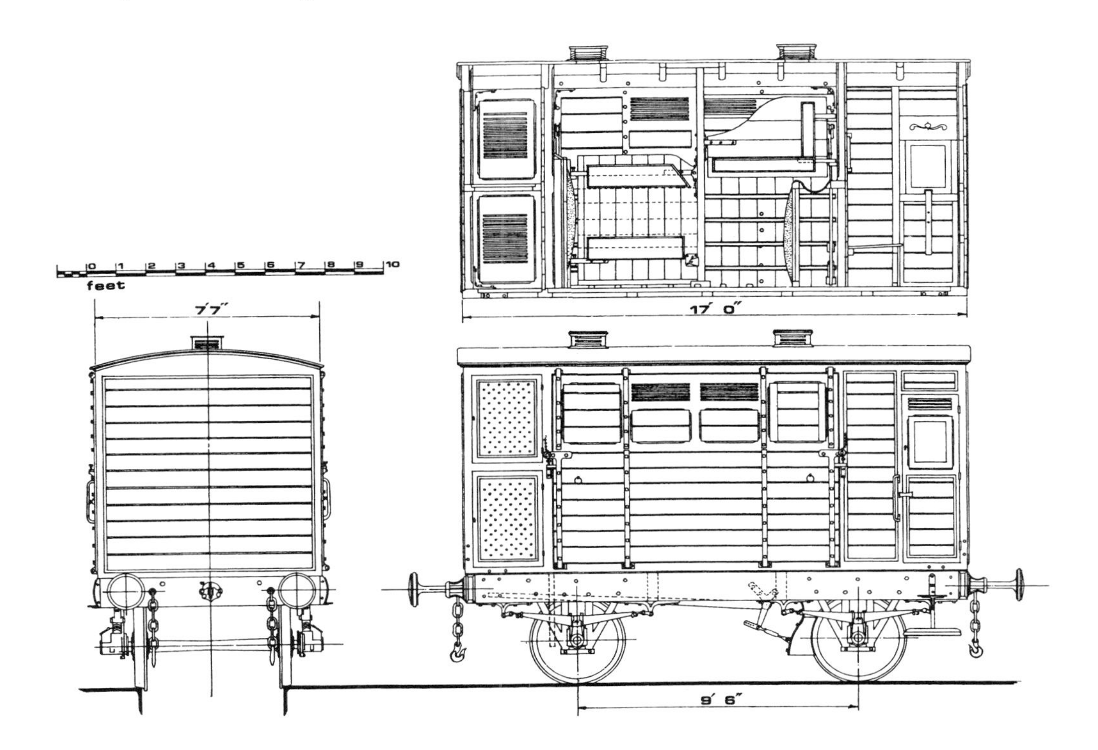

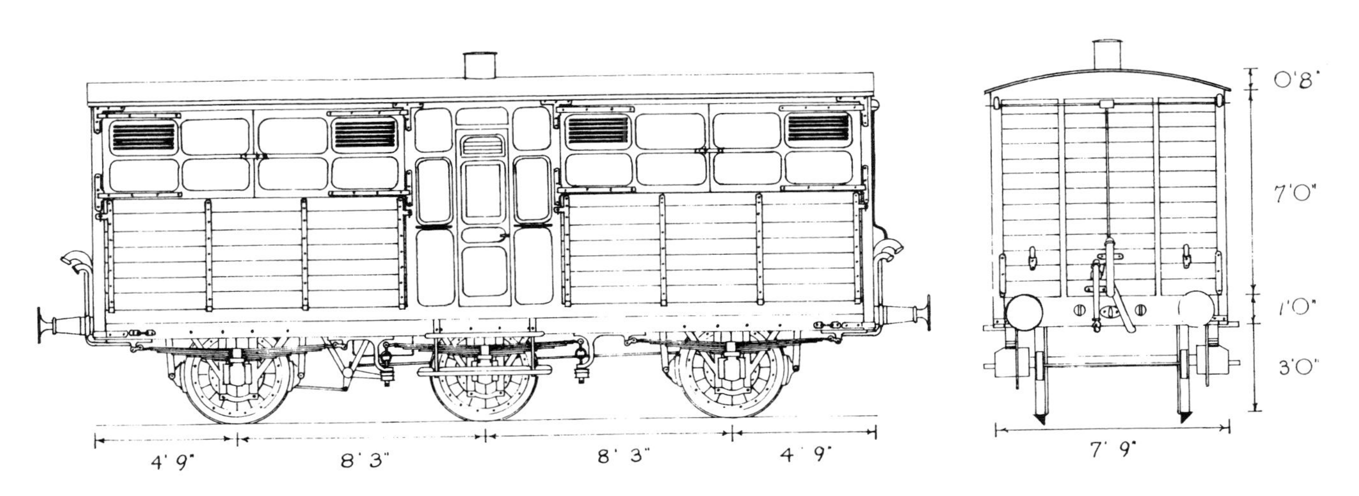

Highland Railway 19ft 8in Horsebox

The second generation of 23 horse boxes to HR Diagram 50, LMS Diagram 56, was designed for the Highland Railway by Peter Drummond in the early 1900s as a replacement to an earlier design. It had both vacuum and Westinghouse brake gear. The lower running numbers will have been renewals for earlier horseboxes withdrawn as life expired, whilst the higher numbers are likely to have been additions to capital stock. There are numerous variations in the detail of the body cladding, with a tendency for increasing amounts of vertical planking in lieu of panelling, as construction practice became more utilitarian for both new build and maintenance repairs with the passing of time.

HR horsebox, possibly No 43783, as the leading vehicle behind an LMS Stanier Black 5 having arrived at Inverness, probably in the late 1930s. Note the panelling on the ends and horizontal planking on the doors, probably a replacement of earlier panelling. (TW Bourne collection)

PROTOTYPE DETAILS

HR No	Built	LMS Nos 1st	LMS Nos 2nd	Ext't
1-6	1903	7521-6	43785-7	9/36
7-11	1923	7527-31	43779-83	2/54
14/20	1914	7534-5	43792	11/47
22-24	1921	7536-8	43777-8	3/56
25	1923	7539	43784	8/55
26-28	1911	7540-2	43788-9	11/47

LMS second series No 43792, formerly HR No 14 built at Lochgorm in 1914 with high proportion of vertical match boarding photographed in 1935. Note dual brake hoses and Mansell wheels. (LGRP)

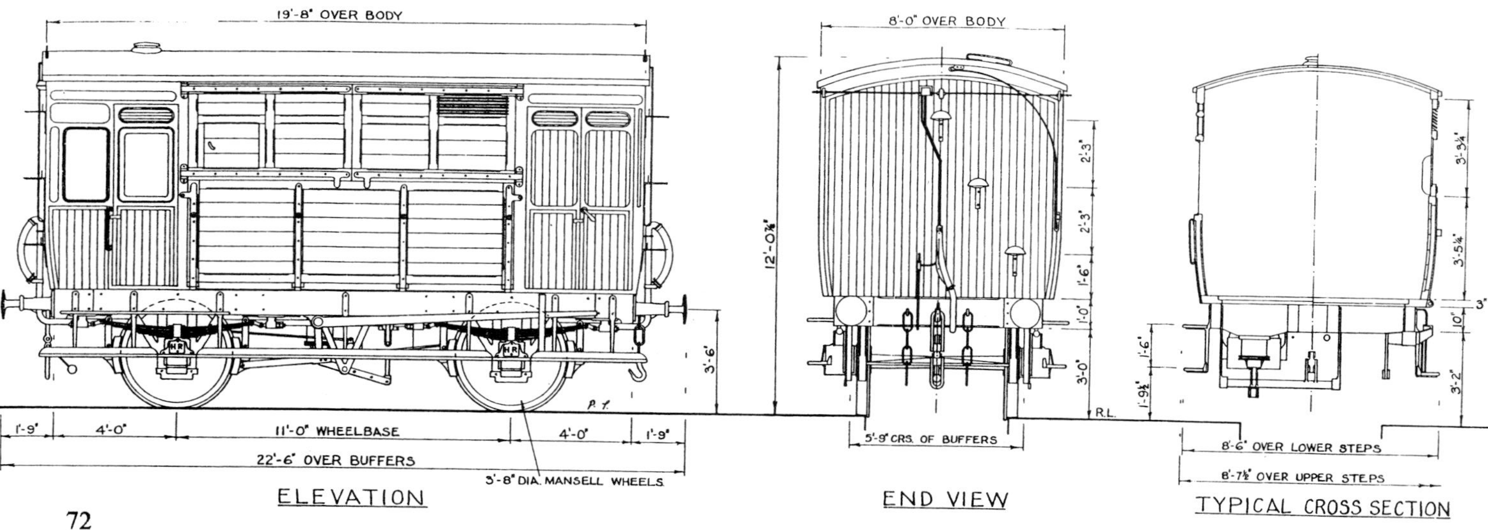

LMS horsebox No M42425M circa 1963. This was built at Derby to diagram 1956 in 1933 and shows the all horizontally boarded sides that superseded the first diagram 1878, which had typical Midland panelled style to all but the box doors. (AG Thomas collection, courtesy HMRS)

LMS Horsebox

The LMS built horseboxes to six diagrams, but their size was the same throughout. The variations necessitating a fresh diagram arose from such differences as the fitting of Westinghouse brake pipes and different lighting systems, as tabulated below. The first, diagram 1878, was however, for panelled sides to the groom's compartment and luggage/fodder store in true Midland fashion, whereas all the remainder had horizontal planking. All were built at Derby, had vertical match board ends, 3ft 7½in diameter disc wheels and 12ft 6in wheelbase, unless otherwise shown. No 42536 was altered to 16 foot wheelbase in 1938.

No M42642 to diagram 1972 built 1937/8 at Templecombe on 18 August 1963. This is generally similar, but has had its wheelbase increased from 12 to 16 feet. It also has self-contained buffers. (AE West, courtesy MS King)

PROTOTYPE DETAILS

Diag	Date	2nd No	Ext't	Remarks
1878	1926	42000-42048	10/61	West pipe, gas lit & panelled sides
1879	1929-33	42099-42408	13/62	West pipe, oil lit
1952	1935	42521-42523	13/62	
1956	1927-35	42049-42098, 42409-42520	13/62	Gas lit
1972	1937-38	42524-42573	3/66	
2125	1948-51	42574-42689	-	16 ft wheelbase

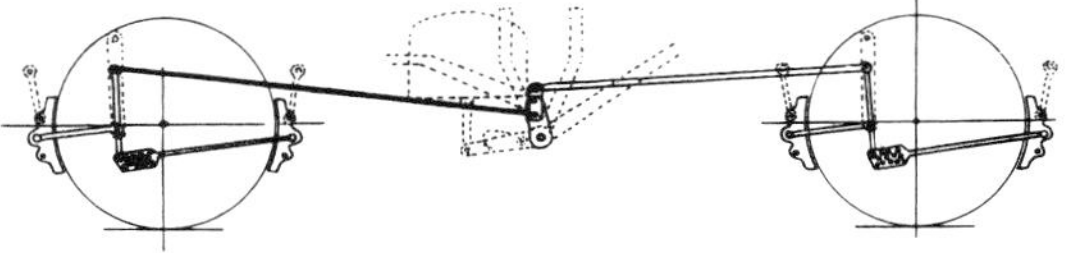

SCRAP VIEW OF BRAKE GEAR FROM OTHER SIDE

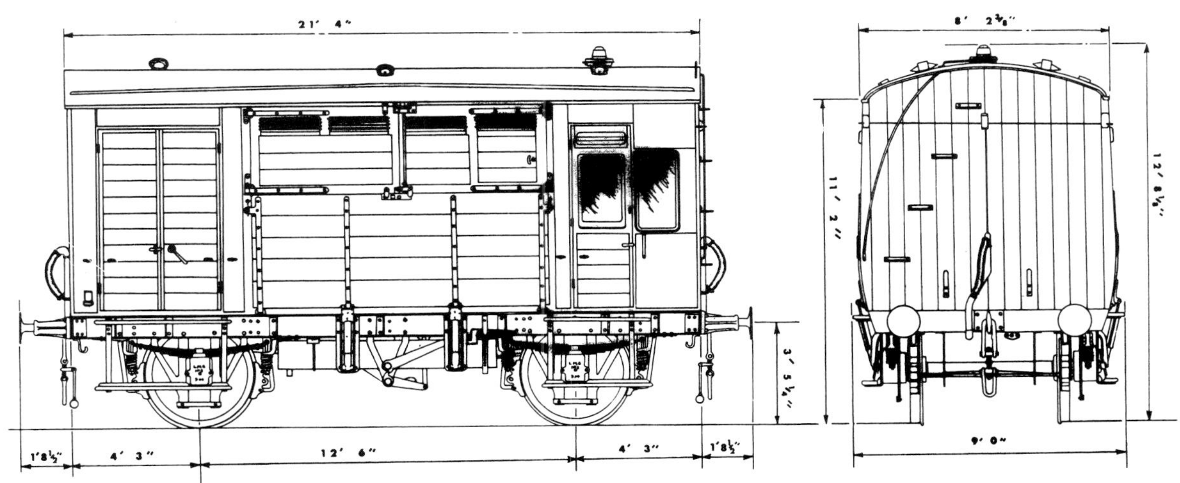

Lancashire & Yorkshire Horseboxes

At the merger with the LNWR the Lancashire & Yorkshire Railway had 152 horseboxes. Of these, 119 were of the types built to diagram 109 and 109A and were virtually the same at first glance. The 1892 type were 16ft 1in long and straight sided, the later development of it introduced in 1901 was 16ft 6in over body and had tumble-home like carriage stock. Building continued through to 1914 and another one was added in 1920 as a replacement due to accident damage. Most carried random numbers as they were built to the renewal account and thus used numbers from older stock. They carried the standard carriage livery of tan and lake without any line between the two colours, which on the drop doors fell mid plank. All were dual Westinghouse and vacuum braked.

Many lasted into nationalisation, still oil lit and in near 'original' condition apart from the change to crimson livery.

No. 158 was built in 1901 to the 'capital' account, thus having a new (higher) number. Until 1909 the brake handles were to the same end. Later builds had a version of the Morton 'cam' brake allowing levers to the right hand end on each side.(BC Lane collection)

PROTOTYPE DETAILS

Diag	Built	L&Y Nos	LMS 1st Nos	LMS 2nd Nos
109	1892-5	117 (46 No)	5934/40/3/5/50 (sample)	43626-43631
109A	1901-20	1, 21/2/5/7/9, 31/3, 54/8, 60/2-5/8, 70/2-4/6/8/9, 158 (74 No)	5817/21/6/9/30/2/9/41/2/4/5/52/8/60/5/6/7/9/72/4/6/8/80/2/4-6/9/90/2, 5904/56/8/9/62/3	43632-43693

A 1911 example in later years as LMS 43675. It bears a paint date 7/39 on the solebar and was probably photographed after the war. (BC Lane collection)

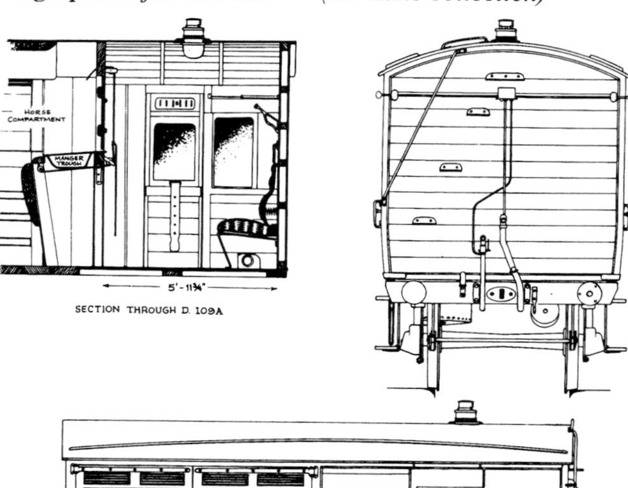

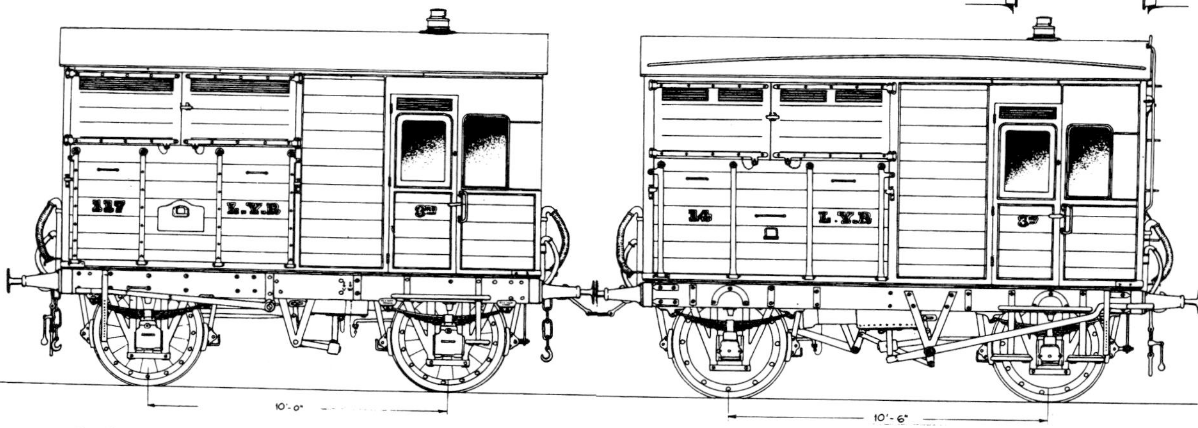

Maryport & Carlisle Horsebox

The first vehicle of this design entered service in 1904. The only M&C horse box listed in the 1932 renumbering was built in 1904 and therefore likely to be of this type, if not No. 4 itself. The LMS numbers for this vehicle were 7907 (1923) and 43735 (1932).

RY Pickering of Wishaw, near Motherwell, Scotland built horsebox No 4 for the small Maryport and Carlisle Railway in 1904. With dual brakes, steam heating pipes and an 11 foot wheelbase its specification was up to the standards of the day. (RY Pickering & Co/HMRS collection W918 & W919)

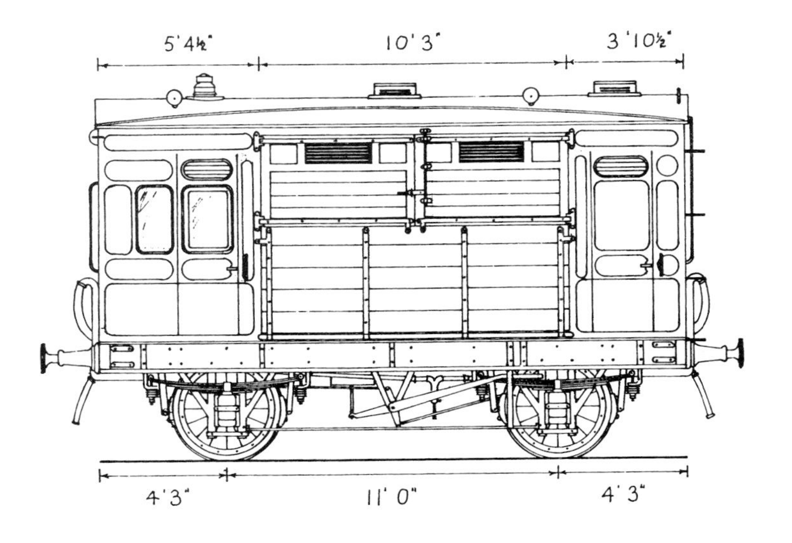

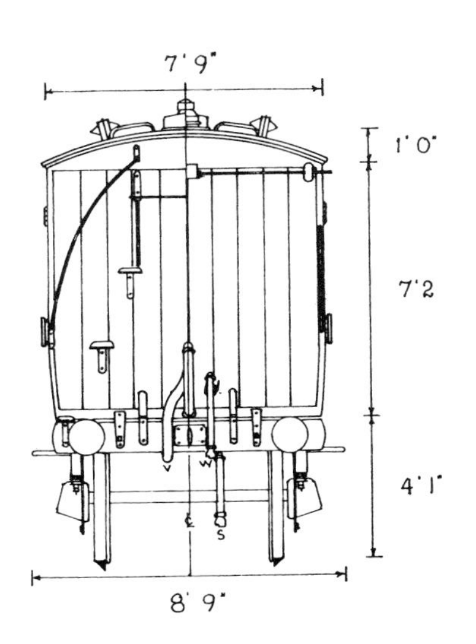

Great Central Horsebox

These horseboxes were supplied to the Great Central Railway shortly after its change of name from the Manchester, Sheffield & Lincolnshire Railway and its extension to Marylebone, London. They were built between 1898 and 1902 to diagram 1X4, later coded 5194 by the LNER. The random numbers allocated suggest that some were renewals, whilst the block numbers are likely to be additions to capital stock. The Cheshire Lines Committee also acquired horseboxes of the same design, as shown in the adjacent table.

PROTOTYPE DETAILS

GC Nos	LNER Nos	CLC Nos	Built
599, 604/11/3/4/6	903/8/15/7/8/20	149/52/4	1900
618/22/4/6/7/9	922/6/8/30/1/3	55-6, 148/53/7	1901
1549-1593	954-998	57, 156	1902

The Gloucester Railway Carriage & Wagon Co Ltd supplied this 17ft 6in long horsebox No 1553 to the Great Central Railway in June 1898. Note the varnished and lined finish. At the ends safety chains and both automatic vacuum and Westinghouse brake hoses can be seen. (P Tatlow collection)

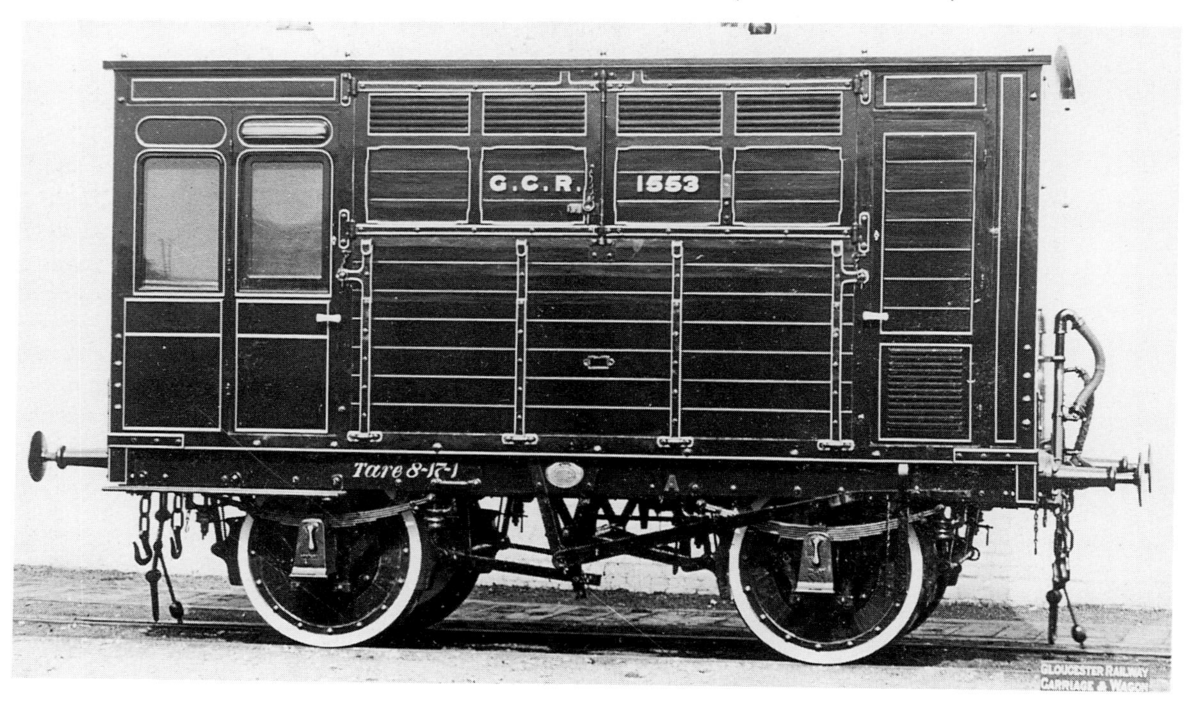

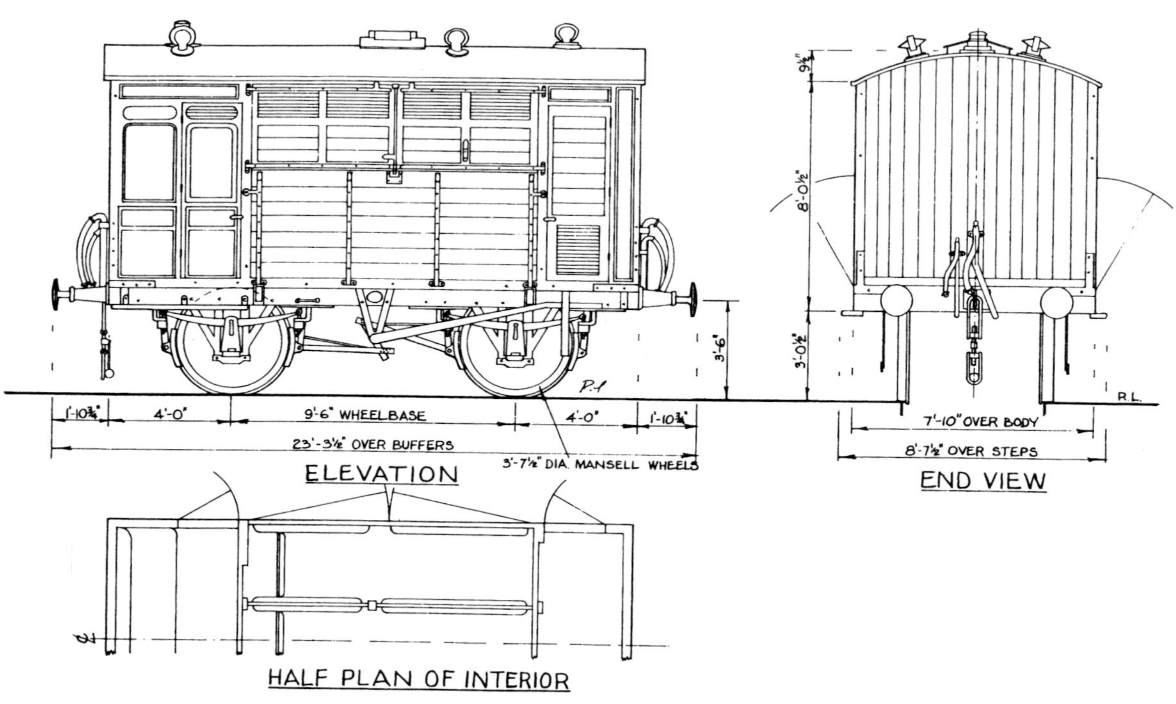

GER 20 Foot Horsebox

Fifty 20ft 2in long horseboxes were built between 1910 and 1913 to GER diagram 28 and subsequently coded 6183 by the LNER. GER Nos were 401-420, 497/9-501/3-8/10/2/523/5-32, LNER Nos 1740-1788, one appearing to have been withdrawn before renumbering. Many were allocated to Newmarket for use by the racing horse owners who had stables there, until displaced by LNER vehicles from 1938, see p 81. No 1768 is reputed to have been made available solely for the use of the King's horses.

Ex-GER 20 foot horsebox now LNER No 1762 at Penrith on 5 June 1950. Note that repairs have been carried out with horizontal boards and some the ventilators in the upper doors have been suppressed, the Westinghouse brake equipment has been replaced by the automatic vacuum system. (ED Bruton)

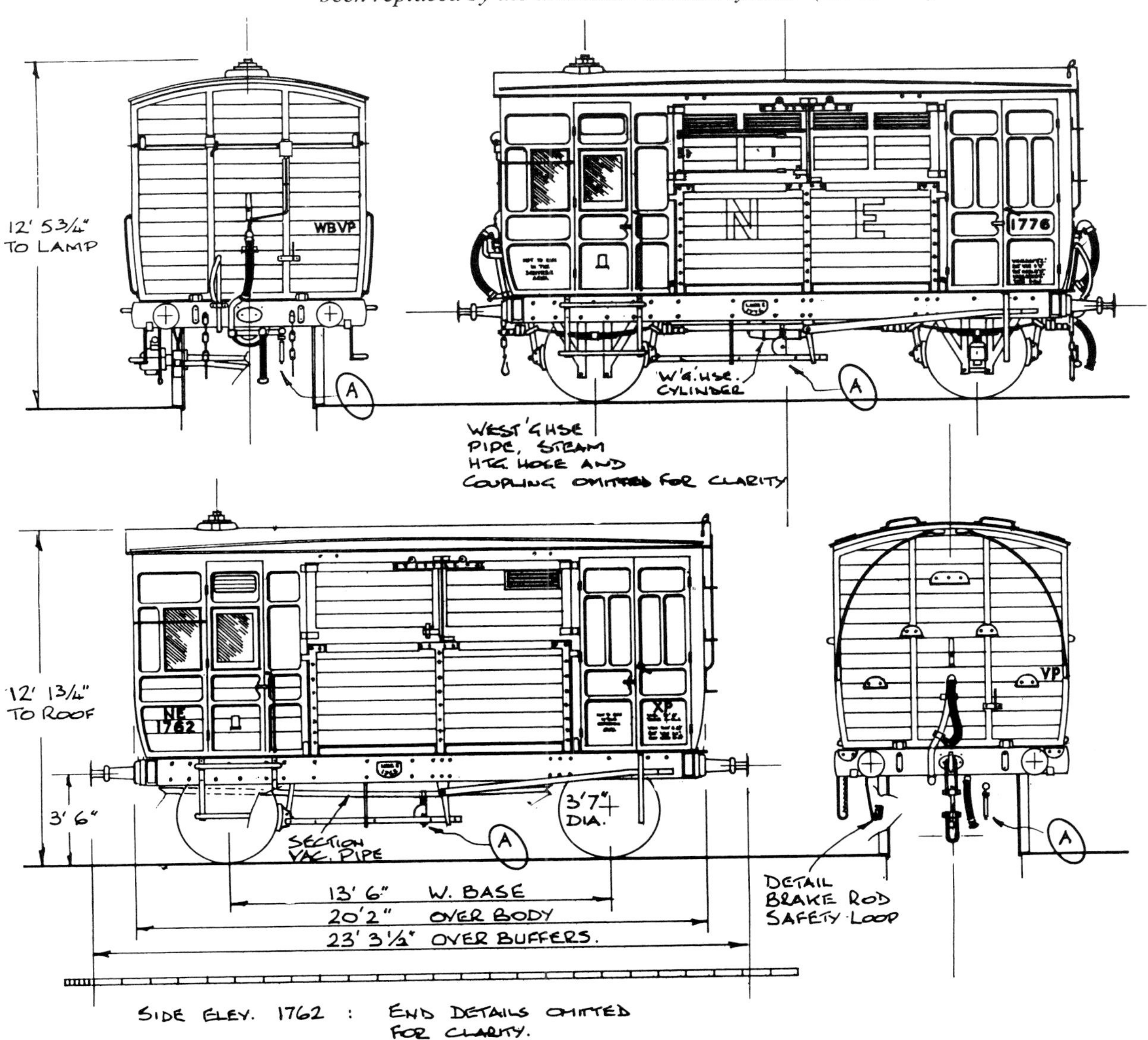

Great Northern Horseboxes

LNER No 780 to diagram 352 in wartime livery at Cowlairs on 21 September 1946. Note old form of brake lever operating to the LHS. (AG Ellis)

There were two basic designs of GN horsebox built at Doncaster over a period from 1882 to 1917. Both were 18 ft 1½in long by 7ft 8in over the body and 10 foot wheelbase with room for three horses. Up to 1897 150 vehicles were produced to diagram 351, LNER code 4238. In these the groom's compartment had a pair of quarter lights with accommodation for up to 10 grooms and attendants, while the fodder box had only a single door. After this date the features were reversed on the 135 vehicles to diagram 352, LNER code 4239 with a single quarter light with seating for only five persons and double doors to the fodder box. Initially dual braking was provided on all vehicles and this was maintained until 1930 after which the Westinghouse brake will have been removed as repairs became necessary. Steam heating seems to have been added during the life of the vehicles.

The CLC also had boxes similar to diagram 352, Nos 246-251 built at Doncaster in 1901.

A view of No E786 in early BR days showing the opposite side of the vehicle. The Westinghouse brake appears to have been removed. (LGRP, courtesy P Tatlow)

PROTOTYPE DETAILS

Diag	Built	Specimen GN Nos	Specimen LNER Nos	Ext't
351	1885-97	118-62/205-15, 2266-86	506-8/11-13/22-9/48-51/8-64/76-84, 648-57	1950
352	1897-1917	1152/3/5/75-8, 1257, 1343, 2783-6, 2882-96	503-5/27-9, 629-31, 695-7, 705-9, 726-9, 751-3, 763-6, 784-7	1952

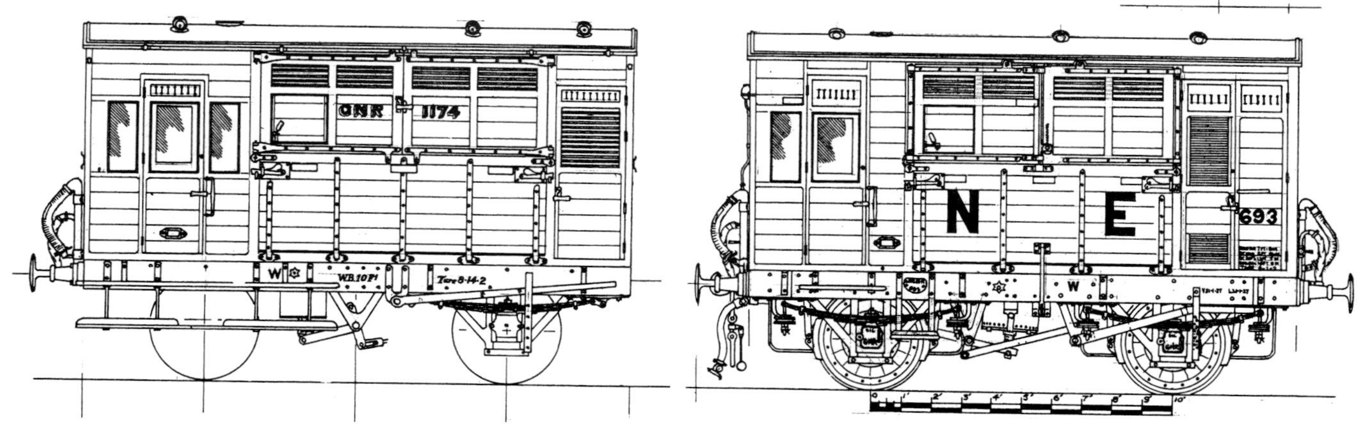

GNS Six Wheel Horsebox

These handsome six wheeled horseboxes were built for the Great North of Scotland Railway between April 1918 and April 1920 for use in the country to be found in the North East of Scotland. They were fitted with both vacuum and Westinghouse air brakes, the latter because it was the company's braking system and the former to enable them to work through to the more numerous other companies which used the vacuum brake. Later, as the vacuum brake became standard on all four of the grouping companies, the Westinghouse equipment was removed. Numbered 9 to 13 by the GNS and renumbered 2108 to 2113 by the LNER, which suggests one has not been accounted for, or was added following grouping. They were coded 7032 in 1938.

A rather decrepit unidentified former GNS six wheel horsebox in BR days not far off retirement. (P Tatlow collection)

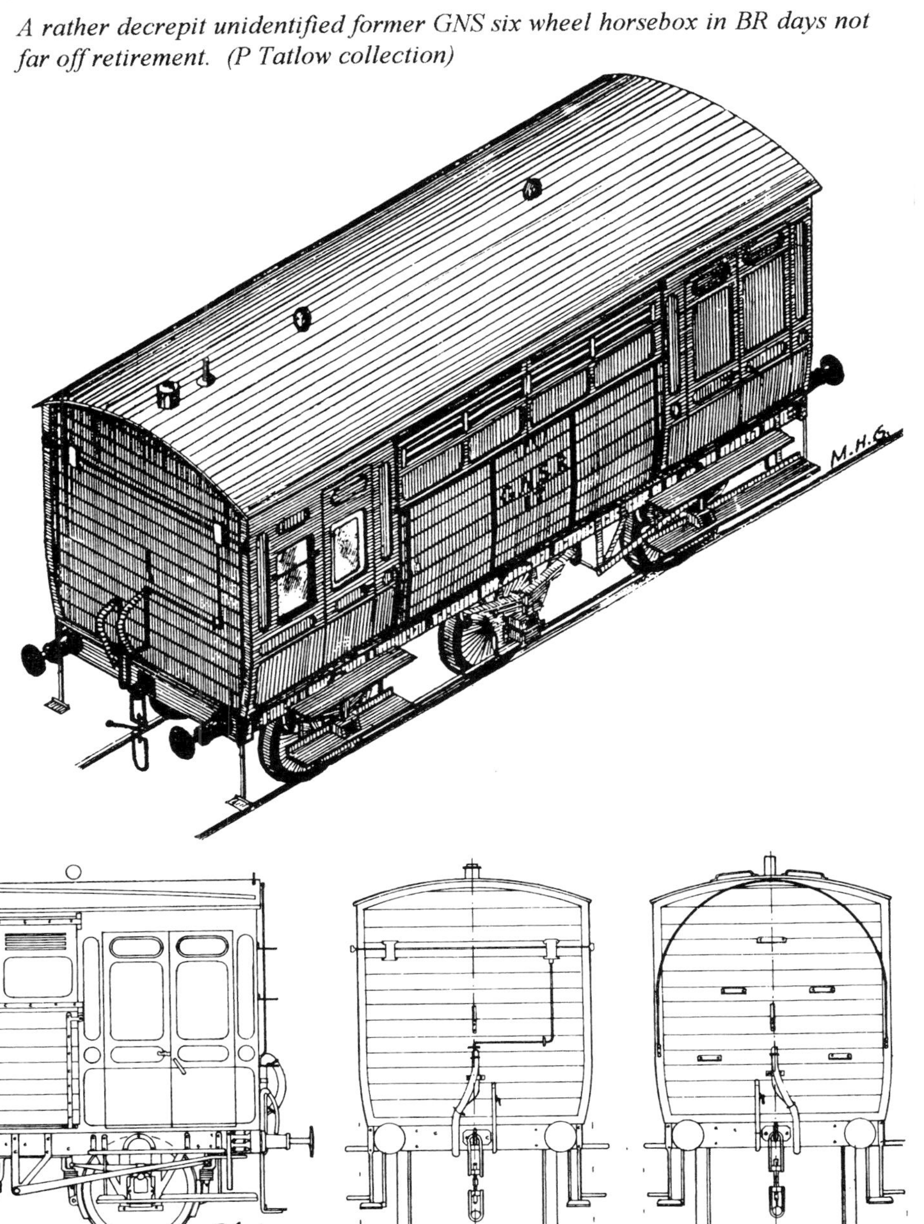

Isometric view of No 13. (late MH Golder, courtesy Mrs M Golder)

4'-0" 7'-0" 7'-0" 4'-0"

9 Nº SOLID SPOKE WHEELS

7'-10½" OVER BODY

8'-9½" EXTREME WIDTH

ELEVATION

COMPARTMENT END

HAY BOX END

Lancashire, Derbyshire & East Coast Railway Horsebox

The Lancashire, Derbyshire and East Coast Railway had eight 16 foot 8 inch long horseboxes numbered 226 to 233. The first four had been built by the Lancaster Carriage and Wagon Co in 1897 and the second batch a year later by Brown Marshall. On taking over the LDEC on 1 January 1907, the Great Central Railway renumbered these 1785 to 1792 in order of age. They were renumbered again by the LNER as 1059 to 1066 following grouping in 1923. Originally dual brake fitted, the Westinghouse brake equipment was subsequently removed and replaced by through pipe only. Although a photograph of one of these horseboxes in the background taken in 1906 exists, regrettably it is not suitable for reproduction. The initials LD&EC, however, can be made out on the second plank of the left hand door and the number at the same level on the right hand door. In their early days they were marked for return after use to: Chesterfield Market Place 2, Langwith Junction 1, Edwinstone 3, Ollerton 1 and Tuxford West 1.

The LD&EC horseboxes were generally similar to the extremely numerous contemporary GER horseboxes. Their GER Nos were 603-957 (LNER 1251-1599) and 425-602, 958-1007 (LNER 1600-1739). LNER Nos 1576 and 1730, of diagrams 6178 and 6179 respectively, are illustrated here. (G Hemingway, courtesy HMRS)

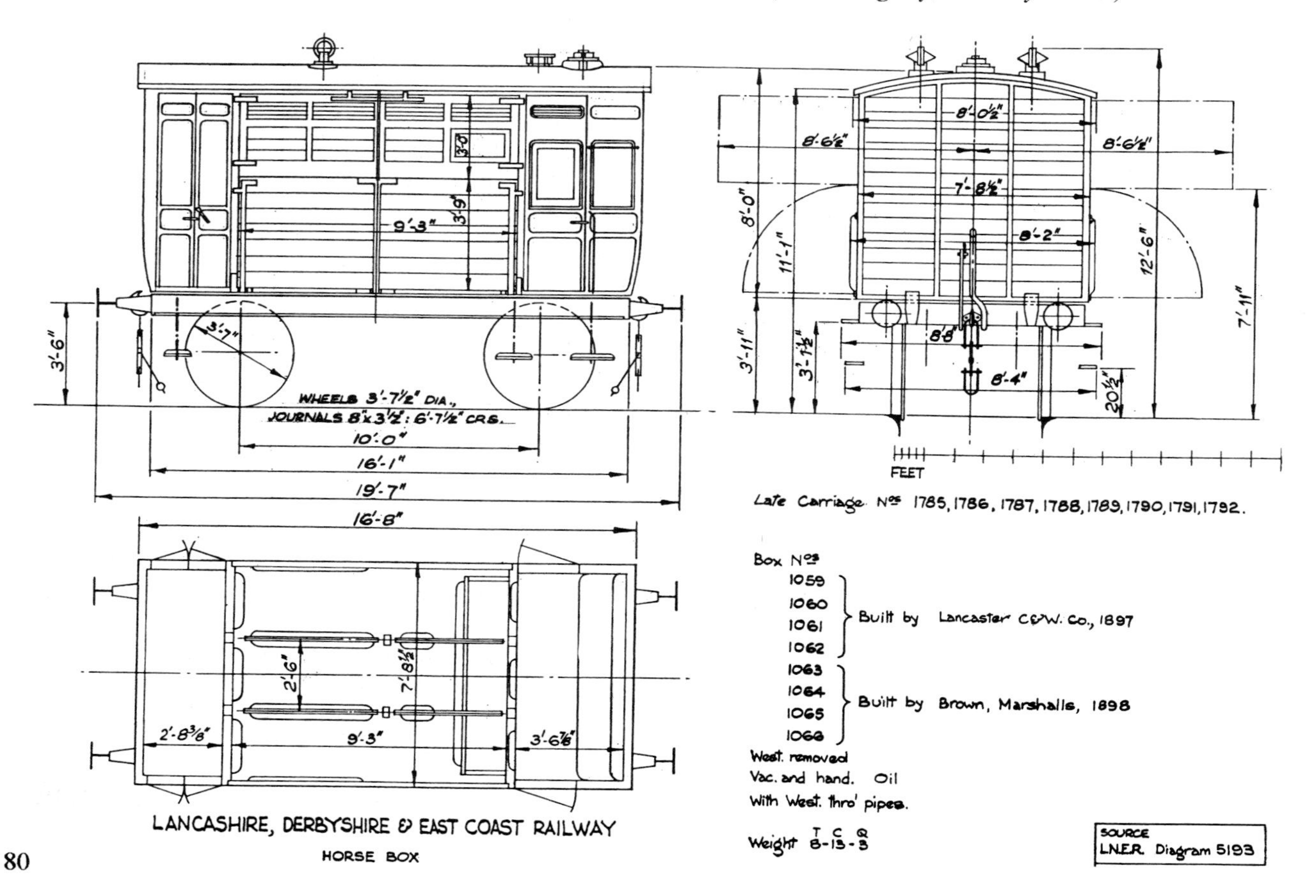

LNER 22 Foot Horsebox

In 1938 the LNER built at York thirty 22 foot long horseboxes to diagram 5, code 8005. These had a central box with two stalls for the horse; a groom's compartment with toilet and luggage locker for tack and fodder. These vehicles were fitted with the usual automatic vacuum brake, steam heating pipe and electric light and will have had the small style of lettering from the outset. All were lettered for return to the destination shown adjacent and many annotated for the use of race horse owners, or trainers. Those shown with an asterisk * are known, at a later date, to have been taken off hire and used in general traffic.

LNER horsebox No E2356 with lavatory for the groom seen here in British Railways carmine livery with small cream lettering. Note that compared with the drawing a different form of hinge has been used on the upper side hung horse compartment doors and that this view is taken from the side with the single vee hanger for the brake lever. (P Tatlow collection)

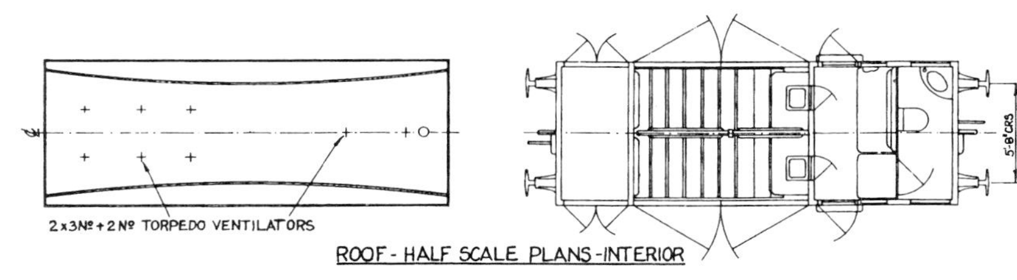

No	For use of:	Return to:
2336		Newmarket
2337		Newmarket
2338		Newmarket
2339	Reg Day	Newmarket
2340	B Jarvis*	Newmarket
2341	GB Barling	Newmarket
2342	JL Jarvis*	Newmarket
2343	JL Jarvis	Newmarket
2344	Frank Butters	Newmarket
2345	JL Jarvis*	Newmarket
2346	Frank Butters*	Newmarket
2347	Frank Butters	Newmarket
2348	Capt C Boyd Rochfort*	Newmarket
2349	Frank Butters*	Newmarket
2350	Hon G Lambton*	Newmarket
2351	CP Kirk*	Kennett
2352	Capt C Boyd Rochfort*	Newmarket
2353	George R Digby	Newmarket
2354	Lord George Dundas*	Newmarket
2355		Newmarket
2356		Leyburn
2357	JG Thompson	Acklington
2358		Malton
2359	Egerton House*	Newmarket
2360		Newmarket
2361	Capt P Whitaker	Newmarket
2362	The Earl of Derby	Newmarket
2363	The Earl of Derby	Newmarket
2364	RJ Colling*	Newmarket
2365	Major WV Beatty*	Newmarket

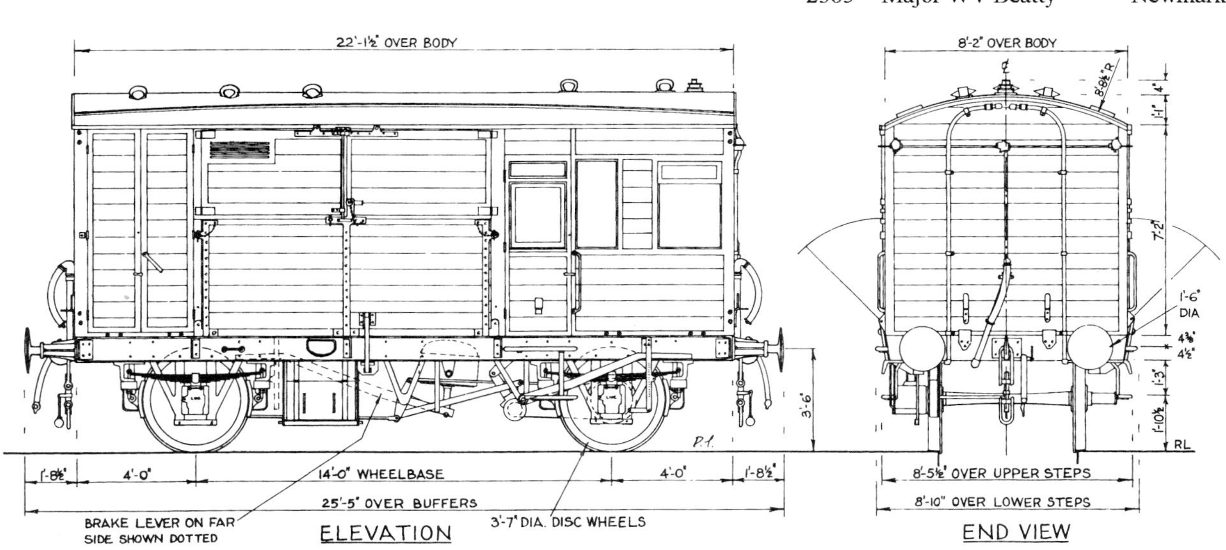

North Eastern Horseboxes

In 1890 the NER introduced a new design of horsebox to diagram 67 with an arc roof. A pair of springs were fitted to the solebars to ease the task of lowering and raising the heavy bottom door. They were provided with a roomy groom's compartment and fodder locker resulting in a length of 19ft 6in. As was usual on the NER, the numbers tended to take those of the vehicles they replaced leading their being scattered over a wide range, unless they were built as additions to capital stock. A selection of those that survived to reach LNER stock are: 34-36, 52-54, 85-87, 115-120, 138-144, 171-173, 182-184, 219-223, 226-36, 274-278, 283-291, 296-299, 301-3, 312-4, 396-445. The LNER continued to use the same numbers

The vehicles of this and the next design to diagram 196 were dual brake fitted, together with through steam heating pipe and lit by oil lamps. Their wooden bodies were panelled. Details of the crimson lake livery and lettering carried in *North Eastern Record, Volume 2*, published by the Historical Model Railway Society in 1997.

NER horsebox No 181 with elliptical roof to Diagram 196, as newly built in 1913. Note door to horsebox let into the eaves of the roof, the left handed brake lever and spoked wheels. (P Tatlow collection)

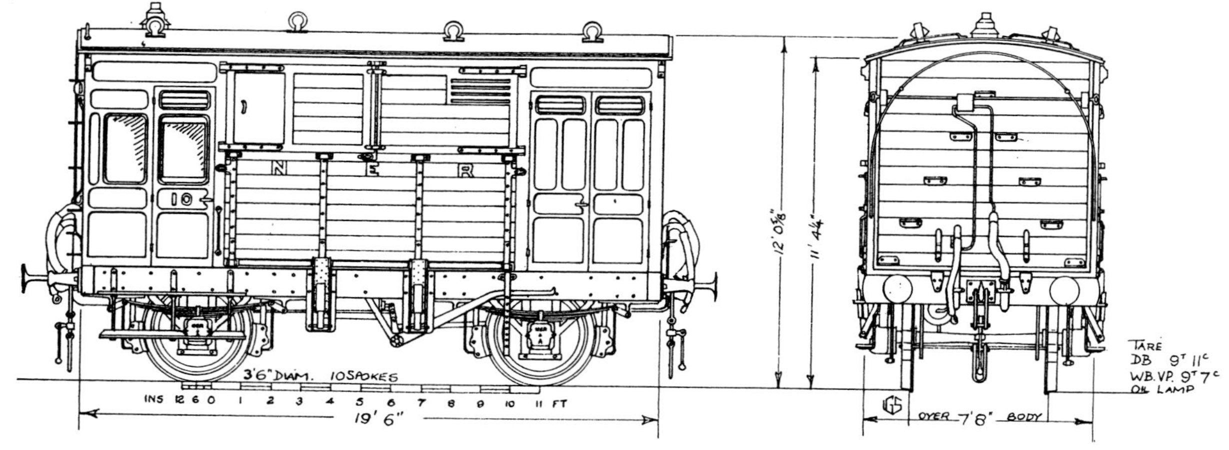

North Eastern Horseboxes

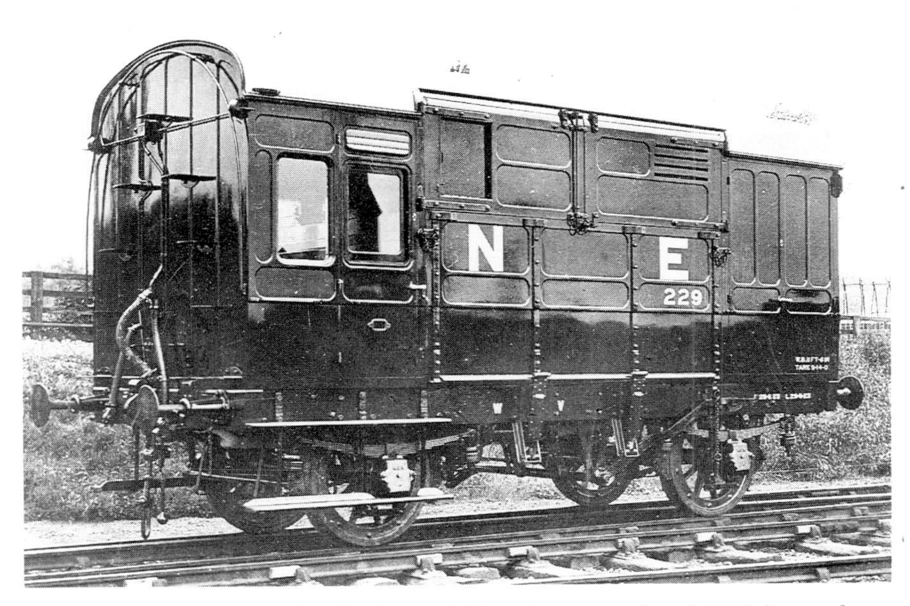

No 229 was one of the last built in 1923 and appeared in LNER livery from the outset. (P Tatlow collection)

From January 1913 the NER built its horseboxes to Diagram 196, with a revised the roof profile in the form of an ellipse, and continued this design until the last batch constructed following grouping in 1923, by which time 250 had been completed. The lower eaves level, compared with the previous low arc roof boxes to Diagram 67, resulted in the large doors in the sides of the vehicle being recessed into the roof, as shown in the illustrations and drawing. Numbers are almost entirely random and only a small selection can be included here, viz: 1913 - 7, 165, 304, 328; 1914 - 84, 174, 309, 335; 1915 - 337; 1916 - 176, 449; 1917 - 192, 350; 1918 - 62, 204, 358, 371; 1919 - 373; 1920 - 5, 86, 383; 1921 - 231; 1922 - 24, 441; 1923 - 437, 229. Under the auspices of the LNER they kept the same numbers.

Later in life No 359, built in 1918, looks somewhat more worn at Leuchars in June 1945. The Westinghouse brake equipment has by now been removed. (AG Ellis)

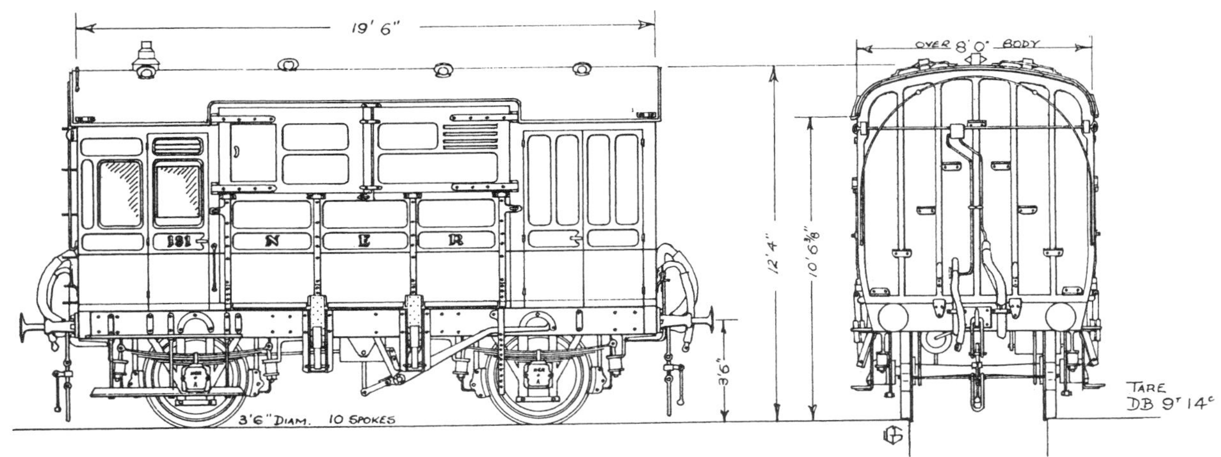

North British 20 Foot Horsebox

The last design of horsebox introduced by the North British Railway in 1911, of which 75 were built by 1920, was 20 foot long by 8 foot 6 inch wide with a low arc roof and was dual brake fitted. They were coded 3039 by the LNER and their numbers were as tabulated.

NB horsebox built at Cowlairs in 1920, photographed as LNER No 1878 probably after World War 2 in the later livery with small lettering. Note the lack of tumble home to lower door. (AG Ellis)

20 foot North British horsebox No 30 in pregrouping livery. (AG Ellis collection)

PROTOTYPE DETAILS

NB No	LNER No
1-8	1801-1808
10-21	1810-1821
22	2028
23-35	1822-1834
36	2029
37-53	1835-1851
61-87	1859-1885
U/k	1954-1955
179	1976
228-230	2025-2027

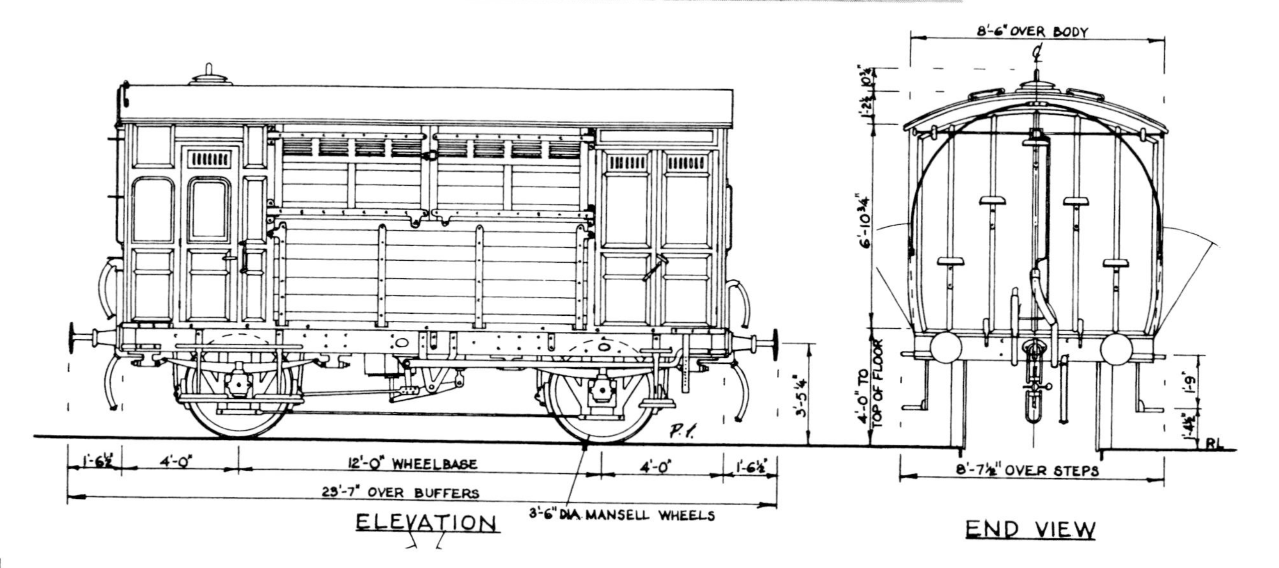

Cambrian and MSWJR Horseboxes

Ten horseboxes were supplied to the Cambrian Railway by the Metropolitan C&W Co in 1892. These were numbered 216 to 227. No 225 was destroyed in an accident near Abermule in 1907 and the remainder were withdrawn between 1922 and 1924 without being renumbered by the GW. Unfortunately no details of the wheels and brake gear are known.

Three very similar vehicles were built by the Midland RC&W Co in 1897 for MSWJR. The main differences were that the later vans had three vents in each panel, the axleguards were of the external W form and the weigh shaft for the brakes was suspended form V hangers attached to the solebars. The numbers were 12, 15 and 18. Nos 273, 283 and 288 were allocated by the GW. The first was withdrawn in September 1928, while the other two had already gone in 1924 without having their new numbers applied.

Two MSWJR horseboxes supplied by Midland RC&W Co in 1897. No 18 on the right hand side shows the vehicle in running condition, while its unidentified neighbour shows the doors open for loading. Note the outside W irons, split spoked wheels and central V hangers. They were fitted with vacuum brake and through pipe for the Westinghouse brake. (ME Morton Lloyd collection)

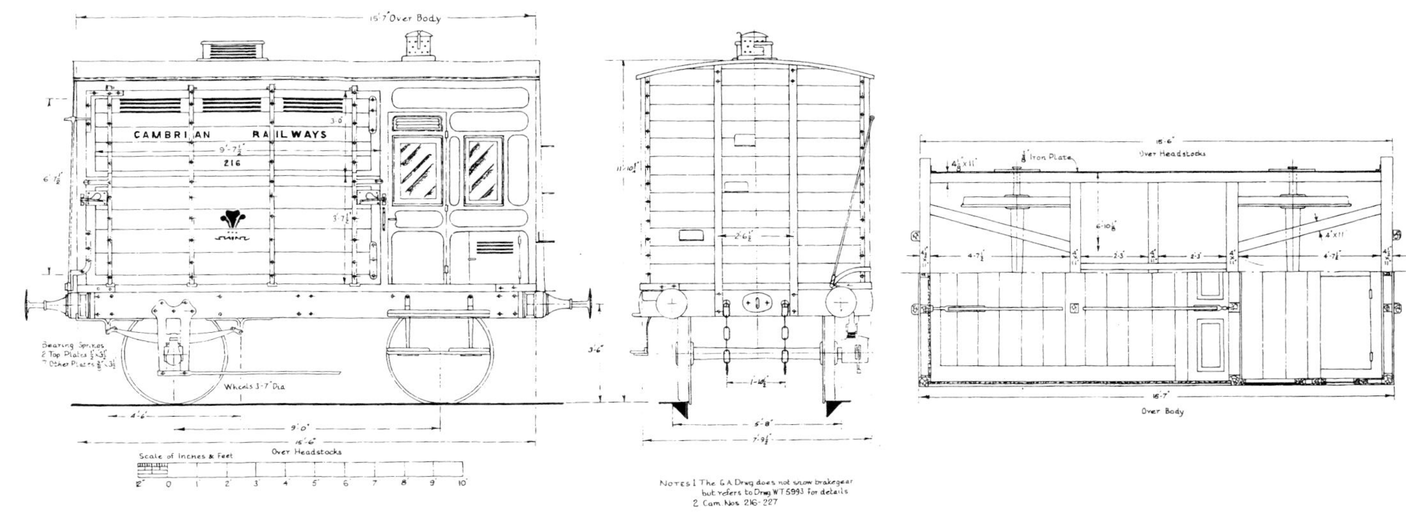

Great Western Horsebox Paco

In 1907 the Great Western introduced a layout for a 21 foot long horsebox which, with a few modifications, it continued to produce for the rest of the company's separate existence. Initially panelled sides and horizontal match boarding was used for the ends, but this soon gave way to flush steel sheeting. Later window bolections and the groom's door vents were dispensed with and finally the ends were made vertical. From time to time various lengths of springs were fitted. Some boxes to diagrams N11 to N14 were originally dual fitted, but all lost the Westinghouse equipment by the 1930s. Gas or oil lighting was applied at various times, all as shown in the adjacent table. Numbering was random, but a selection is also given in the table.

No W268 at St Ives (Huntingdon) on 27 July 1953 is an example of the first diagram N11. Note the horizontal planking to the ends, but its panelling has been sheeted over. It has been fitted with 3ft 6in springs and is painted in BR carmine red with black ends. (AE West, courtesy MS King)

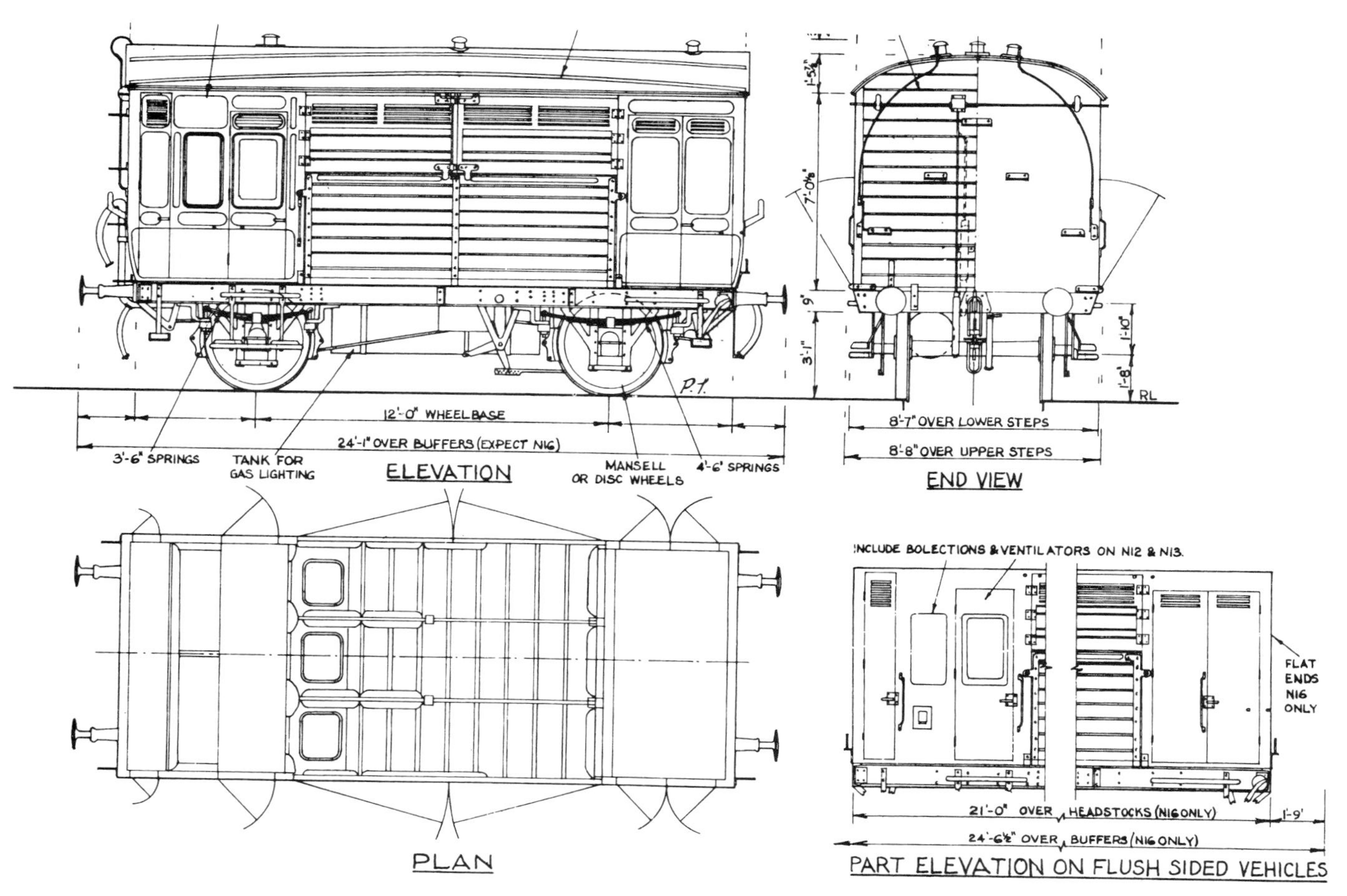

Great Western Horsebox Paco

Some horseboxes were regularly allocated to travelling circuses and this shows No 346 on 5 April 1938 as part of Bertram Mills' train at Ascot, their winter quarters. This vehicle was built in 1922 to diagram N13 with 4ft 6in springs. (HC Casserley)

Although also a vehicle to diagram N13, No W337 has 3ft 6in springs. This is also in BR red and at St Ives (Huntingdon) on the same occasion as No W268. Note bolections round the windows and door vents together with the gas cylinder and Dean/Churchward brake lever below the solebar. (AE West, courtesy MS King)

PROTOTYPE DETAILS

Diagram	N11	N12	N13	N14	N15	N16
Introduced	1907	1914	1922	1920	1930	1931
Number built	78	58	186	3	63	129
Feature	Panelled sides & horizontally planked ends			Only 2 stalls		Vertical ends
Door vents	Yes	Yes	Yes	Yes	No	No
Bolections	Yes	Yes	Yes	Yes	No	No
Lighting	Gas	Gas	Gas	Gas	Oil	Gas
Sample numbers	849-855, 858-861, 863-869	173-175, 192-194, 232-234	146-8, 156-161, 239-241, 247-249, 263-267, 333-337, 893-927	227/30/8	489-493, 500-503, 510-515, 528-531, 563-569, 575-8	582-588, 590-596, 601-606, 608-613, 626-645, 647-685, 689-719

L&SWR 16 Foot Horsebox

To serve the large number of race courses on their systems, together with Army camps on Salisbury Plain and at Aldershot on LSWR territory, all three constituents of the Southern Railway had substantial numbers of horseboxes.

These LSWR vehicles are fairly typical of late 19th century horseboxes and most railways had something similar in size and proportion, but unusually these lasted until BR days. They would not by then be allowed on fast trains and their role is likely to have been limited to ordinary goods trains and stopping passenger trains. Nevertheless, they retained passenger livery until the end.

Three hundred of this basic type were built between 1887 and 1904. The early batches had a single brake lever on one side, acting through independent linkage to the brakes on one wheel only. From 1899 onwards the boxes were fitted with a single lever acting through the V hanger and the vacuum brake linkage. This situation is indicated on the drawing by the far side lever. Later, the near-side brake lever was added to update the vehicle and to conform to a RCH specification.

With the decline in the movement of horse traffic by rail, the Southern Railway built no new horseboxes, but gave pregrouping survivors a face-lift in the 1930s, in this case by removing the beading and sheeting over the side and door of the groom's compartment and the cupboard doors of the horse compartment with steel plates. The ends and drop door were left as original. But the groom's compartment window between the door and the horse compartment was filled in and sheeted.

The running numbers for the 1899 batch, which had brake gear as shown on the drawing, are 298-340 prior to 1912, 5947 to 5989 thereafter and 2727 to 2768 in SR days. No 5979 was broken up in September 1921 and No 2763 not renumbered but withdrawn on 27 May 1925. The whole range of Southern numbers was from 2501 to 2819. The type became extinct by 1957.

L&SWR 16 foot long horsebox of 1899 at Ashford on 30 June 1951 in early BR days, still in SR green with black ends, but with the addition of 'S' in front of its SR No 2727. Note the short lift link brake lever no doubt added to enable it to comply with RCH regulations. (AE West, courtesy MS King)

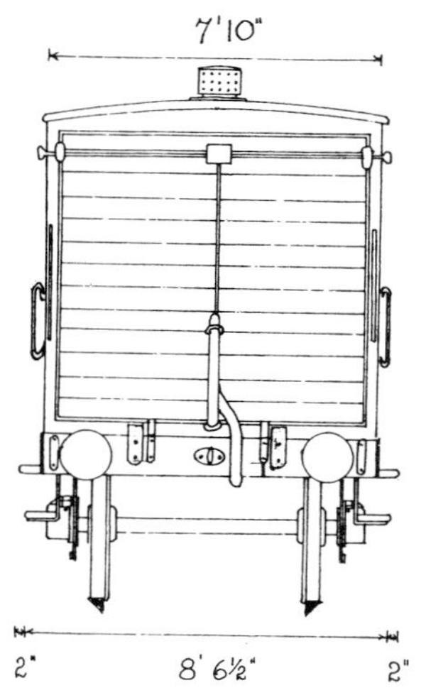

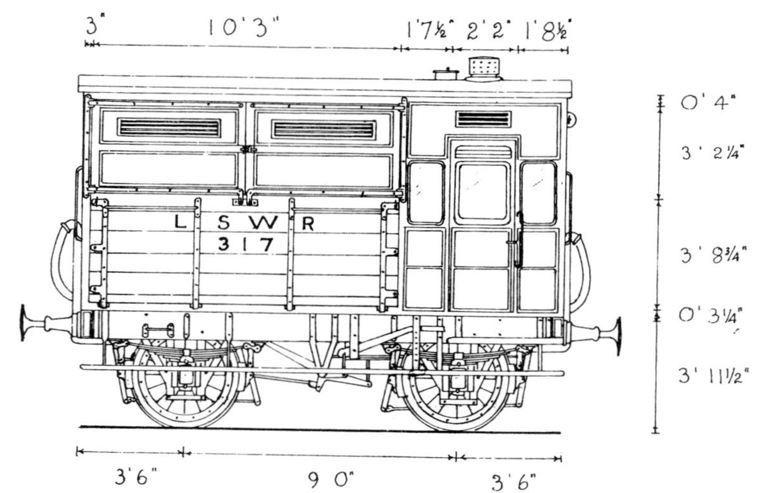

L&SWR 21 Foot Horsebox

These 39 horse boxes were built from 1905 to 1913, as replacements for earlier, smaller boxes. Although many of the bodywork features are retained from the 16 foot box, the 21 foot version represents a considerable step forward, not only in design, but in utility. They would have been acceptable on the LNWR, for instance, which was becoming rather fussy about running vehicles less than 21 foot long in passenger trains. Most of them were fitted with both Westinghouse and vacuum and through pipes for steam heating were added from 1908 onwards.

As with the 16 foot vans, there was a variety of hand brake arrangements, although this time, all varieties worked through the V-hanger and power brake linkage. Those built in 1905 had the hand brake lever on one side as shown and on the other side a mirror-reverse lever. Later variations had either Morton either side-brakes or the Sou'-Western's own either side-brakes. In these cases the direct acting lever pointed towards the hay box.

While oil lighting was the standard arrangement for most of these vehicles throughout their working life, a few were fitted with gas lamps and, of course, gas cylinders, three being so equipped in 1912 and one more in 1914. But it is probable that these had been restored to oil lamps prior to the stock becoming part of the Southern Railway.

Lettering was on the drop door prior to the 1912 renumbering and on the compartment door post this event. Again during the '30s the Southern 'modernised' these boxes by removing the beading from the sides and covering them with steel sheet, leaving only the drop door, as shown on the drawing.

A full set of numbers is not available but some typical 1905 built numbers are 4, 5, 14, 29, 191/3/5, 200/7/10, which after 1912 had 5650 added to them. The SR renumbered them 2820-2/5/36/8/40/3/8/50. No 2844 was the last to be withdrawn in July 1959.

L&SWR 21 foot horsebox No S2831S at Reading South on 7 November 1954. This and the previous vehicle illustrate the SR's modernisation by means of flush sides, suppression of the second quarter light to the groom's compartment and upgrading of the hand brake. (HF Wheeler collection, courtesy SR Carpenter)

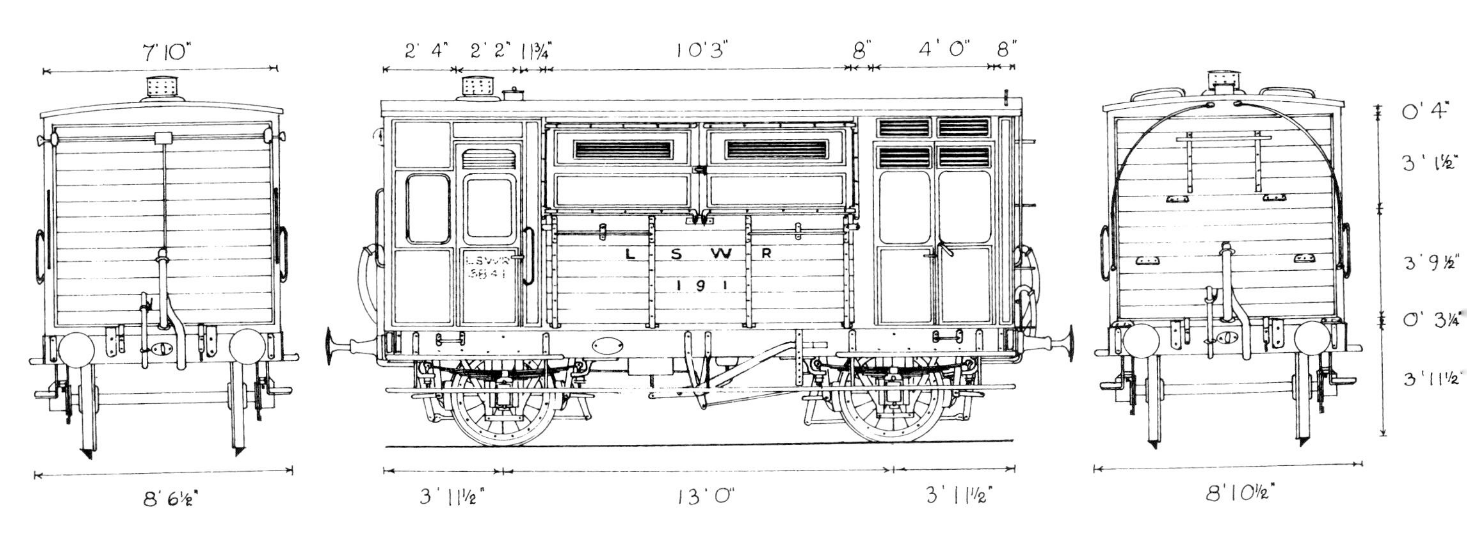

LBSC 18ft 6in Horsebox

These horseboxes were constructed between 1891 and 1906 with no sign of steps or grab rails to access roof to service the oil lamps! LBSC Nos were 5, 13/9, 25, 31/7, 46-8, 58/9, 68, 71/3/9, 90-134/6/7/9, 143/7/9, 154/6/8, 163/4, 174-6, 214/21, 230/7/40/1/4, 251-298, SR Nos 3188-3315. They were originally fitted with dual brake and probably with hand brake lever on one side only. By 1936 the SR had removed the Westinghouse brake gear and fitted a small hand brake lever at RH end on the second side, together with steam heating pipes on surviving vehicles. They also plated over panelling with steel plate to produce flush finish, bottom door landing springs fitted and safety chains removed, steps but no grab rails added! The last had gone by 1958.

The Gloucester RC&W built horseboxes Nos 107-126 (SR Nos 3220-3239) for the LBSC in 1899 of which No 120 is illustrated. These adopted horizontal planking, shown chain-dotted on the drawing below. Note the vacuum and Westinghouse brake pipes, together with safety chains and Monarch patent door controllers to the lower door to the horse compartment. (G Warburton collection)

The Southern Railway refurbished these horseboxes including covering the panel work with flush steel sheet, as shown here of No S3262 in BR carmine red livery at Exmouth Jct on 22 August 1950. (AE West, courtesy MS King)

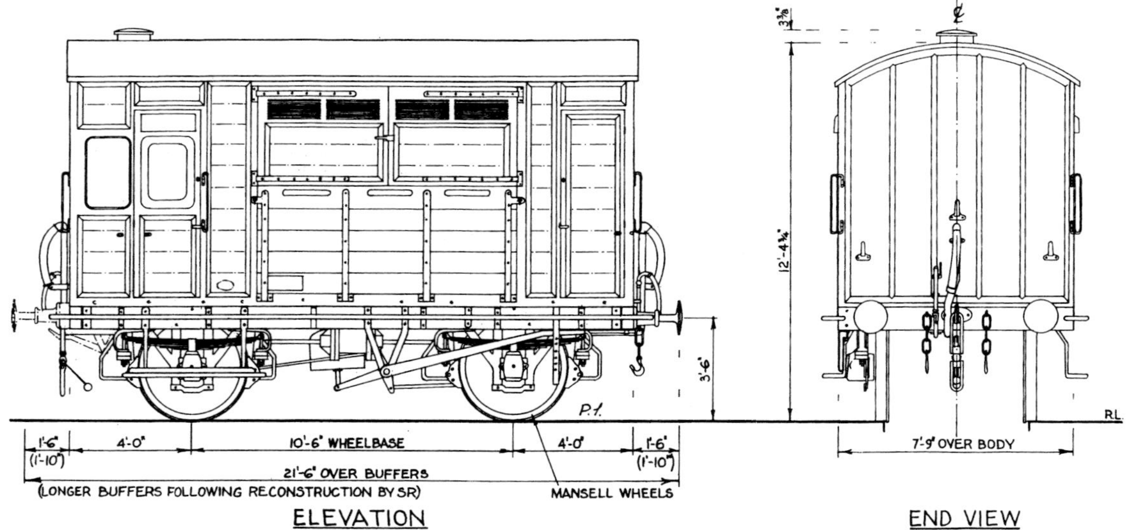

Caledonian Special Cattle Boxes

Details of the Caledonian Railway special cattle vans are set out in the attached table. Nos 53 and 66 to diagram 75 were 18 foot long without the drover's compartment, while the remaining four to diagram 75A were 21ft 6in long with such a compartment. The drawing shows the latter. Note the twin scoop type of roof ventilator typical of the Caley. It is probable that all were dual braked.

No photograph of the Caledonian special cattle van with drover's compartment has come to light. Instead the previous design without the compartment is included and shows some similar constructional features. Note that the left hand ventilator is open and that the vehicle is dual brake fitted and has safety chains. (British Railways)

PROTOTYPE DETAILS

Built	Order No	CR Nos	LMS 1st Nos	LMS 2nd Nos	With'n
01/98	H164	53	6759	-	1931
01/04	H217	59	6765	43997	02/34
01/04	H217	65	6771	43998	U/k
01/98	H164	66	6772	43996	1934
01/04	H217	70	6776	-	1930
01/04	H217	71	6777	-	1929

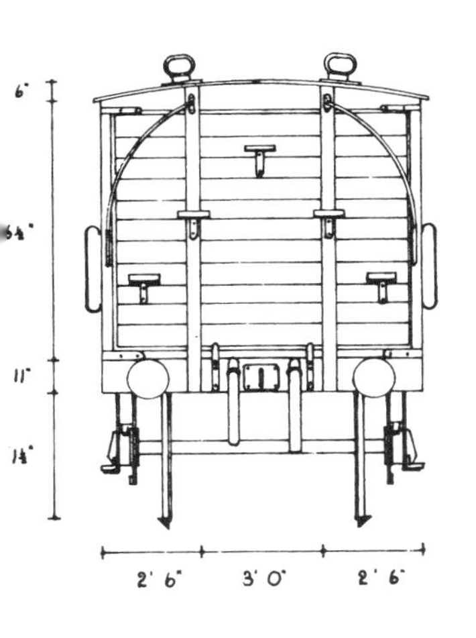

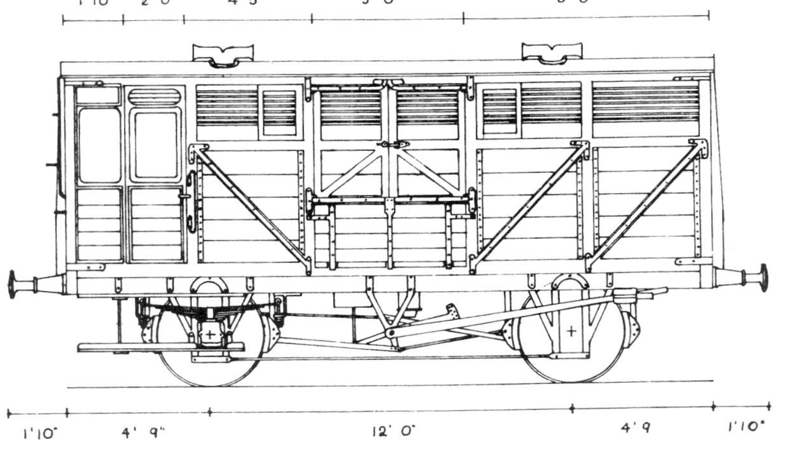

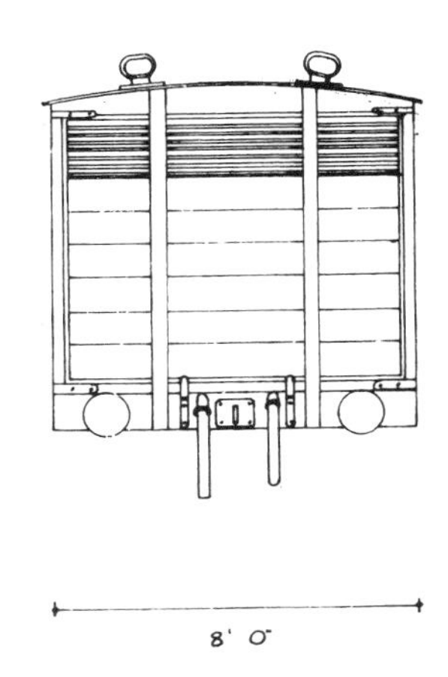

LMS Prize Cattle Van

PCV or SCV, "special cattle vans" are very similar to horseboxes but unlike many horseboxes, these PCVs were built with straight sides. They were equipped with automatic vacuum brake and through pipe for the Westinghouse brake and all were gas lit.

When first built vehicles built to Diagram D1876 were painted crimson lake lined with yellow with both LMS and the number shaded. Later they appeared in unlined red with the running number under the left-hand window and the "LMS" exactly opposite at the other end of the vehicle with "XP" and "W.B. 12' 6"" beneath at the extreme bottom at the right-hand side of the vehicle. Other notable differences were a long brake handle with the ratchet handle against the headstock, which are wood rather than steel. The handle is cranked in an upward V to clear the axle-box when the brake lever is pinned down. Finally, an axle-guard tie-bar is fitted. It is not known if this is a conversion, or whether the first lot from Newton Heath was built like this with the Derby lots as per the drawing.

PROTOTYPE DETAILS

Builder	Year	Lot	LMS 1st Nos (Sample)	L M S 2nd Nos	Ext't
Newton H	1926	227	6713/4/42/50/9, 6850/6/7/72/5/6	43800-43819	12/60
Derby	1927	318	1510, 1805, 8164, 826/31/92/6/7	43820-43834	8/61
Derby	1928	377	1869/71-4, 4931, 5627/47/67/77	43835-43846	1/61

Subsequent construction although of similar style was 24 long with 15ft 6in a wheelbase. The example illustrated here of No 43867 to Lot 598 appears to have been built at Derby in 1931 on a recovered ex-LNWR underframe. (G Warburton collection)

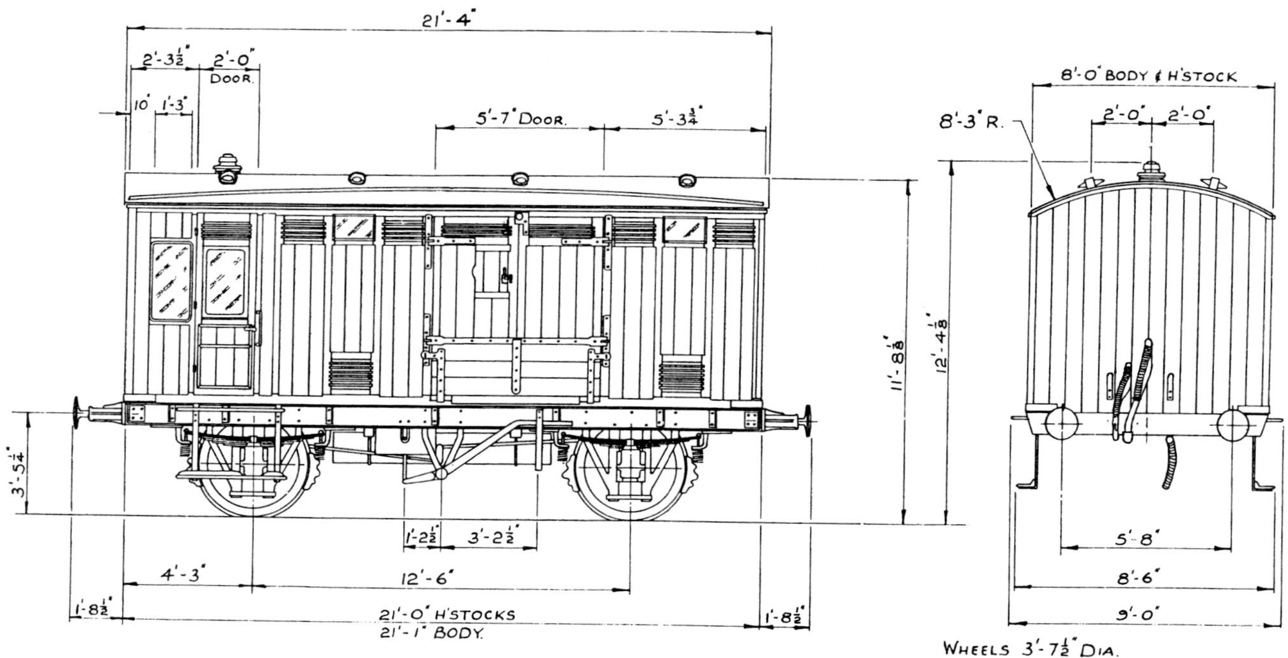

LNWR Prize Cattle Truck to Goods Diagram 26

Although the LNWR classified cattle trucks as goods stock, they were painted brown and No 72331 is seen as such. (HMRS collection V2574)

While still in LMS goods stock prize cattle box No 267403 was photographed about 1930 and would not appear to be grey, so is presumably crimson lake. This vehicle was either withdrawn prior to the renumbering scheme of 1932, or there are more numbers than given above. (RS Carpenter collection)

When built, these special cattle vans were regarded as goods stock and the LNWR numbered them 72329-34, 67403-06, 49477 and 49626. Nonetheless, they were painted dark chocolate with large white lettering. Initially the LMS took these vehicles in to its goods stock and added the usual constant to convert the LNWR number to an LMS number. But, as part of the 1932 renumbering scheme these trucks were removed from the goods stock section and numbered in the passenger list as 'Prize Cattle Van'. From then on until withdrawal they were regarded as passenger vehicles. It is not known whether from 1923 to 1932, as former LNWR brown vehicles, they were repainted red, or alternatively as goods numbered vehicles they may have been painted grey. Thereafter, however, it is more certain that they were red.

Both ends were the same structurally but only the drover's end had the emergency brake indicator. The vehicle has been drawn in 'as built' condition. Few alterations are believed to have been made during the lives of these vehicles. In 1932 the whole block of numbers 43962 to 43969 was allocated to vehicles of this type. The earlier corresponding LMS goods numbers (with building dates) were 272329 ('02), 272332 ('02), 249477 ('12), 249626 ('12), 249476 ('21), 249607 ('23), 249616 ('23) and 249618 ('23). The last was withdrawn in December 1956.

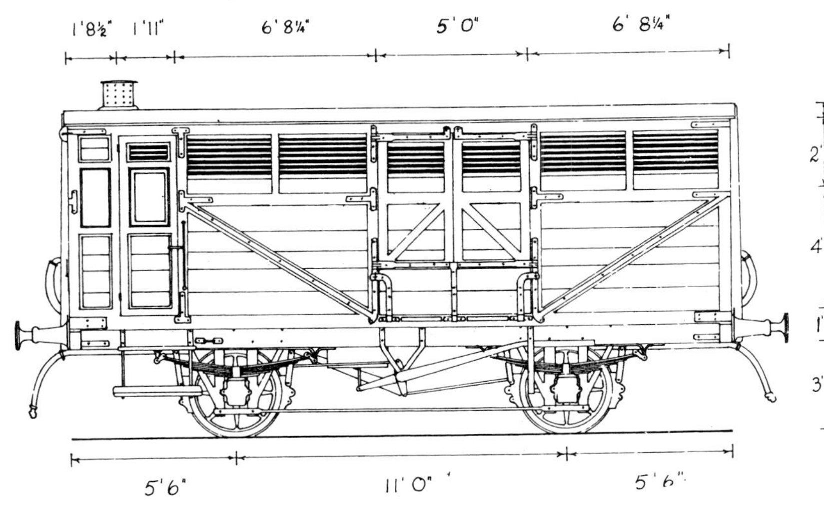

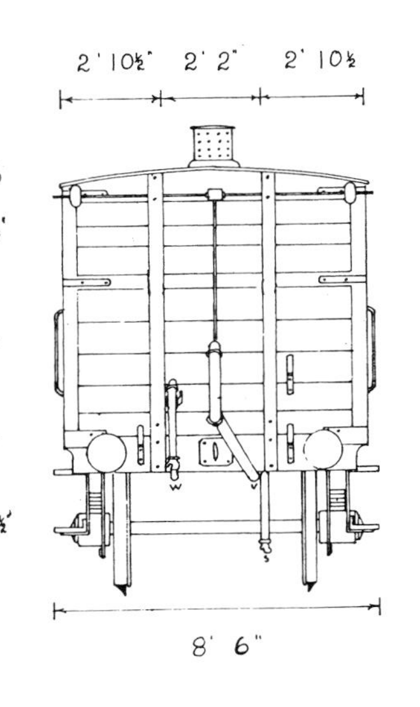

Great Eastern Passenger Train Cattle Box

Whilst ordinarily cattle was conveyed by goods train in cattle trucks, at extra cost animals could be forwarded by passenger train and this was usually only done in the case of prize cattle on their way to or from agricultural shows etc. For such occasions special cattle boxes were provided, such as the example presented here. In 1888 and 1892 the GER had built passenger train cattle boxes without a compartment for the drover. From 1897 until 1914 85 boxes were built which incorporated such a compartment with access to the cattle in the remainder of the vehicle.

All were fitted with Westinghouse brake gear and those built in 1902 and 1910 also had vacuum pipes. Steel underframes were provided for the first three batches and timber thereafter. The LNER retained the GER numbers. Vacuum brake gear was added by the LNER to those without it from the mid 1930s and by nationalisation the Westinghouse equipment was being removed. Withdrawals were in approximate order of construction with 50 handed over to BR with the last half dozen going in 1959.

For further details see *Model Railway Constructor*, p 523, September 1983.

The end view of special cattle van No SC1144 in LNER livery in the late 1930s. (GY Hemingway, courtesy of HMRS & J Watling)

PROTOTYPE DETAILS

Built	GER & LNER Nos
1897	1146-1155
1902	1156-1165
1908	1166-1185
1910	1186-1210
1913	1136-1145
1914	1126-1135

Late in its life ex-GER special cattle van No E1203 at Colchester with the two shutters in the sides open. (J Watling)

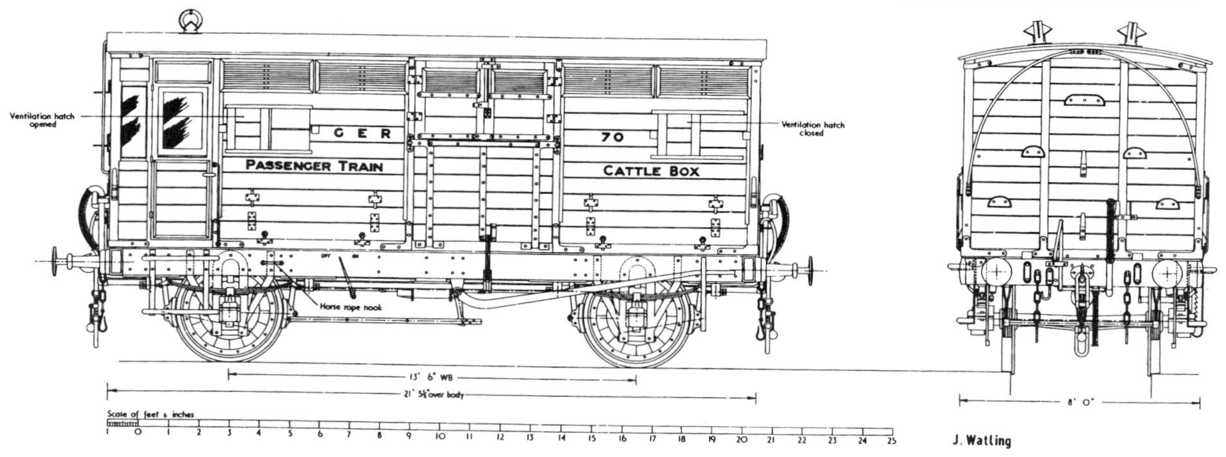

NER and LNER Special Cattle Vans

The LNER built three batches of special cattle van to the NER diagram 242 (LNER 1), based on an earlier NER design to diagram 189 introduced in 1911, also shown on the drawing. The vans had a drover's compartment and large cattle box with ventilated sides and roof ventilators. Initially dual braking was provided, but the Westinghouse equipment is likely to have been removed as this was phased out on the railways. Through steam heating pipes, alarm gear and oil lamps were also fitted. The NER vans were numbered 500/7-17, later 483-493. The diagram 1 vehicles were later were coded 8001.

PROTOTYPE DETAILS

Built	Built at	Nos
1923	York	477-482, 494-9
1924-5	Dukinfield	2201-2220
1927	Dukinfield	2221-2226

LNER special cattle van No SC 2209 from the 1924/5 batch built at Dukinfield was photographed at Sighthill, Glasgow on 15 June 1948. (AG Ellis, courtesy GB Ellis)

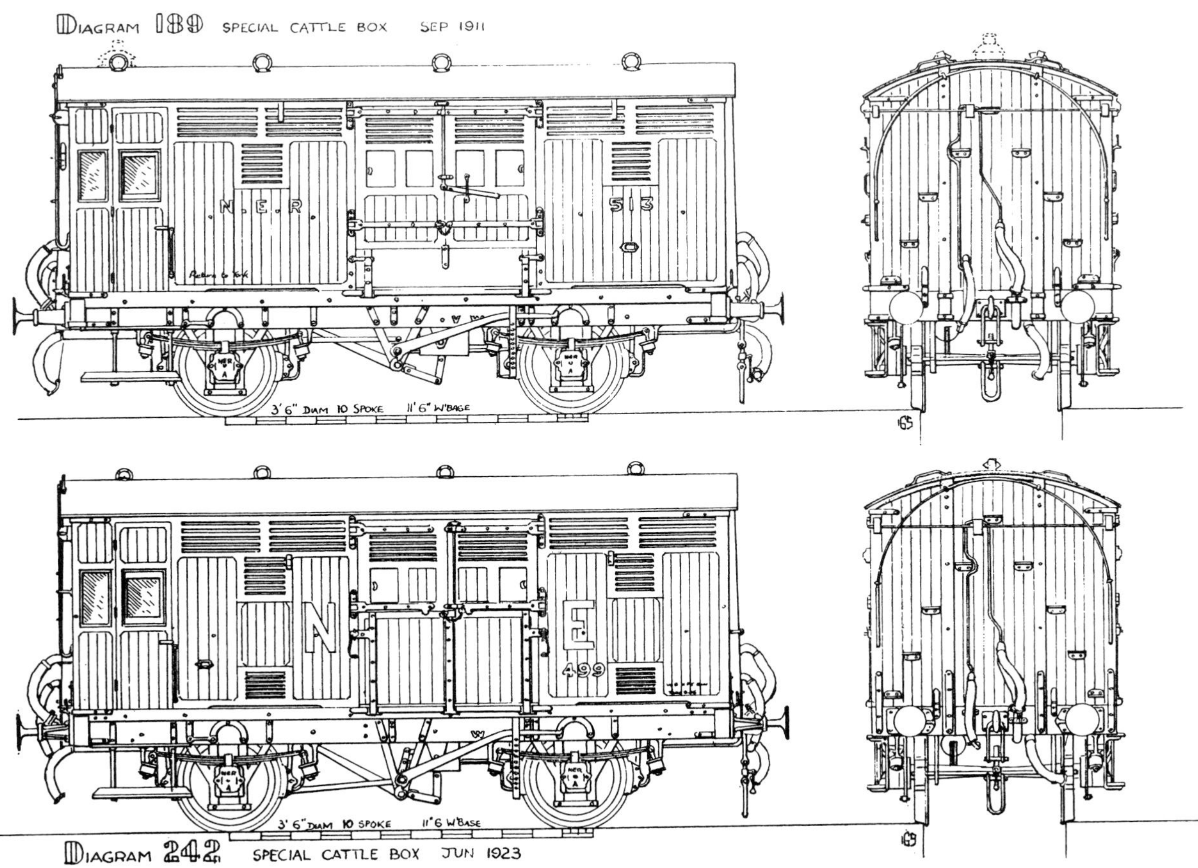

Great Western 6 Ton Special Cattle Van Beetle B and C

Having previously tried special cattle vans without provision for a drover, the GW introduced diagram W7 in 1909 which included a compartment for the person accompanying the beasts. The design was continued basically unaltered until the 6 wheel version produced during the early BR period. There were, nonetheless several minor variations, such as flush areas superseding panelling of the sides, gas or oil lighting and changes in the compartment door ventilators. The first lot (Wagon 639) of vehicles to diagram W7 were dual fitted and coded Beetle B, the second (Carriage 1380) being Beetle C with vacuum brake only. Initially lot 639 was numbered as goods stock and later renumbered. These are listed in the attached table.

PROTOTYPE DETAILS

Diagram	**W7**	**W13**	**W14**
Date built	1909-1926	1930-1931	1937
Comp't sides	Panelled	Flush	Flush
Door vents	4 elements	3 elements	None
End bracing	Cross	Full height	Reduced height
Lighting	Gas	Oil	Gas
Buffers	12 inch dia spindle	12 inch dia spindle	16 inch dia self-contained
Numbers	68464-83 later 981-1000, 200/3/5/6/10/4/6/9/20/2	614-19, 622-5	720-30

Former Great Western special cattle van No 998, coded Beetle B. This vehicle was built to diagram W7 in 1909. Note the bolections around the quarter lights and that the shutters are in the lowered position. (M Longridge, HMRS collection S119-5)

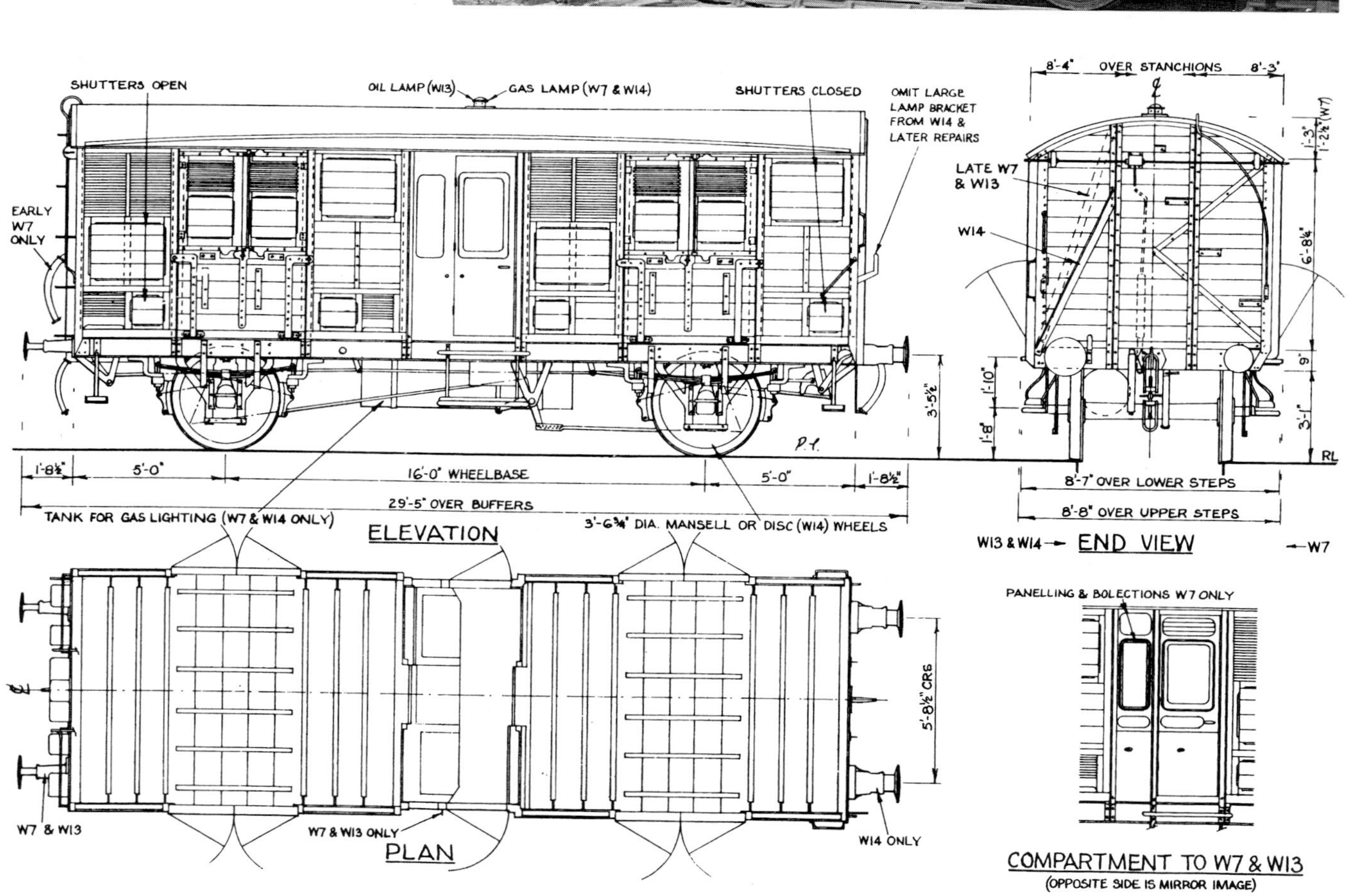

Southern Railway 8 Ton Special Cattle Van

The Birmingham Railway Carriage and Wagon Co supplied 50 special cattle vans, with a compartment for the herdsman, to the Southern Railway in June and July 1930, which were numbered 3679 to 3728. These were equipped with dual braking; steam heating pipes and oil lighting. A further ten, Nos 3729-3738, were built at Lancing Works in September/October 1952 and were equipped with electric lighting and omitted the Westinghouse brake and the end steps. The SR vans were extinct by 1963 and the later vehicles by 1971.

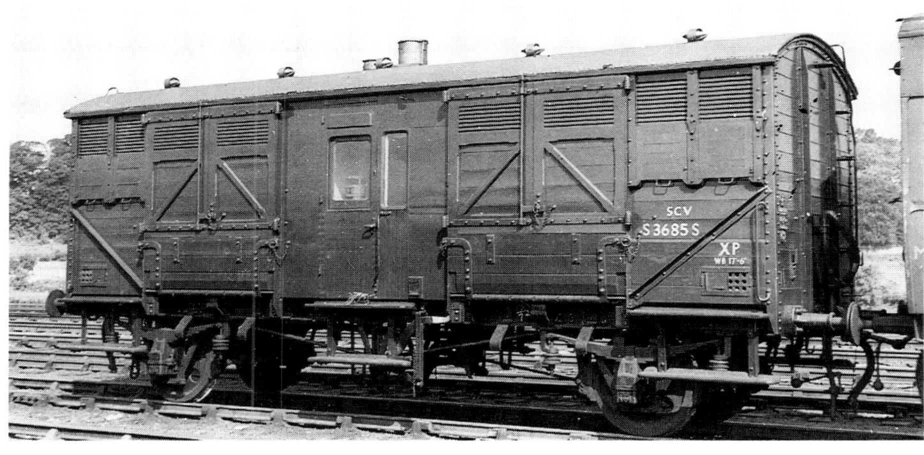

In service at Malton on 30 July 1955 No S3685S of the earlier batch appears to have been recently overhauled and repainted. (AG Ellis, courtesy BC Ellis)

Brand new Southern Railway 8 ton special cattle van No 3683 to diagram 3141, built by the Birmingham Rly Carr & Wagon Co in 1930. Note the wagon sized 3 hole disc wheels, dual brake and steam heating pipe hoses and on the roof the top to the oil lamp. (HMRS collection V1732)

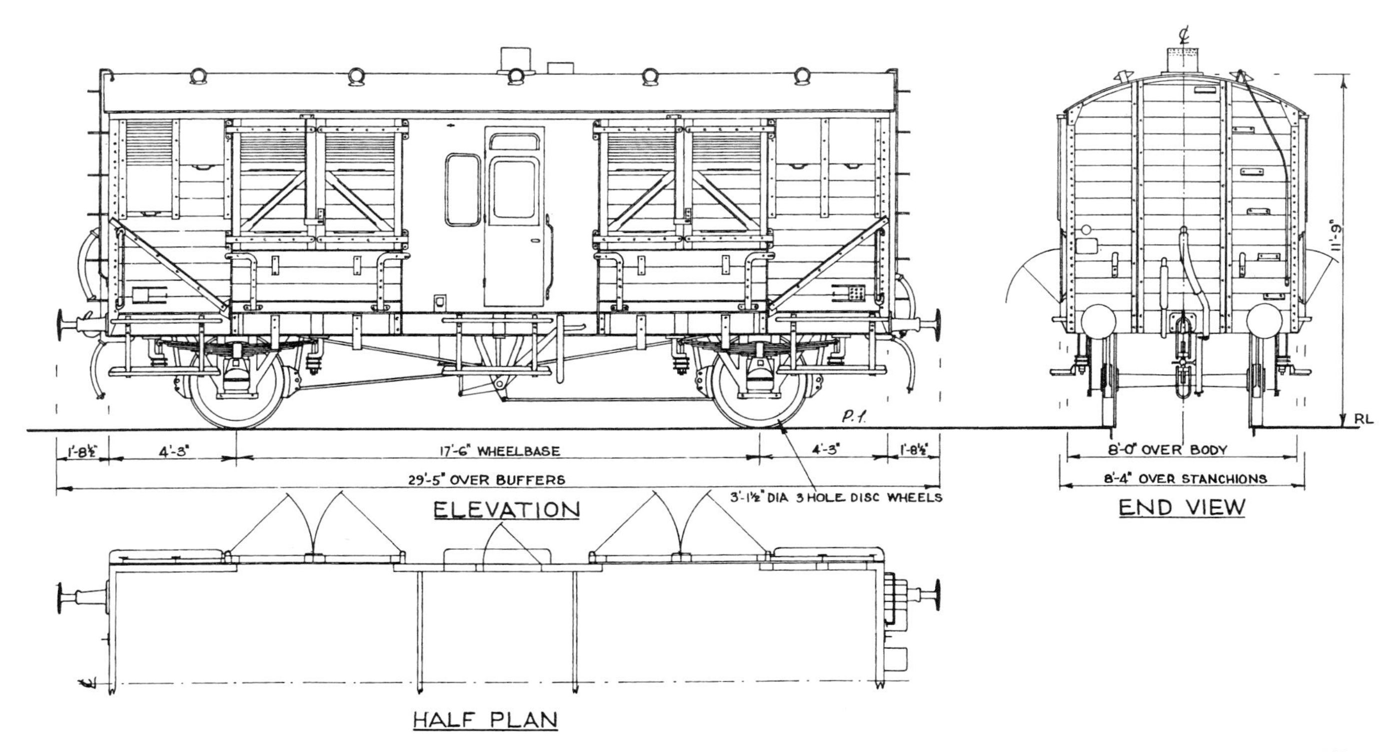

Highland Railway Open Fish Trucks

Originally fish traffic was variously despatched in boxes, barrels, or alive in tanks. The first two were conveyed open fish trucks sheeted over, or, has been suggested, covered in peat turves. The Highland had three types all 18 feet long and, in early days at least piped for through running in passenger trains. The earliest had four plank sides and cupboard doors and curved ends (top drawing). Later full brake rigging and steam pipes will have been added. From 1896, as this type wore out, they were replaced by similar vehicles with straight ends (middle drawing). A variation of the latter had full length drop sides, supposedly to enable them to double up as open carriage trucks (bottom drawing). If not fitted from the outset, lamp brackets will have soon been added.

The Highland numbers were 1874 to 2146. These were initially allocated Nos 7547 to 7845 by the LMS, who subsequently renumbered the survivors 40978 to 40999 in 1932. Accept that those achieving the 2nd LMS No being of the more modern two designs, it is not possible to determine which type any number applies to.

Ex HR open fish truck No M40993 is seen recently overhauled by BR (80 28.5.54). It survived until December 1956. Formerly HR No 2096 built by the company in 1912, its first LMS No was 7795. Alterations include smaller diameter wheels, note joggled keep plates; hand brake lever and push rods; addition of intermediate side stanchions; and removal of Westinghouse brake pipe. (Photo TW Bourne collection, courtesy P Tatlow)

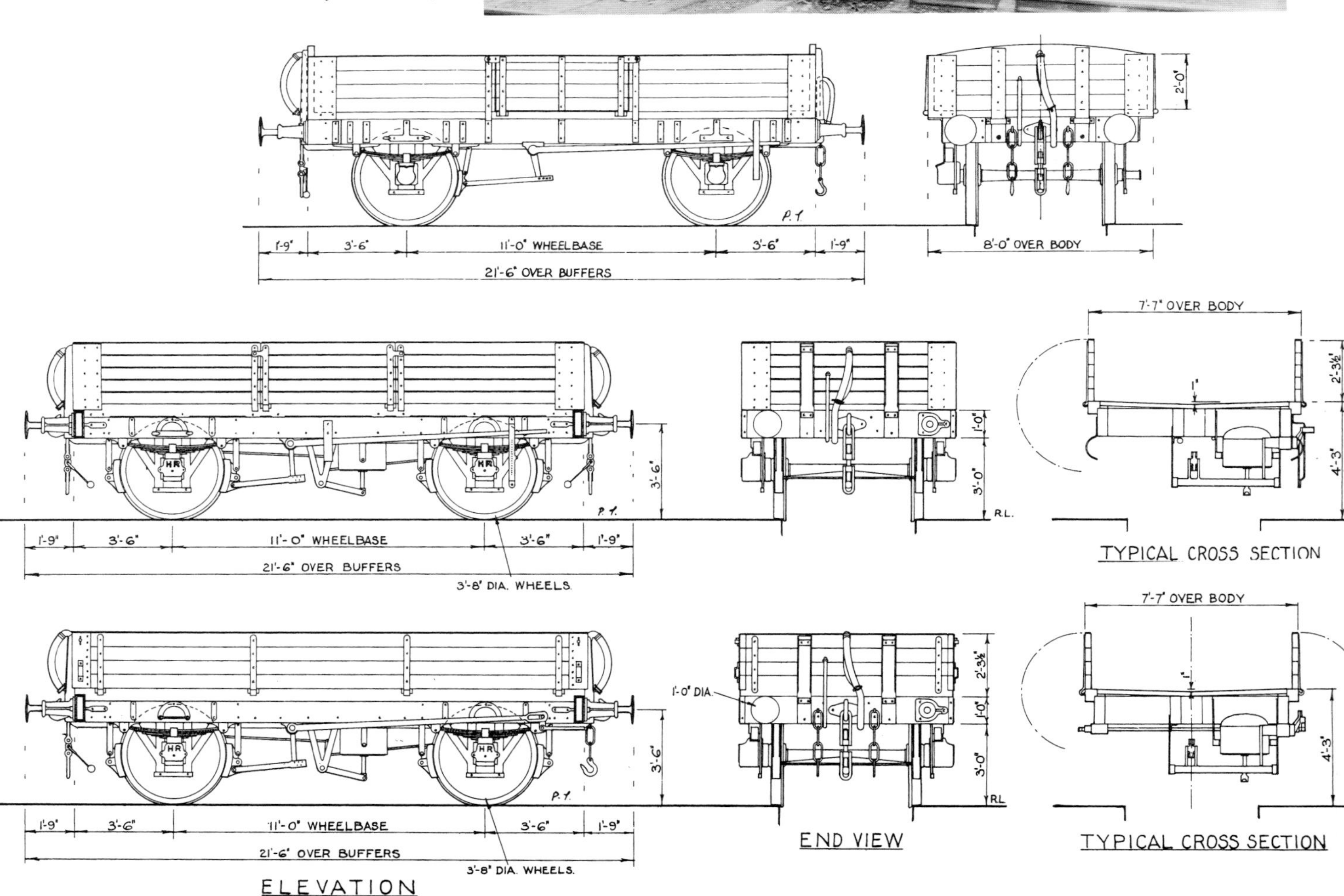

LMS Six Wheel Milk and Fish Vans

This drawing refers to milk and fish vans built to diagrams 1873 and 1874 constructed on second hand Midland coach underframes. When first built those to diagram 1873 and one lot only of diagram 1874 were labelled "Milk Van". Under the 1932 scheme, however, the second lot to D1873 and first of D1874 were numbered into the fish van series, whereas all the others went into milk van series.

The drawing refers to fish vans with six closely spaced boards to the lower sides, but the milk vans had five slats to the sides, although later some of these were boarded up. Diagram 1873 was fitted with through pipe for the Westinghouse brake, as well as full automatic vacuum brake equipment. Otherwise, as far as can seen, there are no other differences between these various batches.

The fish vans were lettered, "To be used for Passenger Train Traffic only" on the bottom plank between the upright and diagonal strapping at the extreme right-hand side. The "LMS" and number were on the doors below the handrail.

PROTOTYPE DETAILS

Diagram	Lot	Built by	Year	LMS 1st Nos (Selection)	LMS 2nd Nos	Extinct by
D1873	112	Derby	1924		38300-38314	6/61
	233	Wolverton	1926	28, 79, 123, 505, 1498, 1913, 3472, 6288/90/4/8/9, 7899	40000-40099	12/63
	364	Derby	1928	6596, 6620/1, 7200/5/31, 7485, 7603, 7726/46, 8020/2/3	38500-38524	12/61
	663	Derby	1933		38545-38549	7/63
D1874	304	Derby	1927	7392, 7400/7/8/10/3/4/9/26/72, 7610	40100-40124	11/61
	442	Wolverton	1929	1563, 1650, 5900/1, 7292-4/6/8/9, 7302/14/6/20	38525-38544	C'70

LMS six wheel fish van No M40029, formerly LMS 1st No 537, towards the end of its life at Hull Paragon on 26 June 1960. (JE Cull)

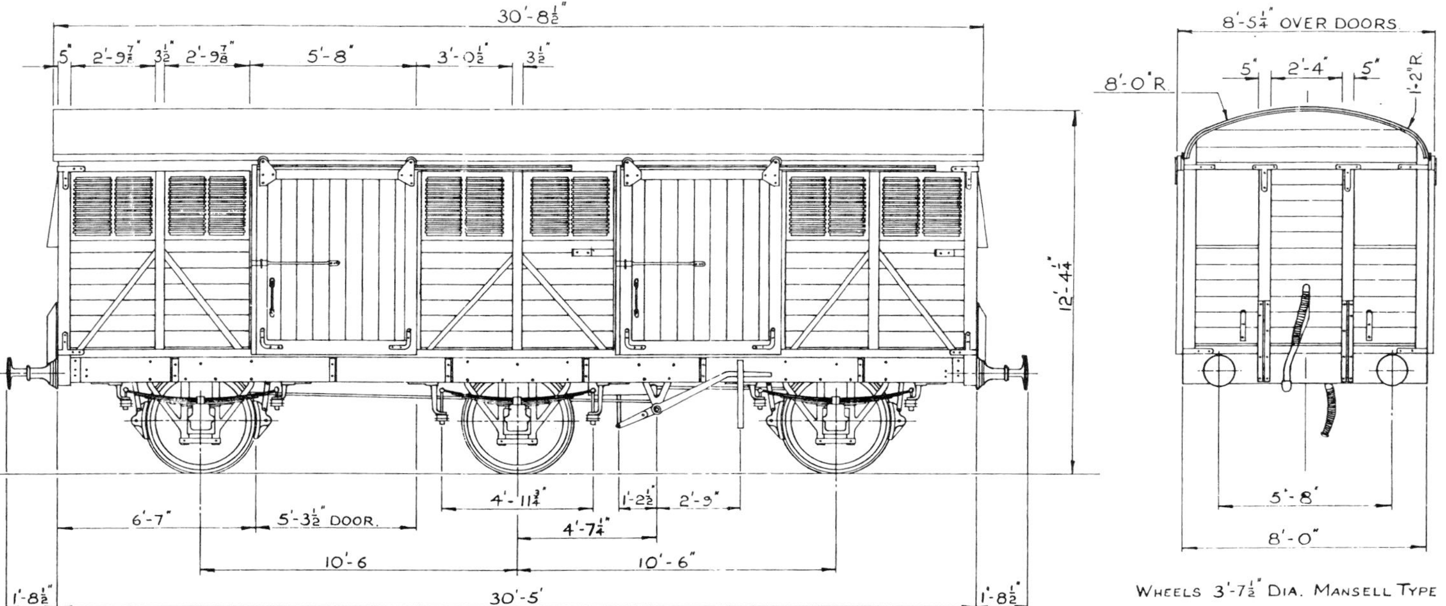

LMS Six Wheel 6 ton Express Fish Vans

As part of the general re-stocking following the World War 2, six wheel express fish vans to diagram were introduced in 1947. Built at Wolverton to D2115, they were similar in style of body construction to earlier 6 ton four wheel 17ft 6in long fish vans, with vertical planks and without ventilators. Numbered in LMS second series, those constructed after nationalisation in 1948 were prefixed M by BR.

LMS six wheel express fish van No 40234. This vehicle is from the first batch built at Wolverton in 1947 and hence painted in LMS livery and coded X-FISH . (SN White collection)

PROTOTYPE DETAILS

Lot	Year	Nos
1428	1946/7	40200-40249
1445	1949	40250-40299
1509	1949	40300-40339

From the last lot to be constructed in 1949 No M40325 was photographed at Birmingham New Street on 1 July 1957. (JE Cull)

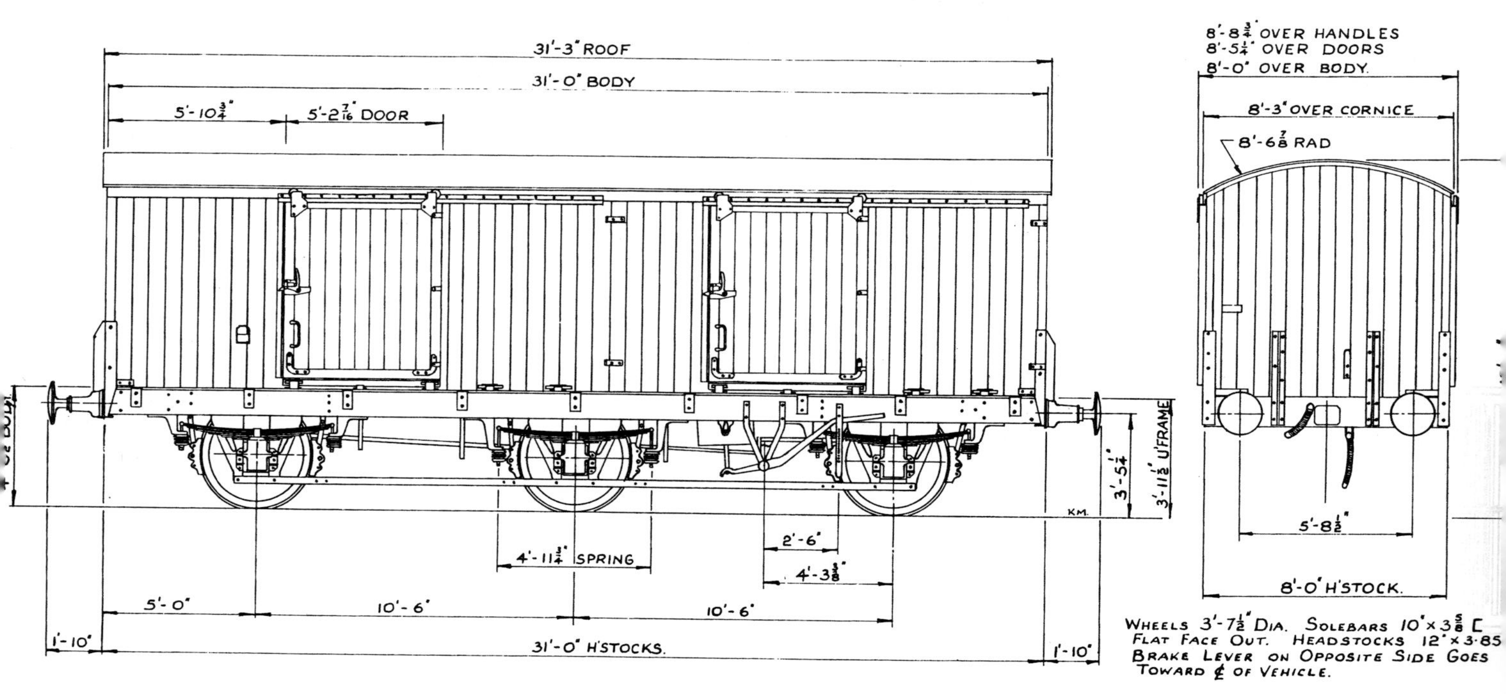

LNWR and North British Open Fish Trucks

LNWR Open Fish Truck to Diagram 468

The LNWR built 248 21 foot long open fish trucks for the conveyance of fish from the ports where it was landed to the towns and cities. Although covered fish vans were later introduced for longer journeys, open but sheeted trucks continued in use on shorter hauls. The floors of the trucks were provided with slats and drainage channels.

The LNWR vehicles were unusual in adopting sliding, rather than drop, doors, although they may also have some of the latter as well. Over the years that they were produced variations in fittings will be found, such as inside and outside W irons, axlebox types, brake rigging etc.

PROTOTYPE DETAILS

Built	LNWR Nos (Sample, add 11000 after 1910)	LMS 1st Nos	LMS 2nd Nos	Ext't
1889-1898	39, 48, 165, 254, 381, 449, 476, 503, 679-758, 979-99	5178-5378	40907-40940	1938
1922	12224-9	5379-84	40942-48	1958

North British 5 Ton Open Fish Truck

The NB built several types of open fish truck over the years culminating with the 16ft 5in long 5 ton design to diagram 165. Some 68 were ordered from RY Pickering in 1920. On becoming LNER property, they were allocated SSA diagram 132B (Code 3054), but re-classified as freight stock. There is doubt, therefore, as whether they were painted brown or red oxide. A cast plate lettered FISH was attached to the side. The tare weight given as 7t 5c 2q, although there would undoubtedly have been minor variations. There were still 12 of this type in service at the end of 1947.

PROTOTYPE DETAILS – Nos

NB	LNER
232 to 299	748001/4/5/8/13/7/22/4/7/9/31/6/46/7/52/3/70/2/7/85/7/8/90/2/7/102/11/4/23/5/6/8/31/2/5-8/41/5/8/51/5/9/60/7/8/73/8/81/99/201/8/18/9/22/3/9/32/40/2/4/53/6/8/64/6/9

An early example of a LNWR open fish truck No 439 with sliding door, outside W irons and safety chains. The vehicle has outside brake pull rods and a horizontal vacuum cylinder, but no hand brake lever and is piped for Westinghouse brakes. (P Tatlow collection)

North British 5 ton open fish truck with falling sides No 297 built by RY Pickering in 1921. The three knobs below the headstocks and solebar door bangers. Note the passenger stock livery and FISH TRAFFIC BY PASSENGER TRAIN ONLY *applied along the top plank. (P Tatlow collection)*

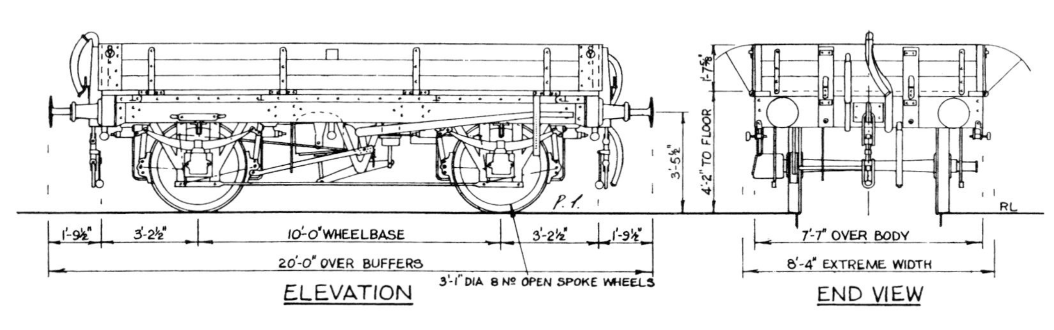

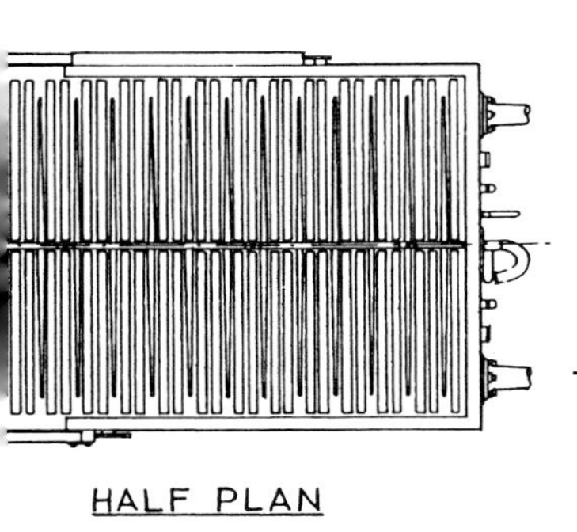

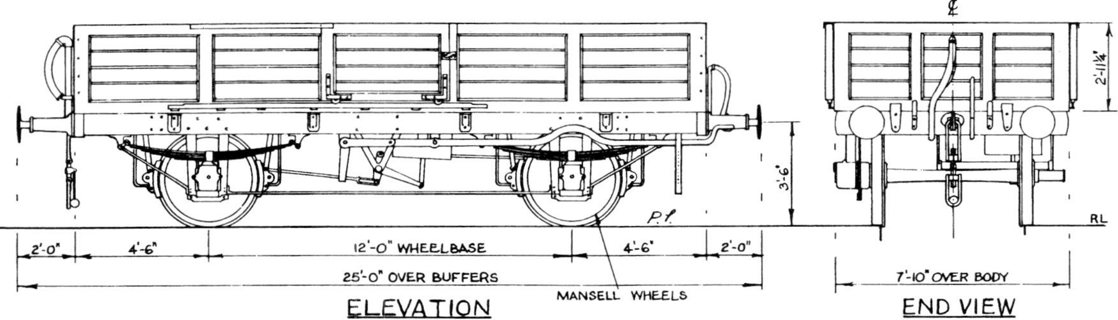

WCJS Six Wheel Fish Vans to Diagram 107

These vans were in construction for West Coast Joint Stock from 1908 to 1910. As produced they were resplendent in lined, chocolate brown, grey roofs, slate waist panels and black running gear. The louvres were varnished wood. They were dual braked to enable them to work on the Caledonian Railway, but, no handbrake was provided. The whole construction is typical of Wolverton and, as might be expected of express stock.

The LNWR, and subsequently the LMS, labelled some of these vehicles for meat traffic from 1913 and full details wil be found in *A register of West Coast Joint Stock*. The vans survived well into BR days but the onslaught of container traffic finished them off, together with many varieties of later fish stock. Many worked on 2.00pm fish train from Aberdeen to London, together with 5.45pm and 7.55pm trains from Aberdeen with individual vans for Carlisle, Carnforth Holyhead, Birmingham, Crewe, Manchester, Preston and Wigan.

The drawing below should be used in conjunction with the LNWR underframes detailed on page 17. There were also six equally spaced torpedo ventilators on the roof centre line and rain strips on each side.

Former West Coast Joint Stock six wheel fish van No 671 built in 1910, seen here as LMS No 4296 in fully lined livery. This had become a meat van in 1913 and in 1933 was, therefore, renumbered by the LMS in the meat van series as No 38893. Note Mansell wheels and slate colour patches on sliding doors upon which to inscribe destinations and other messages in chalk. (P Tatlow collection)

PROTOTYPE DETAILS

WCJS Nos	Year built	LMS 1st Nos	Type	LMS 2nd Nos	Ext't
595-604	1908	4220-4229	Fish Vans	40376-40442	10/58
605-624	1909	4230-4249			
625-694	1910	4250-4319	Meat Vans	38879-38899	5/55
471, 552	1912/'21	4218/9			

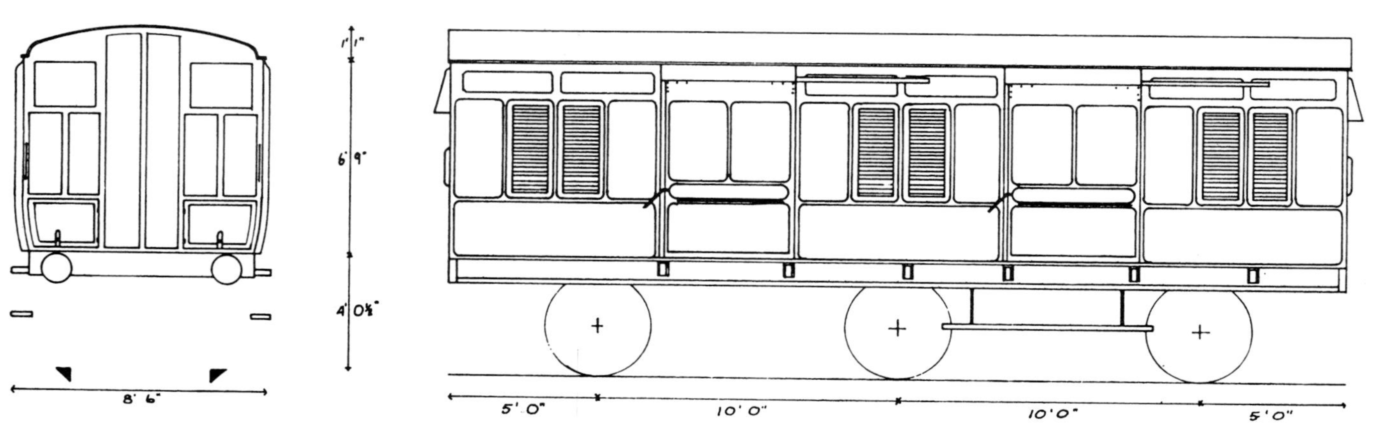

LNWR Six Wheel Fruit Van to Diagram 454

This type of van is all but identical to the later West Coast Joint Stock Fish vans but has a plain high arc roof, similar to the combination trucks. Seasonal fruit traffic was a very valuable revenue earner for the railway, until the motor lorries captured such traffic, and the LNWR obviously thought it worth while to build these vehicles in 1909, rather than add more combination trucks.

On the drawing the straight brake lever is unusual and probably only applied in a few cases. It is thought that some other vehicles were built on second-hand underframes.

PROTOTYPE DETAILS

LNWR 1st Nos	LNWR 2nd Nos	LMS 1st Nos	LMS 2nd Nos	Ext't by
1147-1171	12147-12171	4632-4656	38349-38372	1952

Ex-CR McIntosh 0-6-0 812 class as LMS 3F No 17572 sets off from Perth in about 1930 with a mixed train for the South. Immediately behind the locomotive is a LNWR six wheel fruit van boldly lettered **LMS** *and* **4650** *respectively on the lower panels of the left and right hand doors. Following World War 1, the LNWR used large lettering and numbering on npc vans and the LMS adopted a similar practice on ex-LNWR vans. The end of the brake lever on this vehicle has an upward joggle typical of the LNWR. Behind the fruit van are five bogie gangwayed passenger brake vans, viz: a LNWR 42 foot with elliptical roof and side lookouts; a WCJS or LNWR low arc roof, probably 45 foot long; a CR 50 foot; a LMS 50 foot all-steel; and a MR clerestory, possibly without gangways. These are followed by a long string of a goods wagons and occasional van. (TG Hepburn, courtesy Rail Archive Stephenson)*

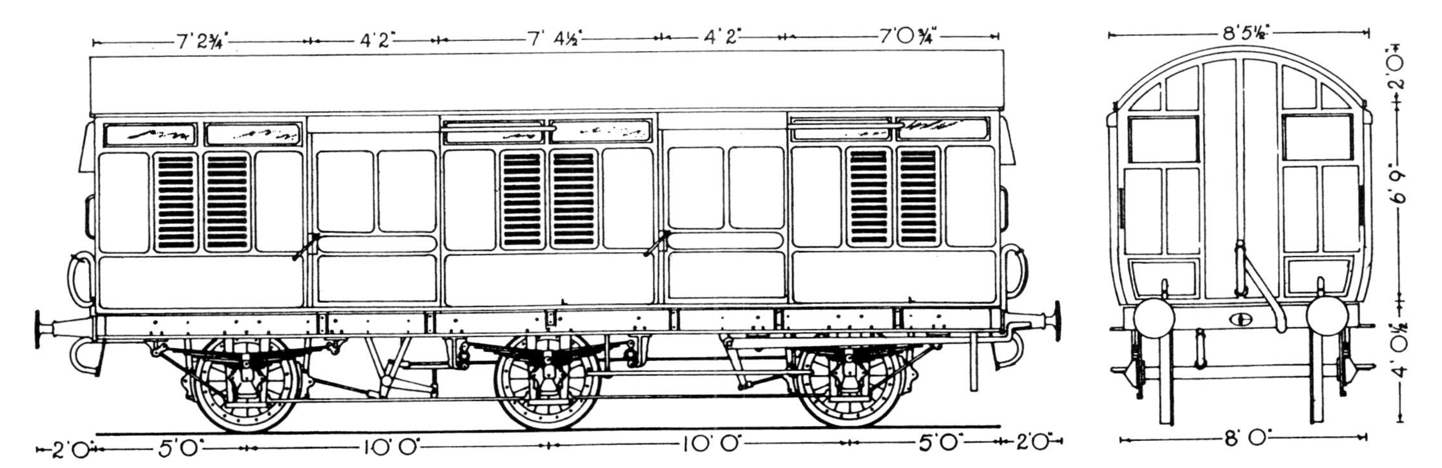

L&Y Fruit Trucks

The Lancashire & Yorkshire Railway had a large collection of passenger luggage vans. The older four wheel type had birdcage roofs and had almost all gone by the grouping. The company were masters of rebuilding old carriage stock into vans rather than spending capital on such 'secondary' vehicles. Twenty 'Fruit Vans' were ordered in November 1912 and were typical of the process. They had been three compartment third class brakes. The interior was gutted and some doors were fixed while the centre compartment door was made into a double.....at 2ft 2in the doors were each the 'passenger' size while the original van doors remained the 2ft size. Horizontal guard rails were fitted in the old passenger area and the guards brake equipment was removed. They carried the normal LYR carriage livery and were never repainted in LMS colours, the last being withdrawn in the mid 1930s.

Above - *No. 54 as converted. The 'fruit' title was an LYR derivation for freight just as other railways used code names for vehicles. (BC Lane collection)*

Conversions often had detail differences and this example has kept its gas lamps, footboards and the doors are not in exactly the same location. In LMS days, the vans worked far from 'home' ground carrying anything from pigeons to parcels traffic. (BC Lane coll.)

PROTOTYPE DETAILS

L&Y Nos	LMS 1st Nos	LMS 2nd Nos
36 - 55	5663, 5909, 5968-75/86-9/91/3/6-9	38492 - 9

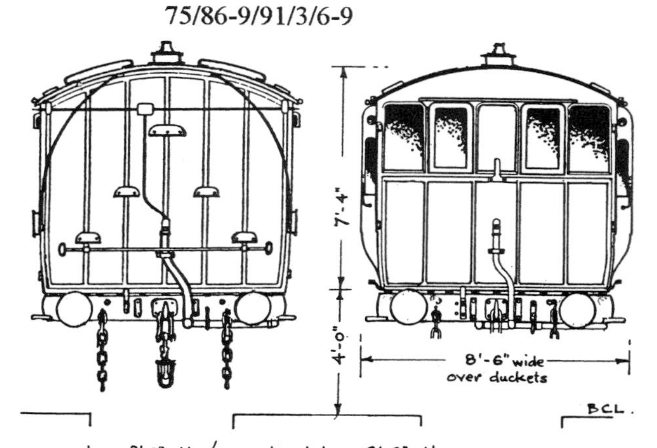

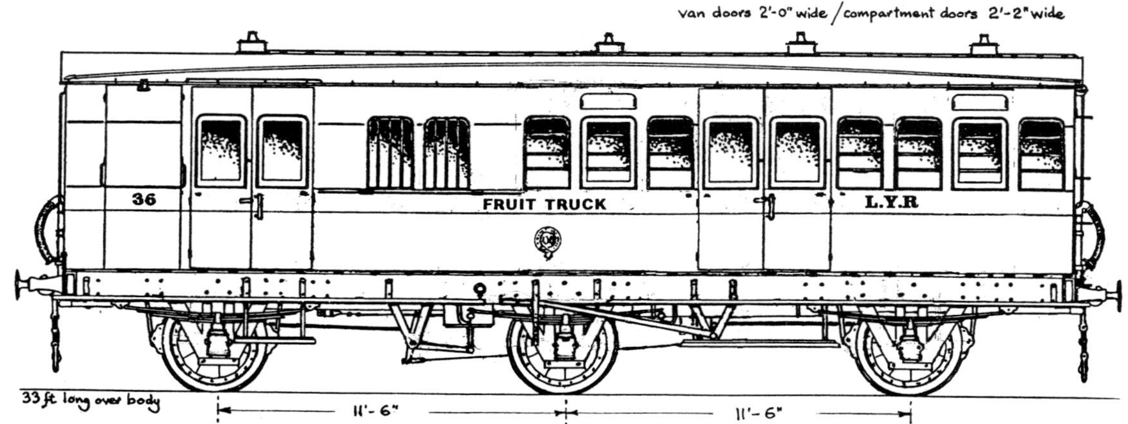

L&Y Four and Six Wheel Milk Trucks

Ten 25 foot long milk trucks were built by the Lancashire & Yorkshire Railway to diagram 111 in 1898 to Lot Y13 on recovered four wheel carriage underframes and numbered 22 to 31. They acquired new 5ft 6in springs, oil axle boxes and buffers with automatic vacuum brake equipment. The body framing was inside with horizontal boarding on the outside which was the reverse of what was shown on the official diagram. The pregrouping livery was the same as carriage stock, tan for the upper portion of the sides with carmine lake below. Standard gilt transfers for the LYR letters and numerals were used but the MILK TRUCK lettering, 'To Carry 6 Tons' and 'Tare 7.3.1' were painted in yellow. The milk traffic came largely from the West Lancashire, Fylde and North Lancashire districts.

A further four vehicles were added, on recovered 6 wheel underframes in 1912 and up to five milk trucks would be attached to early morning trains to Manchester, returning with the empties as available.

All were taken over by the LMS and three of the four wheelers survived to be renumbered in 1932 as 38630-2 (the first having carried LMS No 5981, but many never carried their 'first' LMS numbers). The last of the four wheeled vans was withdrawn in 1938. The six wheeled examples lasted to nationalisation and travelled far from home ground. No. 38634 was recorded at Willesden in 1949.

The LYR official photograph of No 25 does not show the difference in livery colours, as the orthocromatic film emulsions were 'blind' to reds and browns. There was no line between the two colours but the beading around each section was picked out in orange. Ends were dark brown. (BC Lane collection)

A close up view of a train at Manchester Victoria station ready for loading. The slate panel can be seen on the third board down. (BC Lane coll)

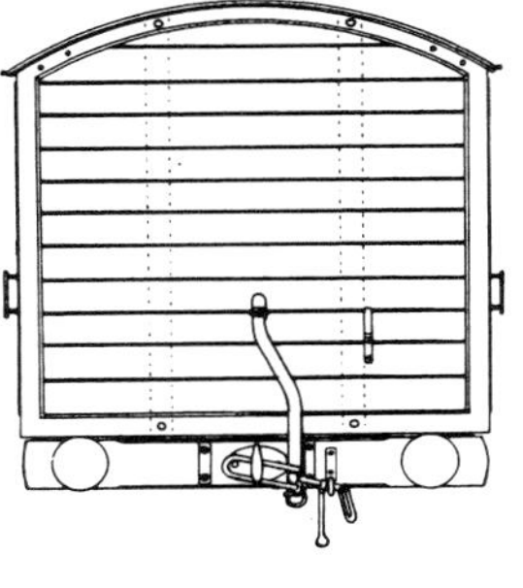

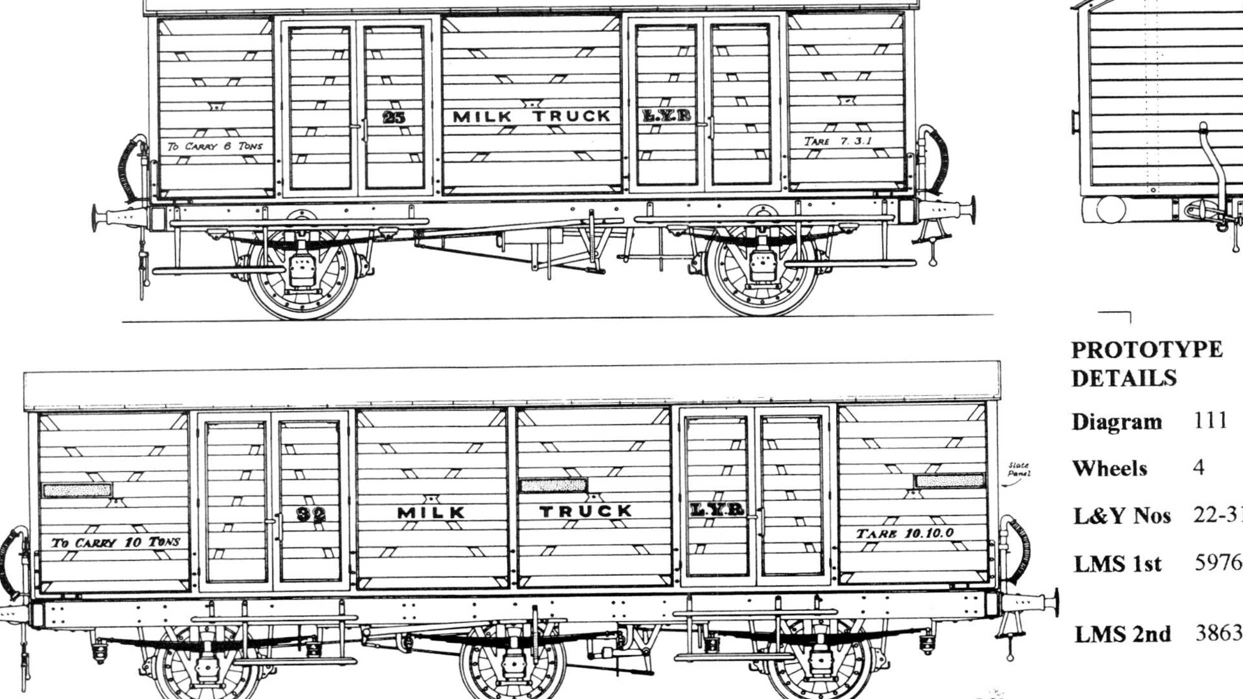

PROTOTYPE DETAILS

Diagram	111	117
Wheels	4	6
L&Y Nos	22-31	32-35
LMS 1st	5976-85	5990/2/4/5
LMS 2nd	38630-2	38633-5

MR and S&DJR 5 Ton 25 Foot Fruit and Milk Vans

Both vehicles are structurally identical and the S&D batch were constructed as part of one lot passing through Derby works. As built, both had the ring-type door handles shown on the S&D drawing, but the Midland one, to Diagram 419, had the more usual tee-head handle fitted at a later date. The Midland vans had the eight roof ventilators. The S&DJR enjoyed less lavish station facilities than the Midland and probably for this reason specified an oil lamp in the roof with, of course, steps at one end of the vehicle for access to the lamp.

The hand brake provided by the Midland consisted of one short and one longer lever acting through the power brake linkage. The S&D lever operated a separate linkage to the left hand wheels. On taking over S&D stock, the Southern classed their share of these vans as passenger luggage vans PLV and the word LUGGAGE would be painted just over the bottom bead in the bottom right hand corner. It is thought that they would have scrapped theirs before the outbreak of World War 2.

These vehicles present an opportunity, if the period is picked correctly at say mid 1930, to have one red LMS, one blue S&D, one blue SR and one green SR.

Midland fruit van No 38470 in LMS condition in the late thirties showing the foot board cut away to accommodate the hand brake lever. Some repairs have been carried out to the panels resulting in the amalgamation of the waist and lower panels. (RA Mills)

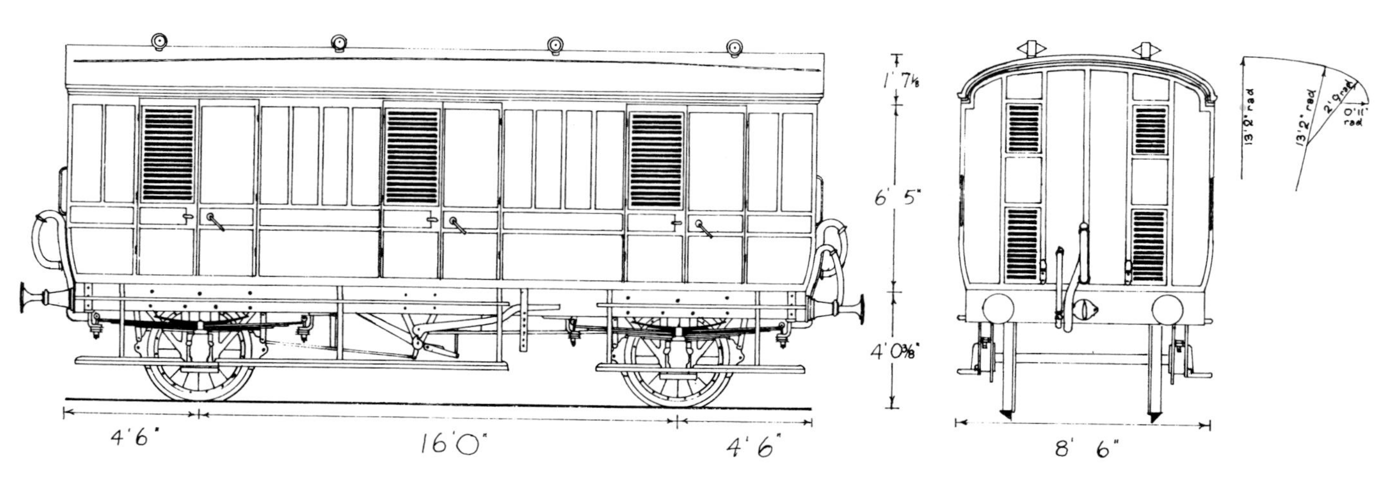

MR and S&DJR 5 Ton 25 foot Fruit and Milk Vans

PROTOTYPE DETAILS

Lot	Built	MR Nos	LMS 1st Nos	LMS 2nd Nos	Extinct
476	1900	551-575 + u/k	1705-1729	38415-38436	12/51
523	1902	S&D 7-18	(1-11) u/k + (12-17) to SR	1710-1715	12/36
531	1902	207-212	1569-1574	38437-38441	10/49
572	1904	243-272	1575-1604	38442-38471	10/45
881	1918	192, 196, 310-8, 535	1555-62/4/8, 1605-13/98	38472-38491	10/55

No 38482 is an example from Lot 881 built in 1918 with rounded corners to the panels and was photographed at Cardington on 22 March 1940. Note also the three separate sets of steps, one to each pair of doors and bottle shaped buffer housings. (AE West, courtesy MS King)

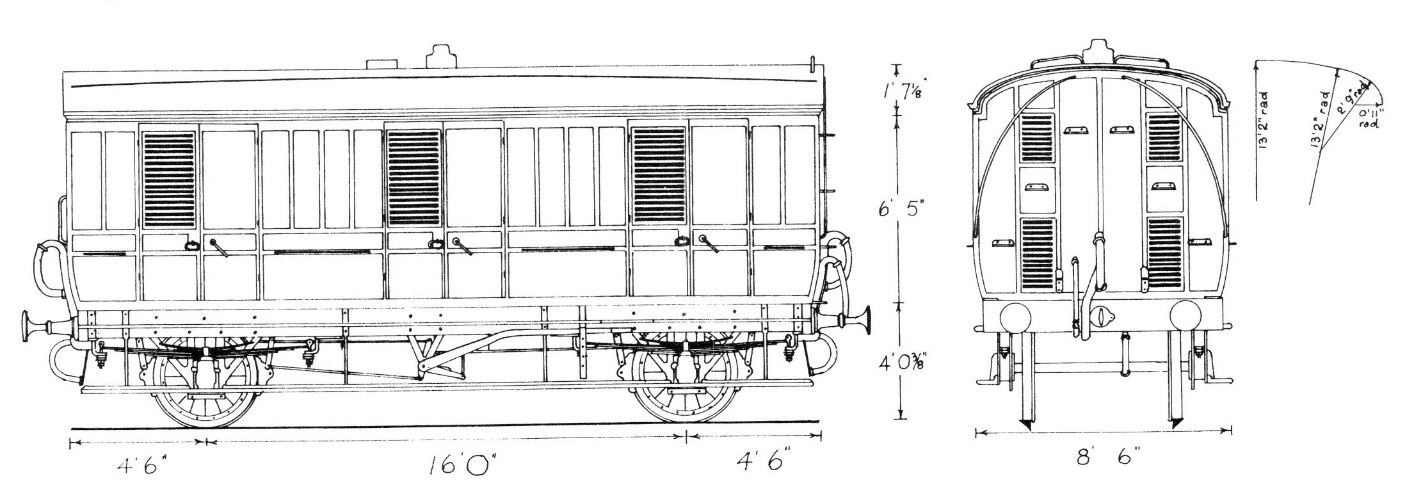

North Staffs Four Wheel Milk Vans

Although the majority of the NSR's revenue must have been derived from industrial activities in the Potteries and Burton-on-Trent districts, its rails also traversed a considerable agricultural area from which it received milk in large quantities for transport to the conurbations, especially to London and Manchester. Other workings include dual-fitted milk vans between Uttoxeter and an unknown destination on the North Eastern main line. The NSR built distinctive vehicles for the traffic, with both four and six wheel types, but there is considerable variety amongst each type. The earliest of the milk vans so far traced dates from 1876, and it is not known what vehicles were used earlier, if indeed the traffic existed prior to this date.

It is believed that at least some of these milk vans were built on second hand underframes of various lengths between 20 and 25 feet between 1889 and 1895, with a further batch between 1907 and 1909. The bodies were constructed with 7 or 8 planks surmounted by a louvred section.

PROTOTYPE DETAILS

NS No	Built	LMS 1st No	Remarks
056/7	1907	6070/1	LMS 2nd No 38638/7
174-7	1891-3		
178			Became calf van No 0178
179/81/9/94/5/9	1893		
196	1907		
297	1876	06060	22ft body, LMS 2nd No 38639, Withdrawn 2/38
302	1909	6092	
303/4	1908	6078/9	
318/9	1908	6080/1	319 became 38640
325	1889		
332-5	1890/1		
344-55	1894/5		

A derelict grounded body from a North Staffs four wheel 20 foot milk van in a field near Stoke of which measurements were taken and the drawing below prepared. (FW Shuttleworth)

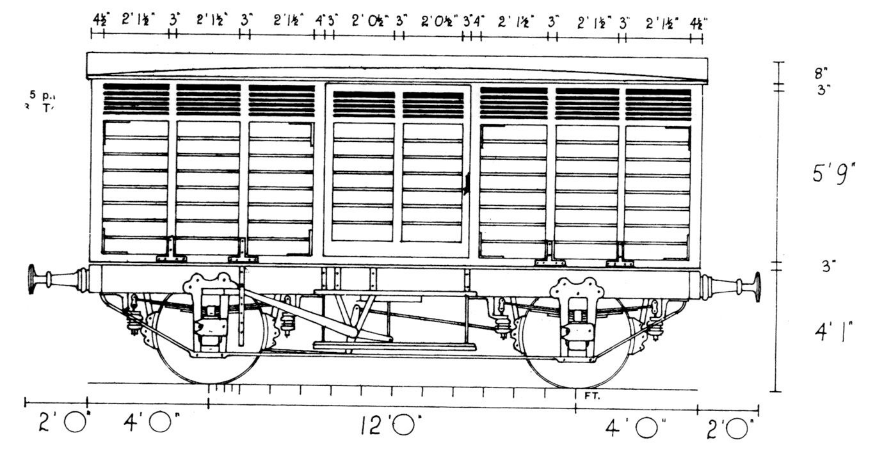

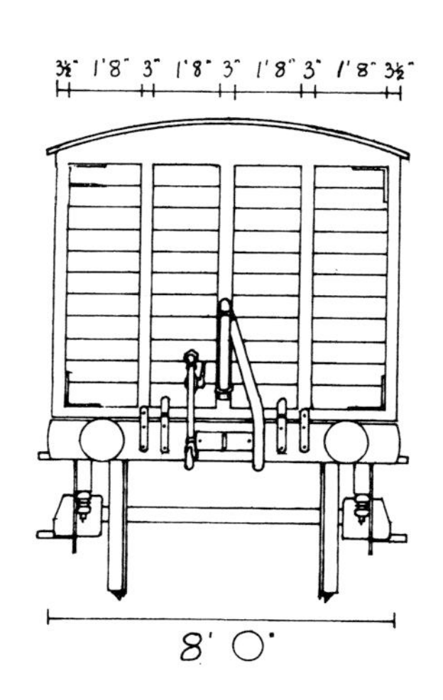

PROTOTYPE DETAILS

NS No	Built	LMS 1st No	LMS 2nd No	Extinct
357-62	1896/7	6005/23-5	38641-4	10/40
375-80	1906	6056-61	38649-52	4/46
294-301 /5/20	1909/10	6089-91/4-100	38653-60	8/46
174-9	1911	6107-12	38661-6	9/47
302-4/18 /21-3/30	1911-4	6113-6/30-3	38667-74	6/56
319/24/5/31	1916/7	6134-7	38675-8	7/55
60, 92, 262/5/6/70, 326/65/6/72	1921	6002/3/140-5	38679-88	2/57

North Staffs Six Wheel Milk Vans

Early examples of NS six wheel milk vans probably had slatted sides, but some time prior to 1906 a change was made to fully boarded sides. Up until 1906 vans had shallow side louvres and from 1911 they were made much deeper. Those built in 1916 and 1917, probably together with all subsequent construction, had outside sliding doors instead of the previous inside type. The drawing is a composite showing shallow louvres and slated sides on the left, while the right hand side has deep louvres and fully boarded sides. Some vehicles were dual fitted. Nos 174 to 179 were supplied by Metropolitan Carr & Wagon in 1911.

North Staffs six wheel milk van No M38672M built in 1914 with deep louvres and inside sliding doors and seen here at Crow Road, Lanarkshire on 20 September 1956 awaiting scrapping. (FW Shuttleworth)

An example of a North Staffs van with outside doors is depicted of No 38679. Note the outside W irons and tie rods connecting each headstock and horn guides throughout. WO Steel collection, courtesy RJ Essery)

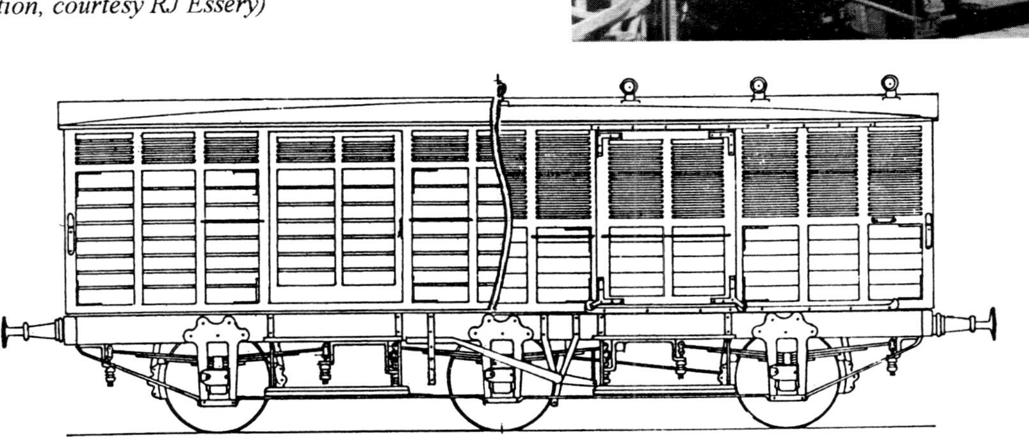

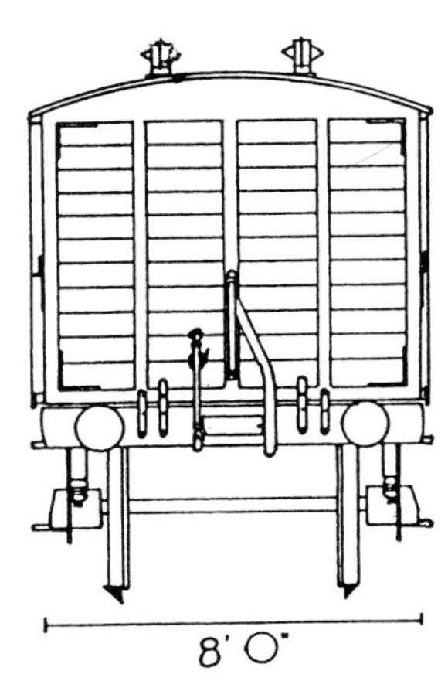

LMS and Great Western Six Wheel Palethorpes Sausage Vans

The drawing of the LMS 6-wheel van represents the first of the several designs of vehicles built during the 1930's for the Palethorpe's Company of Dudley, following the expansion of their business. The insulated vans were fitted with end ladders and roof hatches to give access to ice boxes, together with a dynamo, battery and regulator boxes to supply the fan to circulate chilled air around the product being conveyed.

It is thought that these vehicles were used on regular balanced workings. In the early 1930's a new railway siding was built at their factory and this could accommodate two or three vehicles at a time. The vans, specially designed to carry their products packed in cardboard boxes and generally weighing 36lb, were labelled and secured at the factory and then checked and stamped by railway officials. On arrival at the siding, they were sorted and loaded by both Palethorpe's and railway employees. The boxes were placed in different sections of the vans depending upon their destination. These, when fully loaded, were withdrawn at different times of the day to be attached to mainline passenger trains. Both the LMS and GWR supplied stock (to different designs) and the destinations were only the larger stations such as Bristol, Cardiff, Bangor, Crewe, Manchester, Stockport, Carlisle, Glasgow, Edinburgh, Newcastle and Leeds, etc.

At these stations, the boxes were collected for delivery to Palethorpe's customers by local railway delivery vans. Some traffic was sent by express passenger train and then transferred to local trains. The railway companies provided wicker hampers for the goods, which were distributed to the east and south coast by this method.

Extensive use was still made of British Railways in the 1960s for the transport of Palethorpe's goods to areas not covered by their own road transport and daily vans are dispatched to South Wales, Scotland and the North Country.

The LMS vans were crimson lake, while the GW was milk-chocolate back-ground colour. Both used pale blue lettering, with a bunch of pink sausages on the right.

The GW supplied two vans, obviously to the same specification, at the same time with only minor differences, such as Dean/Churchward hand brake gear, oval buffers and small dimensional differences.

LMS six wheel Palethorpes Royal Cambridge sausage van No 38732, the first of the series and in pre-war livery. (SN White collection)

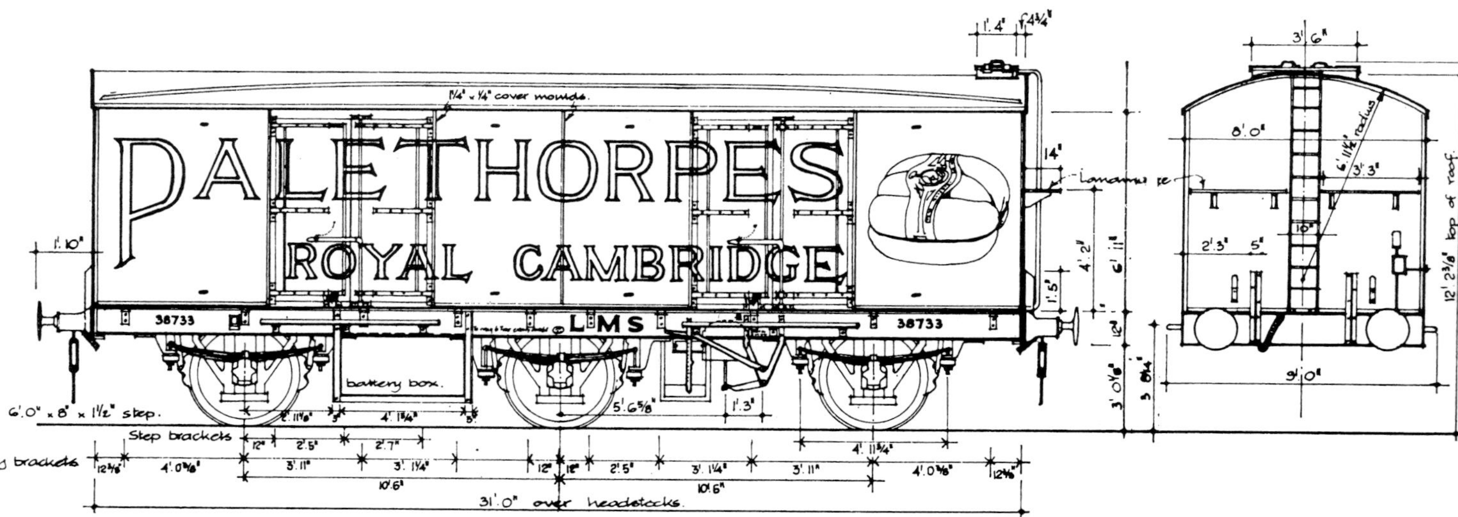

LMS and Great Western Six Wheel Palethorpes Sausage Vans

PROTOTYPE DETAILS

Company	Diagram	Lot	Builder	Year	Nos	Extinct
LMS	1955	986	Wolverton	1936	38732-5	10/66
GWR	O47	1584	Swindon	1936	2801/2	U/k

A similar van No M38735 at Stockport (Edgeley), but now in simplified livery with Pork Sausages instead of Royal Cambridge. (JAGH Coltas)

Below – *A Great Western example of a Palethorpe's van No W2801W at Worcester Shrub Hill on 8 May 1962 marshalled in a passenger train between a coach and cattle truck. Note shallower headstocks, spindle buffers, tie rods between W irons and OK axleboxes. (JE Cull)*

Four Wheel 2,000 & 3,000 Gallon Milk Tanks

It could be argued that, once established in the early days of the development of railways, non-passenger coaching stock types and form remained static and merely reflected current improvements in detail. One exception to this, however, was in the field of the conveyance of milk, when from 1927 2,000 and 3,000 gallon glass lined tanks were introduced initially by the LMS and GW, largely replacing milk churns. They were soon followed by the LNER.

These tanks were at first mounted on four wheeled underframes, but the riding of the vehicles was found to be unsatisfactory at the speeds then operated and initially a longer wheelbase of 13 foot was tried by all companies, including the Southern. Nonetheless in the end they were all remounted on six wheeled underframes between 1936 and 1938. The LNER's seven redundant four wheeled underframes to Diagram 122 were converted into Lowfits to wagon diagram 144, Nos 221175-221181 in 1938. The tanks were owned by the dairy companies and were mounted on railway owned underframes. When new, or recently overhauled, the tanks were brightly finished in the dairies' colours, but these quickly became so grimy that they were frequently indistinguishable from tar tanks.

PROTOTYPE DETAILS

Coy	1st Nos	2nd Nos	Diag	Built at	Year	Tank	Size	Remarks
LMS	644-9	44006-11/6-9/32-5	23	Derby	1928-31	United	2,000	Rebuilt as diagram D1992 in 1937-8
LMS	638-43	44000-5/12-5/22-31	24	Derby	1927-9	United	3,000	Rebuilt as diagram D1993 in 1937-8
LMS	25, 1840	44075-7	24	Derby	1929	Nestles	3,000	Rebuilt as diagram D1993 in 1937-8
GW	2001-12		O38	Swindon	1927	United	3,000	Rebuilt as diagram O44
LNER	4301-3/11		121	Stratford	29/30	United	2,000	Rebuilt as diagram 222
LNER	4304-4310		122	Doncaster	1928	United	3,000	Rebuilt as diagram 184

An LMS four wheel United Dairies 2,000 gallon glass lined milk tank built at Derby to diagram 23 at Annan. Compare the short hand brake lever on this LMS vehicle with the LNER's longer version. Instability at speed led to all four wheel milk tanks being rebuilt on six wheel underframes during 1937/8, in this case to diagram D1992. (R Anderson collection)

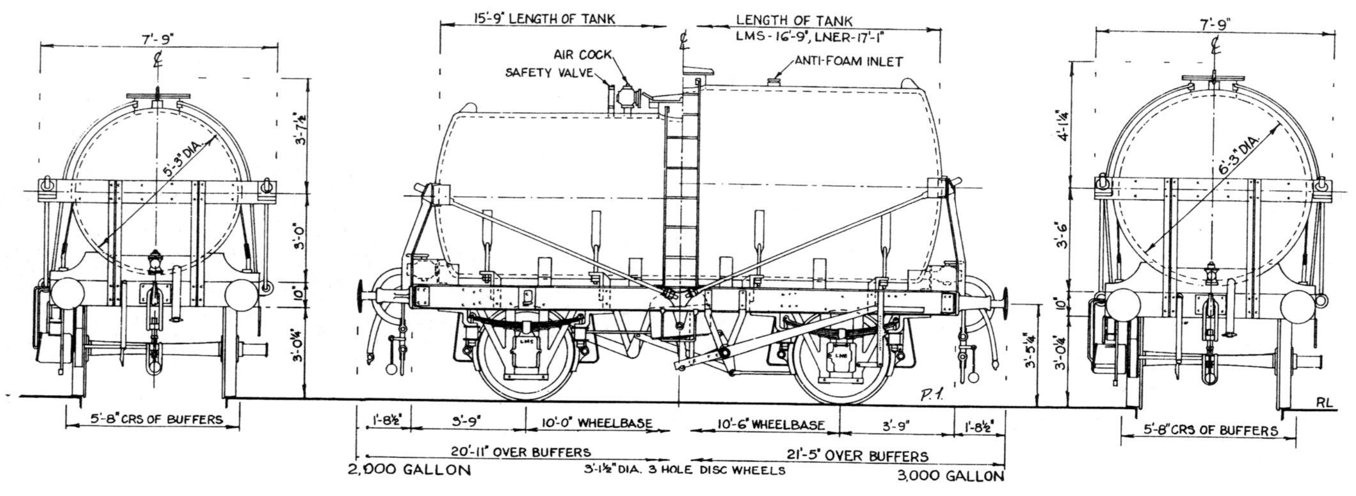

Four Wheel 2,000 & 3,000 Gallon Milk Tanks

A line of the initial batch of six LMS four wheel 3,000 gallon milk tanks Nos 638 etc built at Derby in 1927. These were likewise converted to six wheelers to diagram D1993 late in the 1930's.

The GW Tanks were similar but had a 1ft 6in deep fascia boards behind the holding down straps, RCH split axle-boxes and the diagonal ties finished inside the solebars, rather than outside. (HMRS collection V395)

LNER 3,000 gallon glass lined milk tank No 4306 (or 8) for United Dairies built in 1928 at Doncaster as first mounted on four wheel underframe to Diagram 122 for the Ingestre to East Finchley traffic. Later these tanks were also remounted on new six wheeled underframes to Diagram 184 and the old frames reused as Lowfit wagons. (P Tatlow collection)

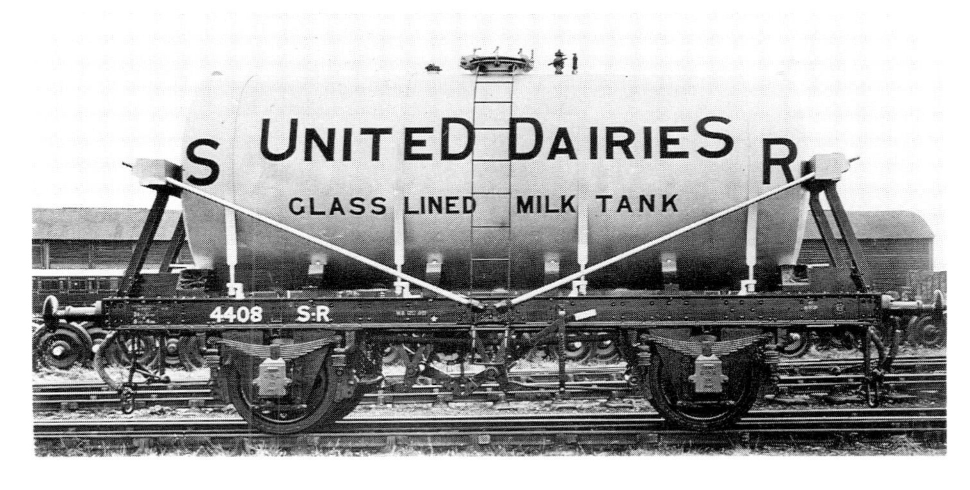

By the time the Southern Railway entered the field, the tendency to derail at speed had been recognised and the length and wheelbase was increased to produce a vehicle 21ft 6in long, as shown in this view of a 3,000 gallon tank in white with black lettering and underframes for United Dairies No 4408 built at Lancing in 1931. Nos 4404-9 commenced operations on the 6.5 pm between Sherborne and Waterloo. (HMRS collection V3179)

LMS & LNER Six Wheel 3,000 Gallon Milk Tanks

From 1931 all subsequent milk tanks were mounted on six wheel underframes and, as noted, in due course those already on four wheel chassises were either re-mounted, or reconstructed on six wheels.

As well as glass lined (Glass) tanks, stainless steel Staybrite (SS) and aluminium (Alum) tanks were introduced by the dairies, as shown in the following tables. In addition to the clad cork slab, or cork asbestos compound and cement insulation, separate covers over the upper half of the tanks were tried to shield the tank from the effects of direct sunlight, but in due course appear to have been removed.

An early Express Dairies glass lined milk tank No 2 mounted on an unidentified LMS six wheel underframe. Note the cover over the upper half of the tank with air scoop at the end. Only four bolsters have been provided. This was found to be inadequate and was subsequently increased. The tank barrel, including the cover, of Express Dairy vehicles were cobalt blue livery, lettered grey edged in white, with the remaining parts black. Later, all above the solebar was painted blue and the lettering was all white. By 1953 the blue was a slightly paler shade. (P Tatlow collection)

United Dairies (Wales/West?) milk tank mounted on an LNER six wheel underframe No 4315, later renumbered 70347, built at Dukinfield in 1934 to diagram 184. Note the turn buckles to the holding down straps and the absence of tie bars between the axleguards. (WO Steel collection, courtesy RJ Essery)

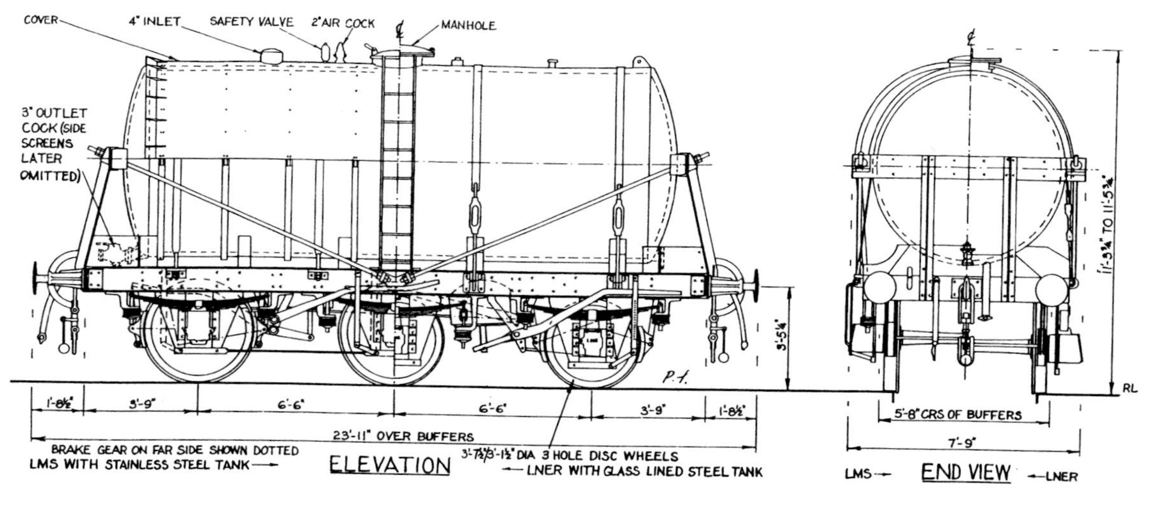

Six Wheel 3,000 Gallon Milk

Some milk tank liveries

Dairy	Tank	Lettering
Co-op Wh Soc	Dark green	White edged black
Express Dairies	Deep blue	White
London Co-op	Signal red	Gold
United Dairies	White	Vermilion
West Park D	Chocolate	Cream
BR period	Stainless St	White on black

LMS 2nd Nos	Diag	Built at	Year	Tank owned by
44091-2/6	1991	Derby	1931	Nestles
44000-5/12-5/20-31	1993	Derby	1937-8	United
44075-7	1993	Derby	1937-8	Nestles
44036-69	1994	Derby	1937-41	United
44078-90/3-5/7-107	1994	Derby	1931-2	Nestles
44150-2	1994	Derby	1937	CWS
44170-201/30-5	1994	Derby	1931-46	Express
44250-2	1994	Derby	1932	Cow & G
44253-65/76-85	1994	Derby	1934-42	Not listed

LNER 1st Nos	LNER 2nd Nos	Diag	Built at	Year	Tank owned by	Type of Tank	Remarks
4315-7	70357-9	184	Dukinfield	1934	UD(W)		
2415-23	70400-8	220	Dukinfield	1935	Express		
4304-10	70347-53	184	Dukinfield	c1936	United	Glass	Tanks reused from 4 wheeled u/f
4312-4	70354-6	184	Dukinfield	1937	United	Glass	Altered from 4 wheeled u/f. Cased
2444-7	70568-71	323	York	1943	Express	SS	
-	70572-7	325	York	1944	MMB		
-	70578-83	333	York	1946	United	SS	

SR Nos	Diag	Built at	Year	Tank owned by	Type of Tank	Remarks
4410-3	3153	Lancing	1932	Express	Alum	Casing
4419-24	3155	Lancing	1932	United	Glass	
4427-8	3156	Lancing	1933	Express	SS	Casing later removed
4429-32/55-66	3157	Lancing	1933/43-4	United	Glass	
4433-4	3158	Ashford	1935	Express	Glass	
4404-9	3159	Ashford	1937	United	Glass	Rebuilt from 4 wheelers
4435-54	3161	Ash/East	1937-44	Express	SS	

GW Nos	Diag	Year built	Tank owned by	Remarks
2071-3	O36	1932	CWS	
2043/57, 2504-9	O38	1932/5	United	
2528-30/40-3	O38	1933	CWS	
2567-72	O38	1936	IMS	6 alum + 4 enamelled steel tanks
2512-7/31-6/87-92	O39	1934/7	UD(W)	
2587-92	O39	1937	United	
2547-58, 2935	O41	1935	L Co-op	Twin 1,500 gallon tanks
2561-3/93-8	O42	1935-9	Express	Cased
2002	O44			Rebuilt from O23
2581-6	O47	1936	United	
2932-5	O49	1940	L Co-op	Twin 1,500 gallon tanks
2947-52/8-63	O51	1942/3	United	
2553-6	O52	1942	Express	
2995-3000	O52	1944	Cow & G	
1958-60/3-5	O52	1945	MMB	
1955-7	O53	1944	CWS	
1951-4	O53	1944	Aplin & B	
1968-77	O54	1946	Express	Cased
1978-83	O55	1946	Cow & G	
1986-95	O55	1947	MMB	
1984-5	O55	1946	Aplin & B	
3001-22/33	O57	1946	United	
3023-8/120-3	O58	1947/50	Cow & G	Twin compartment

Great Western & Southern Railway Six Wheel 3,000 Gallon Milk Tanks

Although the six wheel 13 foot wheelbase, generally 20ft 6in long, underframe was adopted by all four of the grouping companies, numerous detailed differences will be found between their respective products. The LMS used coach sized wheels, whereas all the rest relied on 3 hole steel disc wagon wheels. Variations will also be found in the axleboxes, springs and hangers, brake gear, access ladders and platforms, inclined tie rods attachment to the solebars, bolsters and holding down straps. Further milk tanks were built by BR following nationalisation in 1948 by the London Midland and Western Regions.

Independent Milk Supplies Ltd tank No 14 mounted on GW underframe No 2570 to diagram O38 built in 1936. Note the OK axleboxes, flat strip tie bar between axleguards, Dean Churchward brake gear and fully exposed holding down straps. Vehicles to diagram O49 and subsequent had ordinary lever hand brake. (PE Matthews collection, courtesy HMRS)

Former SR United Dairies glass lined milk tank No S4409 to diagram 3159 preserved at Didcot. The tank was originally fitted to a 21ft 6in long four wheel underframe at Lancing in November 1931 and remounted on a new six wheel underframe built in February 1937. Note the secondary stays to the end stanchions, the holding down straps passing beneath the lagging and the large secondary bearing springs. (G Warburton collection)

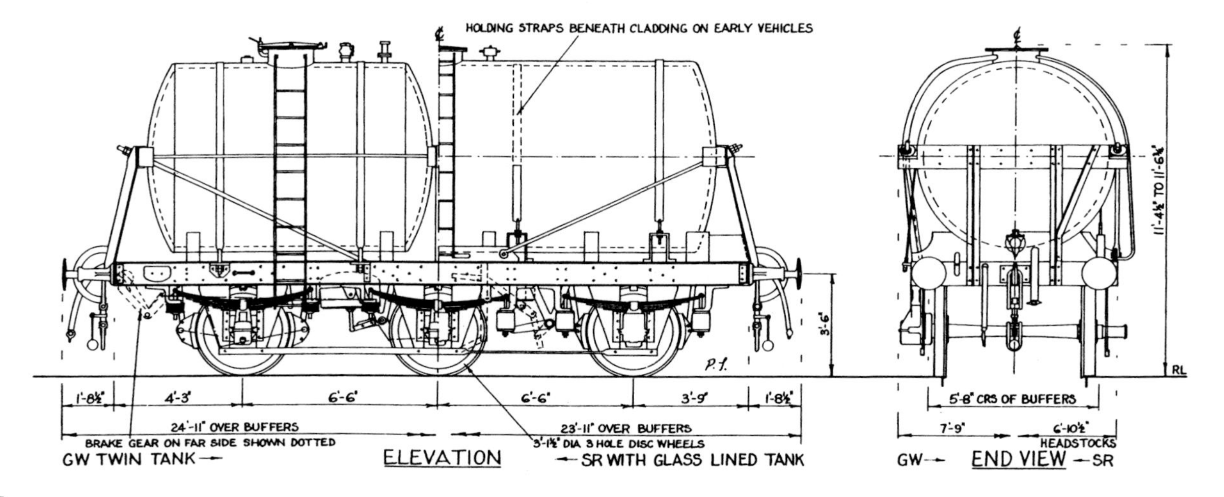

Great Western 10 Ton Fruit Van Fruit C and D

Much fruit traffic was generated for the Great Western in the Vale of Evesham. Purpose built ventilated fitted fruit vans for use on passenger trains were introduced on the GW in 1890, but retained goods stock livery and numbers until around 1916. 10 ton 22 foot long twin double door vans to diagram Y3 were produced in 1911 and 1912. Coded FRUIT C, unless dual fitted when the suffix became D. A further batch to a revised modernised design with end ventilation bonnets and vertical planking to the doors to diagram Y9 appeared in 1937. All adopted the Dean/Churchward brake linkage and were gas lit

PROTOTYPE DETAILS

Diagram	**Y3**	**Y9**
Date built	1911-1912	1937
Side door	Horizontal planks	Vertical planks
End vents	Louvres	Hoods
Numbers	85926-86000, later 2426-2500	2803-2832, 2847-2866
Dual brake	79946-79970 later 2401-2425	-

Former GW Fruit C or D to diagram Y3, now in departmental service as No DW 150159 for use as tool and equipment van by the thermic welders of Cardiff District. Thermic welding is the on-site welding of rail joints. Note the cross bracing on the ends and framed doors. (G Warburton collection)

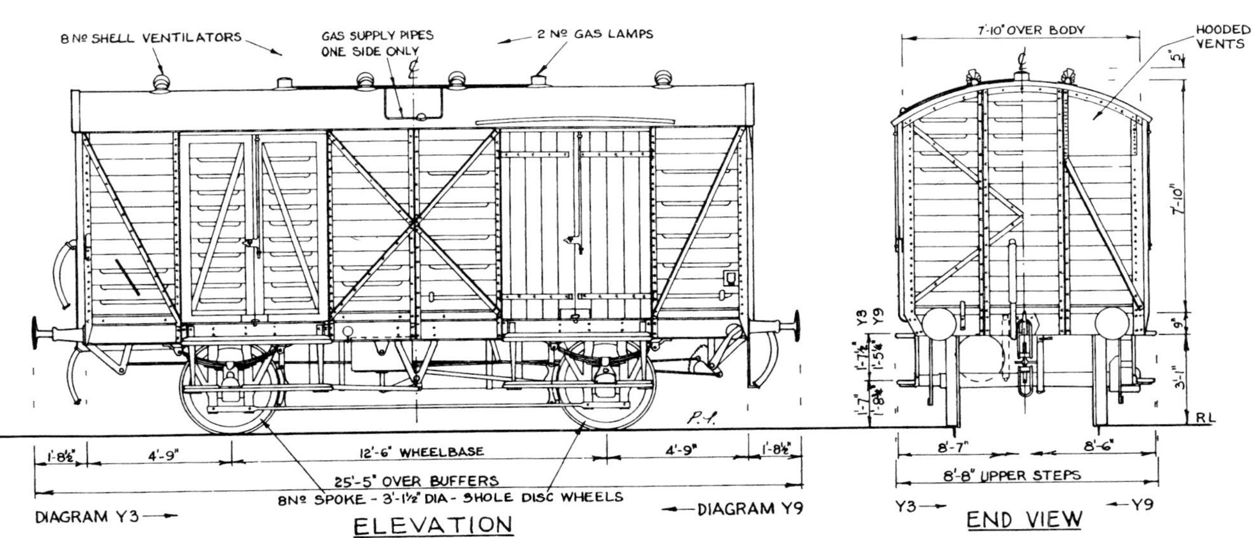

Great Western 10 Ton Fish Van Bloater

At first fish landed at our ports was conveyed to the centres of population in open fish trucks. By the second decade of the 20th century, however, a change was made to covered vans. Following batches of single and two door types, a design with three doors per side was introduced in 1916 and production, with minor differences tabulated below, continued for 12 years. These were coded BLOATER and suffixed A if dual fitted. The Westinghouse equipment was, however, removed between 1930 and 1935. The sliding doors run between the double skin of the sides. All were gas lit.

With the decline in the fish trade a number of vans were reallocated to parcels traffic from 1935 and further transfers were made in 1941/2, but all reverted to fish vans between 1943 and 1947. Further details on these vans will be found in *Great Western Journal* No 7, 1993.

PROTOTYPE DETAILS

Diagram	**S8**	**S9**	**S10**	**S11**
Date built	1916-1919	1919-1922	1925-1926	1928
Roof vents	None	Shell	Shell	Shell
Side vents	Louvres	Louvres	None	None
End vents	Louvres	Louvres	Louvres	Hoods
Buffers	Oval spindle	Self-contained	Self-cont'd	Self-cont'd
Numbers	2139-2213	2214-53, 2601-29, 2268-88	2650-2699	2700-2749
Dual brake		2114-2138, 2254-2267	-	-

GW 10 ton Bloater fish van No 2603 to diagram S9 at Birmingham Snow Hill in 1947. Note that some planks, chamfered to provide ventilation, have been replaced by plain planks. (PJ Garland, HMRS collection M20138)

Renovated for use as a parcels van is No W2219W seen here at Birmingham New Street on 8 July 1959. The body has been reclad and the doors replaced with the later horizontal style of planking. (JE Cull)

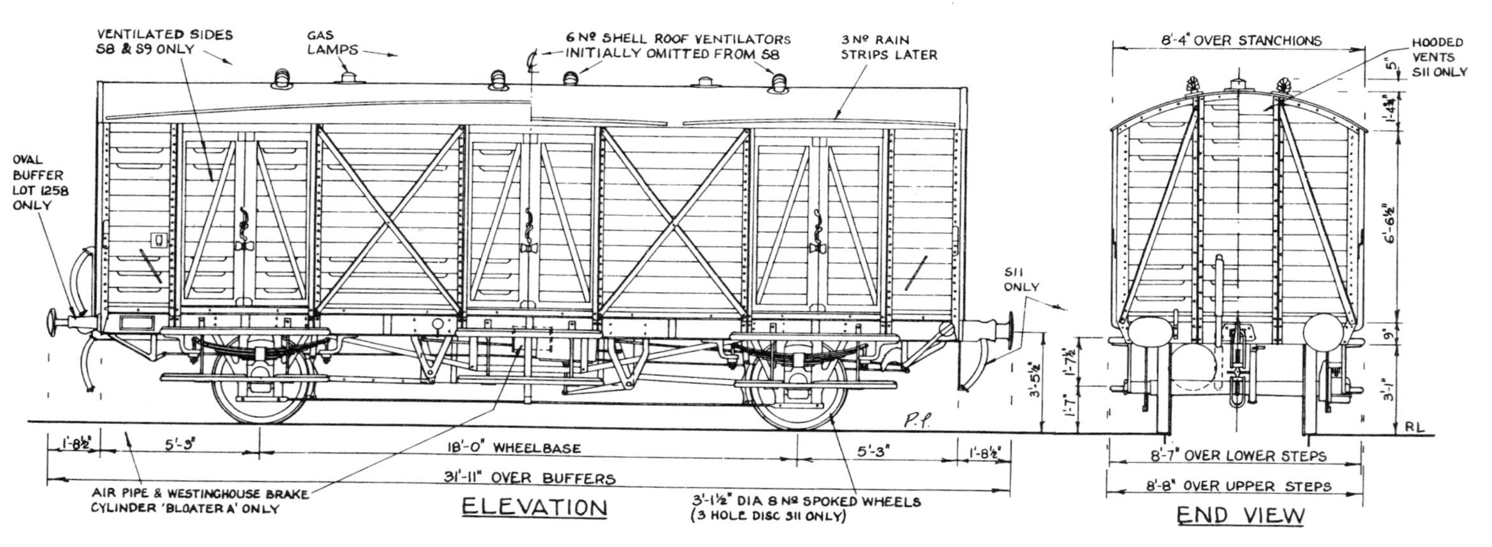

Great Western Outside Framed Siphon G Milk Van

Although described as milk vans, the 50 foot long bogie vehicles to diagram O11, with four sets of double doors per side and gangway connections, were capable of use for many types of passenger rated traffic. Only the first two lots had 10 inch deep solebars, the remainder being 9 inch deep. Lot 1211 had flat bar trussing, lot 1264 multi-round bar and the rest angle section. The first three lots had gas lighting and the remainder electric. Most started life on 9 foot wheel base American bogies, but subsequently some were changed for other types. For details see Slinn JN, *Great Western Railway Siphons*, HMRS, 1986.

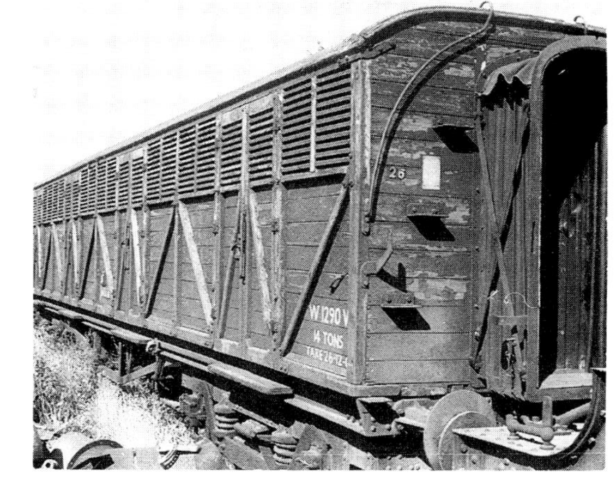

Left: *Out to grass in Woodham's Yard, Barry circa 1962 is No W1290W with angle iron trussing still has it American bogies. (JM Hodgetts)*

PROTOTYPE DETAILS

Lot	Built	Nos	Extinct
1211	1912/13	1462-1481	9/57
1264	1915/16	1442-1461	1/59
1316	1922/23	1345-1364	7/62
1347	1925	1290-1309	12/62
1368	1926	1271-89	12/62
1378	1926/27	1240-69	12/62

Below: *GW outside framed Siphon G No W1457W showing the multi-round bar tie rods and 9 inch deep solebars of Lot 1264 built in December 1915. Its original 9 foot coil spring bogies have been replaced by the 7 foot wheel base type. (PW Bartlett collection)*

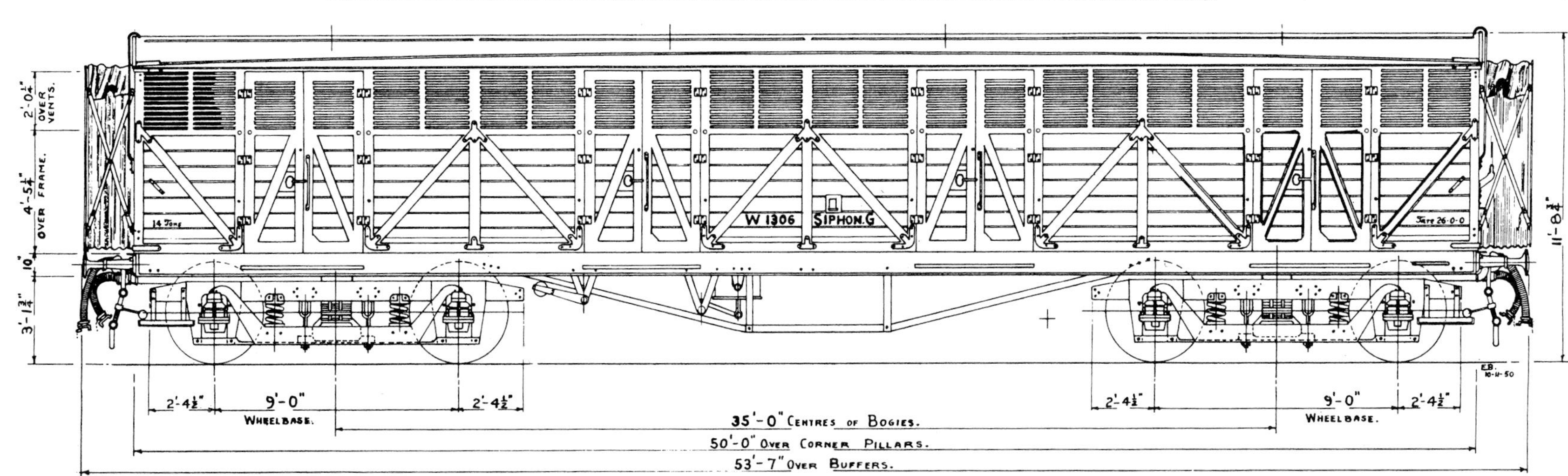

L&SWR Six Wheel Special Milk Van

Sixteen 7 ton six wheel vans were built between 1907 and 1909 for the conveyance of milk from the country to Vauxhall, one stop short of Waterloo, where much milk for the metropolis was handled. They were fitted with 6 foot long springs; a double skin roof ventilated by six torpedo roof vents; ventilation louvres along lower side panels; gas lighting; dual brake and steam pipe. In Sou'-Western days the whole body was painted salmon pink. The waist panels on the sliding doors were of slate. During 1918 and 1919, nine were converted by fitting end doors to carry aeroplanes. They were all withdrawn from revenue earning service by November 1941.

PROTOTYPE DETAILS

1st LSW No	2nd LSW No	SR No
5, 111/28/9/35/41/3/7/63/98, 205/18/23/4/66, 324	5005, 5111/25/6/32/7/9/41/53/82/9/96, 5200/1/30/85	1636-42, 4560-8

The first LSW 32 foot six wheel special milk van No 163 as initially fitted with only four roof ventilators. This vehicle is in all salmon pink livery, the purpose of which was to reflect sunlight and thereby keep the contents cooler. (HMRS collection V1141)

A former LSWR milk van No Ds 1414 now in departmental service as a mess van for the Signal & Telegraph. (Coutanche collection)

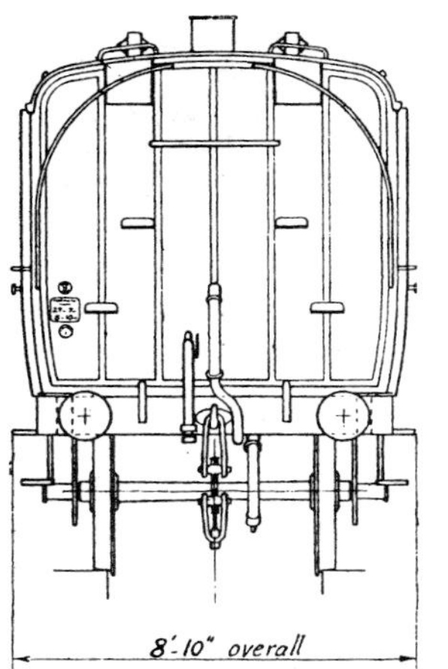

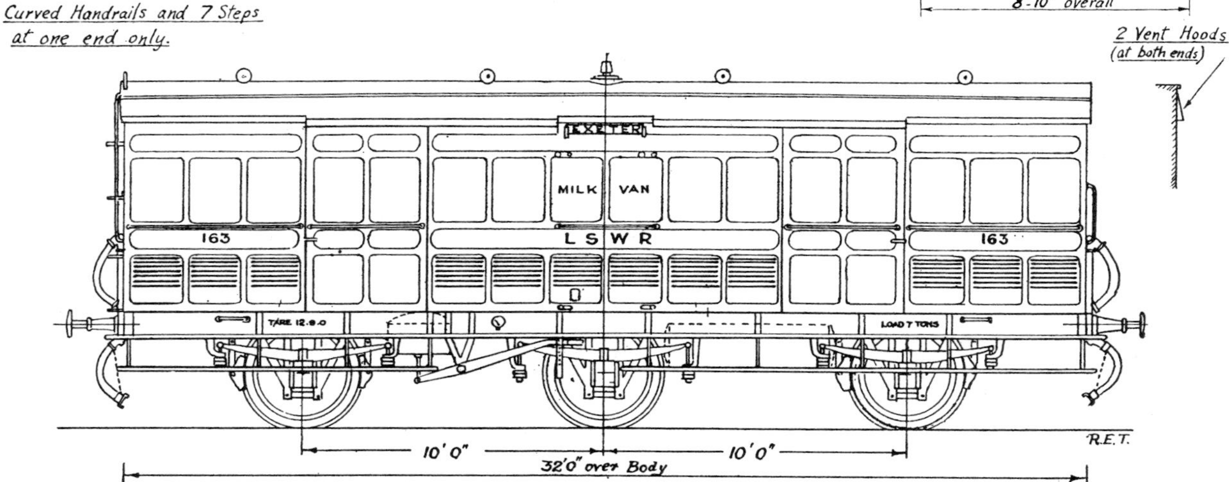

Metropolitan Railway Milk Van

These vans were built by Birmingham Railway Carriage & Wagon Co to a Metropolitan Railway drawing dated 8 June 1902. This also notes that train line conduits and receptacles were added in 1920, together with jumper containers under the left hand buffer at the London end in November 1927. Following withdrawal from revenue earning service in 1936, No 3 became a breakdown tool van for which it was renumbered No 700 and painted grey. Subsequently it has been preserved and is on display at the London Transport Museum, Covent Garden, London.

On Sunday 26 May 1963 0-4-4T No L44 hauls a special train at Neasden including preserved Metropolitan Railway milk van No 3 leading. (LUL)

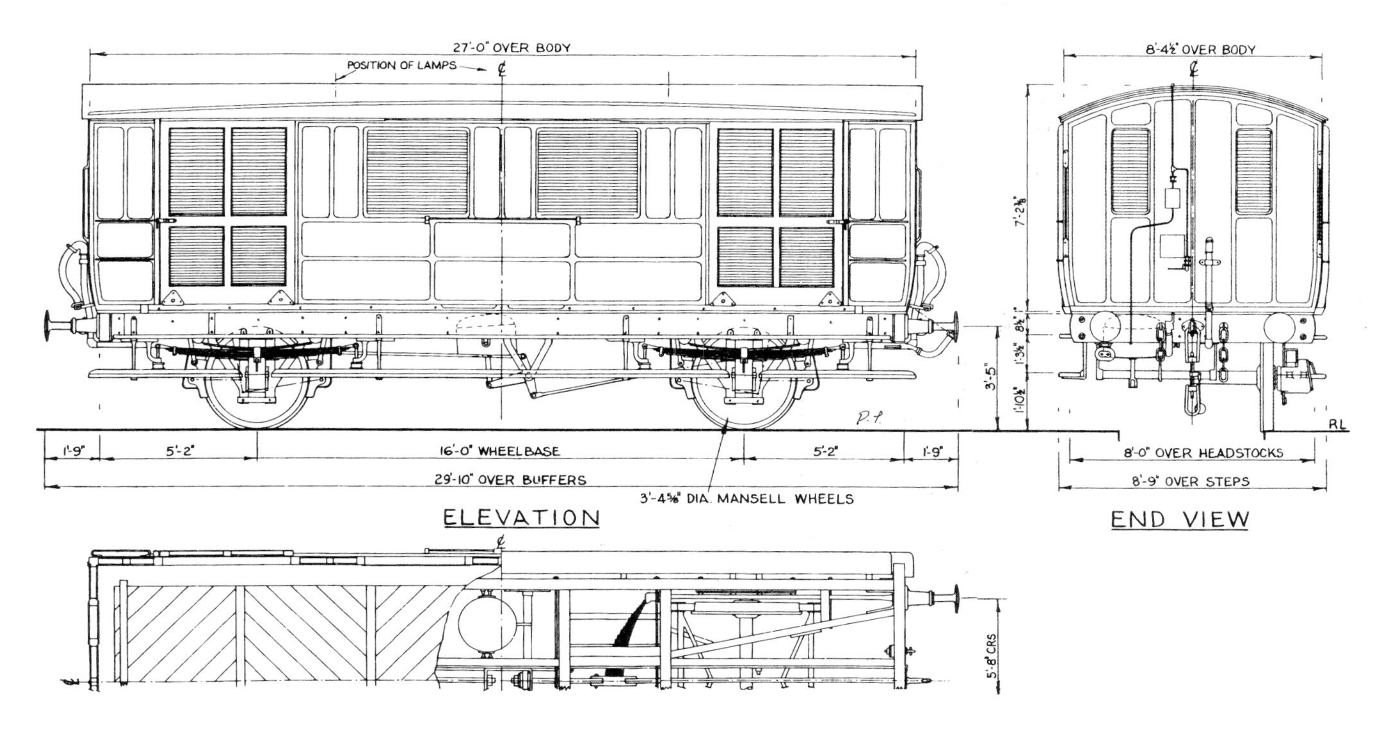

Highland Railway Directors' Saloon

In 1901 the Highland Railway built at its Lochgorm Works, Inverness a bogie saloon for the use of the directors and for hire to private parties at other times. It was given the No 59, this becoming No 18615 on the inauguration of the LMS. Under the 1932 renumbering scheme it was to have been No 823, but it never carried this prior to being re-designated as an engineer's inspection saloon and given the No 45042 in 1934. Dual braked and initially oil lit, steam heating was added in 1909. It was withdrawn prior to 1947.

When built in 1901, the HR directors' saloon No 59 was painted in Peter Drummond's dark olive green livery with white waist and upper panels lined in gold. It is likely to have been repainted in all green before the LMS took over and applied lined crimson lake. (WDG Chalmers collection).

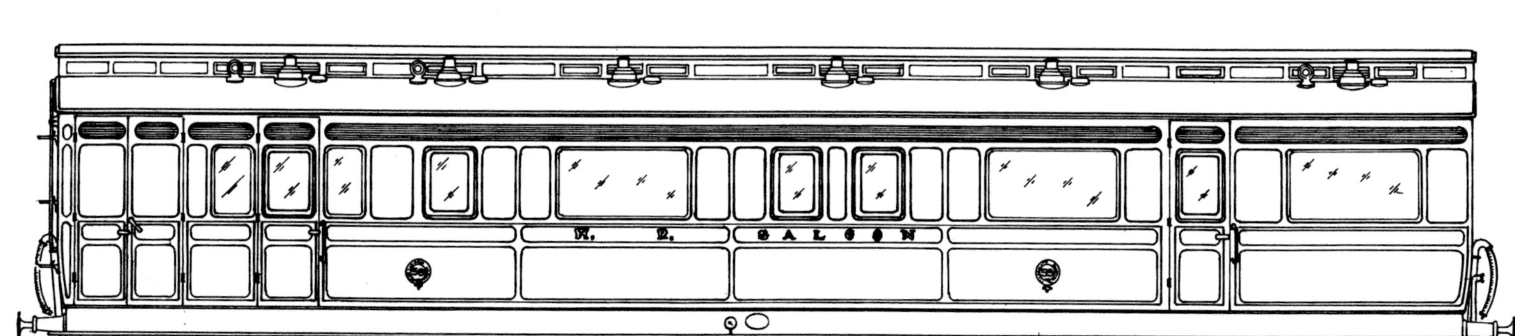

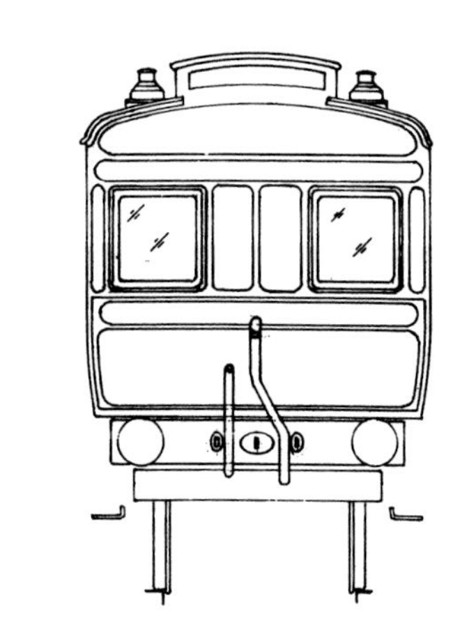

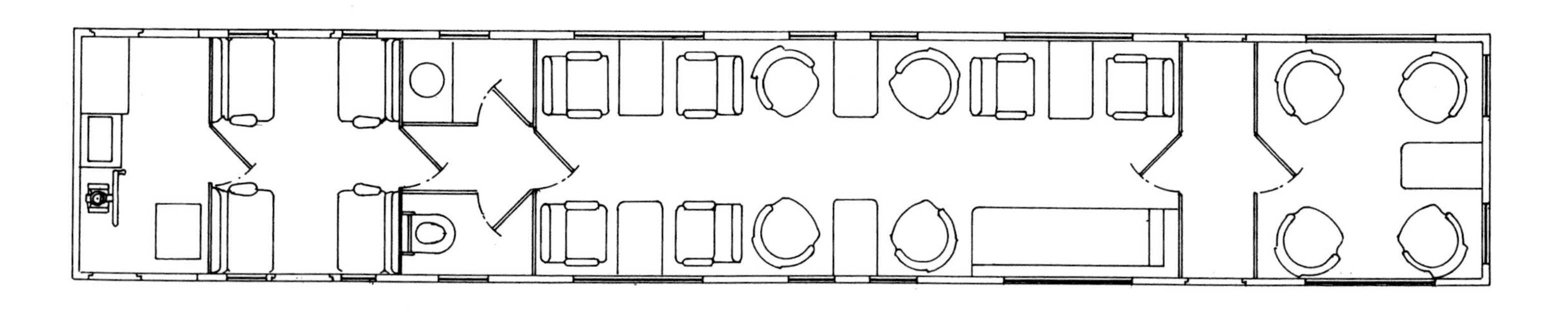

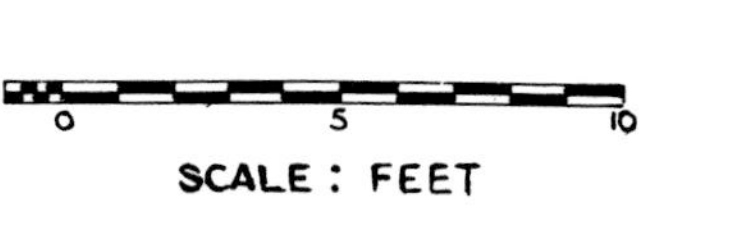

LMS Engineer's Inspection Saloon

Inspection saloons are an ancient institution on the railways; the very earliest railways used them for all sorts of special duties including the transportation of high ranking officers. The Chief Civil and District Engineers' duties often required them to make on site inspections of the track and structures, particularly in determining priorities during the preparation of the annual budget and to attend to any serious incident along the line. The additional burden thrust upon these gentlemen during World War II probably led to the construction at Wolverton of 14 saloons to a new design between 1940 and 1947. The drawing shows the production version diagram D2046.

To ease the task of inspection, large observation windows were provided in the ends and vacuum operated steps to enable the engineers to descend to track level for closer examination. The steps are interlocked with the brake system to prevent the coach being moved unless the steps are in the raised position.

For the greater part of every trip the coach is propelled by the locomotive and additional side control springs are fitted to the bogies to damp out any unpleasant oscillations due to this unusual leading position.

Large supplies of water and gas in cylinders are carried for cooking purposes, etc., and the coach is normally manned by a guard and a steward, a small compartment being provided for their use. The inspecting engineers were provided with a small brake valve and a system of bells to enable them to communicate with the footplate staff should they wish for a change in speed or a stop to be made.

For an illustration, see Jenkinson D & Essery RJ, *LMS coaches – An illustrated history 1923-1957.*

PROTOTYPE DETAILS

Diag	Lot	Year	Nos
2045	1221 Part	1940	45043
2046	1221 Part	1940	45044/5
	1264	1941	45046-8
	1327	1942	45028-30
	1356	1944	4520/1/6
	1432	1947	45035/6

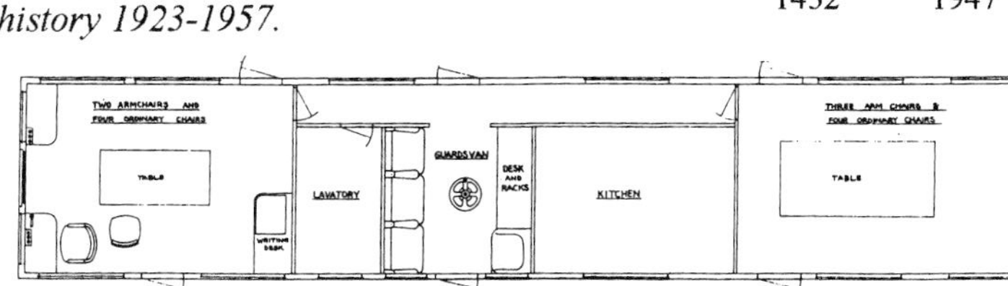

PLAN – HALF SCALE

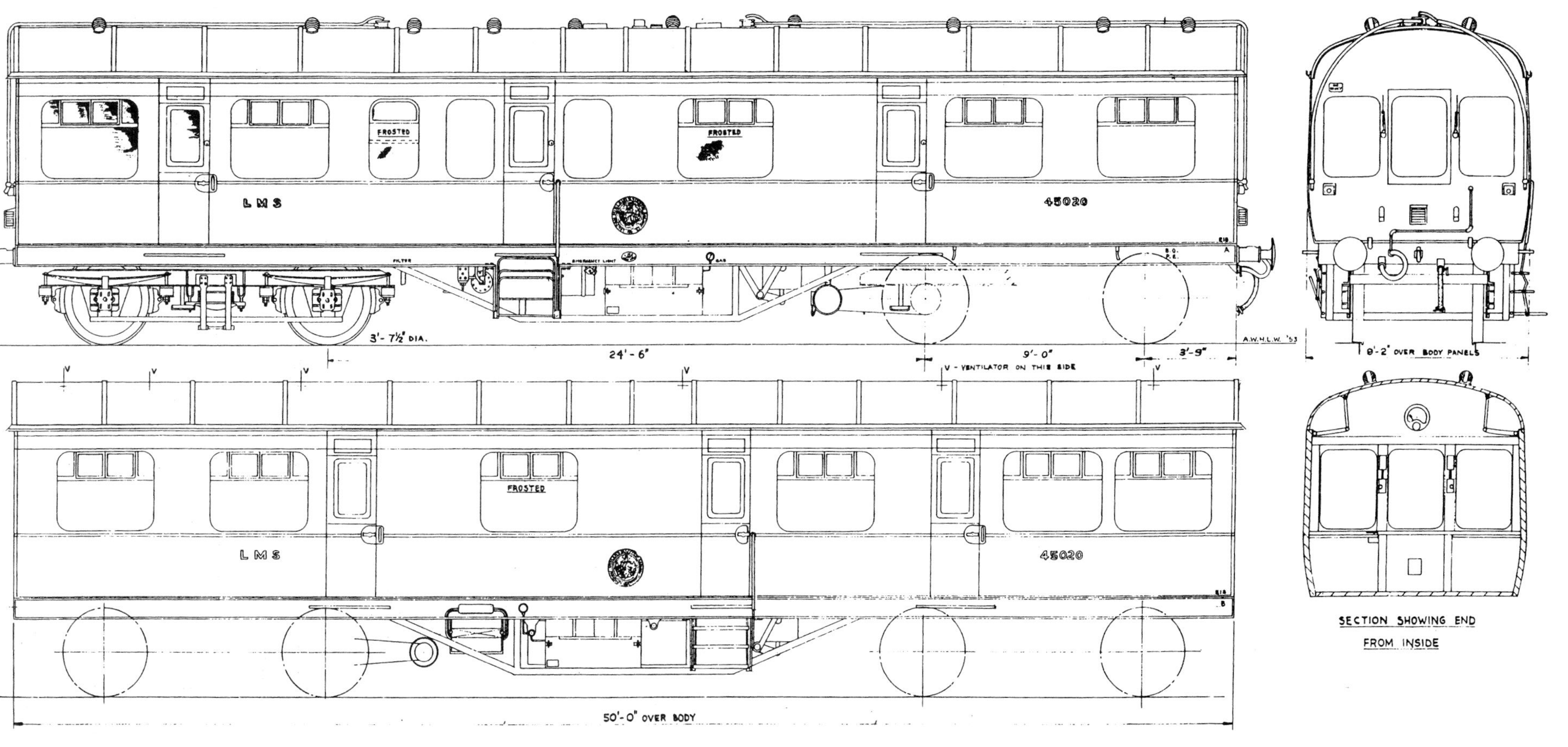

LMS Twin & Triple 18 Foot Tank Travelling Gas Holder Trucks

With the advent of carriage lighting by gas, the railway companies built travelling gas holder trucks to convey the product of their producer plants, usually at the railway's works, or other central location, to various out-stations to service carriage stock. The presence of three link couplings on some early examples indicates that they were intended to be conveyed in goods trains, but in the end it was recognised that these gas tanks were best forwarded by passenger rated trains and duly fitted with automatic brake and through steam pipe. Even with the change to electric lighting, gas continued to be required for kitchen cars and in some cases station lighting.

The LMS built small batches of gas holder trucks, usually on recovered underframes already equipped to coaching standards. The most numerous design was the twin 18 foot tank to diagram D1815, which utilised a LNWR 21 foot underframe. Two further vehicles (D1825) were a variation of the theme with three tanks, as shown in the LH end view. An illustration of the latter will be found in *An illustrated history of LMS wagons Vol 1* plate 270. In pre-war days, the LMS appears to have painted gas tanks unlined crimson lake and applied coach style insignia.

PROTOTYPE DETAILS

Lot	Built at	Year	No of tanks	No built
311	St Rollox	1927	2	3
416	Derby	1928	2	2
514	Derby	1930	2	2
563	Derby	1930	2	3
566	Derby	1930	3	2

Two views of LMS twin tank gas holder truck No 279472, the only known number, at Tredegar in 1937. This clearly shows the LNWR origins of its 21 foot underframe, built in 1913. Note the coach style lettering.
Care was needed in shunting gas holder trucks to avoid shifting the tank on the bolsters and the risk of consequent damage to the gas pipe connections. (JP Richards, HMRS collection AAJ312 and AAJ311)

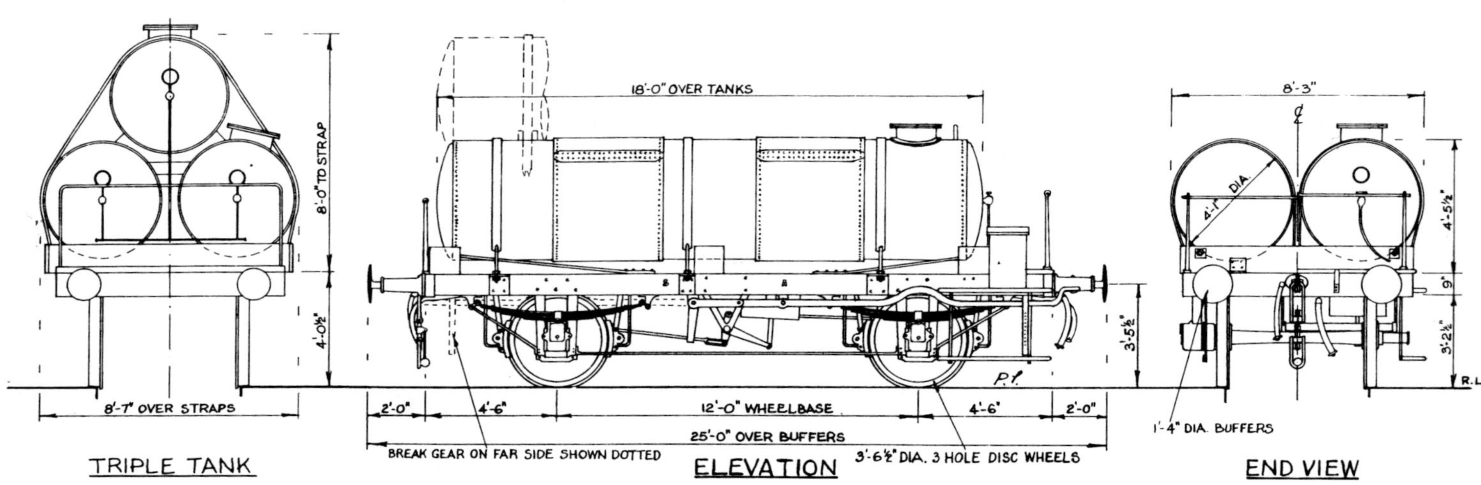

Ex-L&NWR C&W Stores Van Converted from Brake Van to Diagram 385

These two vans were converted from the later standard type of six wheel full brake built between 1889 and 1898. The duckets were removed, as was the drop light guard's door. The door opening had then been widened to take a pair of doors and the remaining gap filled in solid and panelled over. At the same time, top lights had been cut in the sheeting. It is just possible to see in the photographs the original framing behind the glazing. The work may have been carried out by the old LNWR, but in any event are likely to have entered departmental service for the LMS prior to 1933 and there may have been others. Nos 279902 and 279960 were particularly long lived and lasted respectively until being withdrawn in July 1968 and December 1971 and subsequently broken up. No 279982 was similarly derived from a diagram 385 vehicle, but retained its ducket and guard's door.

Ex-LNWR six wheel parcel van converted from brake van to Diagram 385 seen here in departmental service as No 279902M. (FW Shuttleworth)

No 279960 also in departmental service. (FW Shuttleworth)

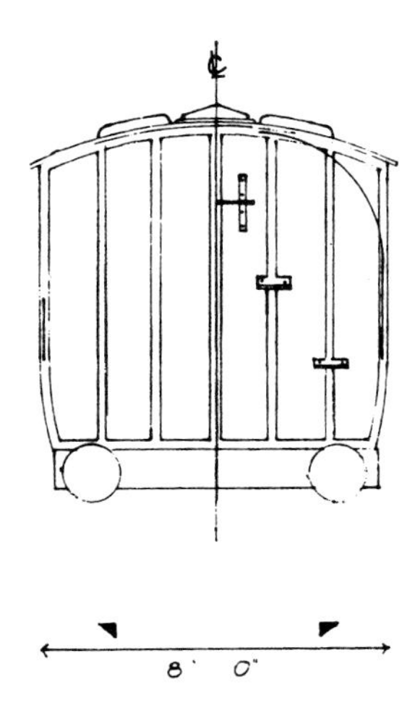

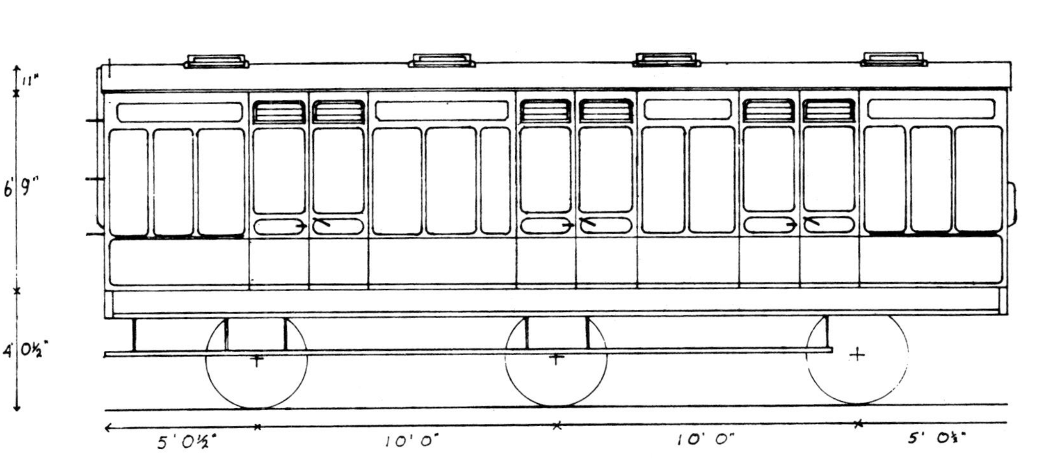

GW Twin 15 Foot Tank Travelling Gas Holder Trucks

The twin tank travelling gas holder trucks to diagram DD5 were introduced in 1883. Their telegraph code was CORDON and, as departmental vehicles, they were painted grey with white lettering. Built over a period of many years, they were subsequently either modernised or fitted with new underframes, resulting in numerous differences in detail. For instance, the means of applying the brake by hand included Dean Churchward gear, lever and screw pillar. Early vehicles had the flanges to the solebars facing inwards, while later construction was with the flanges outwards. Mansell wheels may have been fitted when new, but steel disc wheels appeared later. For further details, see *Great Western Journal* No 1.

PROTOTYPE DETAILS

Nos	**Built**	**Length** (ft-in)	**Wheel base** (ft-in)	**Springs** (ft-in)	**Wheel dia** (ft-in)
1-5	1883	18-6	9-0	3-6	3-6
6/7	1883	18-6	9-0	3-6	3-0
8-11	1887-8	19-0	9-0	3-10	3-0/3-1
12-15	1888-9	19-0	9-0	3-10	3-1/3-6
16/7	1891	19-0	9-6	3-10	3-1/3-6

Twin tank travelling gas holder truck is No 3 was built in 1883. It has outside actuated clasp brake blocks and Dean Churchward hand brake gear, together with inward facing solebar flanges. The tanks were remounted on a new underframe in 1952. For obvious reasons gas holder trucks were not permitted to pass through the Severn Tunnel. (M Longridge, HMRS collection S113-15)

No 13, seen here at Marlow, was built in 1889 has the brake blocks applied by an internal mechanism and lever hand brake. The flanges of the solebar face outwards. It had new tanks fitted in 1925. (JJ Davis, HMRS collection ACD002)

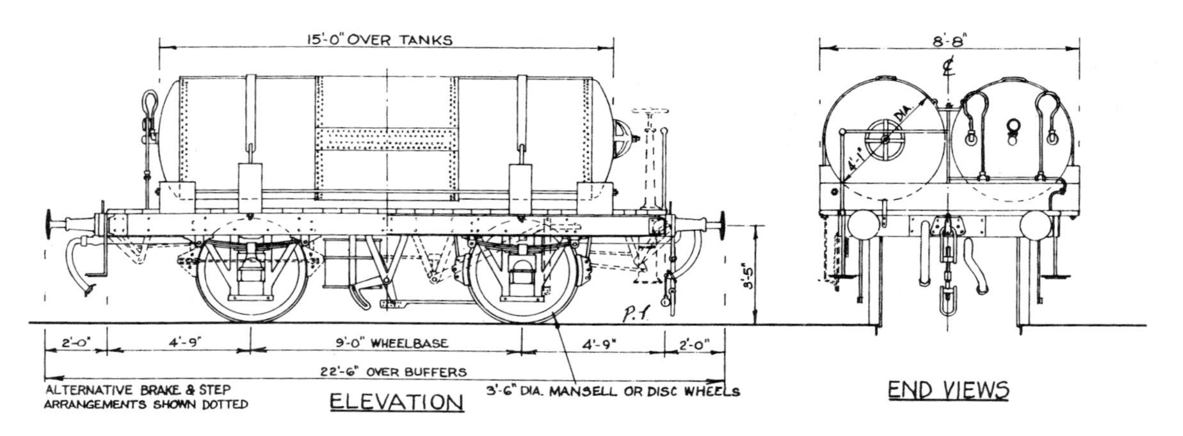

APPENDIX – Statistics for 31 Dec 1922

Company	Post Office	Luggage/ parcels/ brake van	Carriage truck	Horse Box	Misc.	Total
LONDON, MIDLAND & SCOTTISH GROUP						
London & North Western (incl L&Y)	60	1,447	1,139	817	460	3,923
Midland	16	581	348	385	341	1,671
North Staffordshire	0	16	24	47	106	193
Furness	2	23	12	27	27	92
Stratford & Midland Junction	0	1	0	10	0	11
Maryport & Carlisle	0	12	4	3	1	20
Knott End/Wirral	0/1	2/0	0/0	0/0	0/0	2/1
Caledonian	15	247	120	171	171	724
Glasgow & South Western	8	159	17	82	155	421
Highland	9	103	50	27	303	492
TOTALS	**111**	**2,591**	**1,714**	**1,569**	**1,564**	**7,549**
LONDON & NORTH EASTERN GROUP						
North Eastern (incl Hull & Barnsley)	13	235	248	461	71	1,028
Great Northern	18	276	192	332	49	867
Great Central	1	103	109	177	632	1,027
Great Eastern	14	465	152	539	471	1,641
North British	0	219	221	229	549	1,218
Great North of Scotland	2	75	17	23	196	313
Mid-Suffolk/Colne Valley	0/0	1/2	0/0	2/1	0/0	3/3
TOTALS	**48**	**1,381**	**939**	**1,764**	**1,968**	**6,100**
GREAT WESTERN GROUP						
Great Western (incl absorbed coys)	31	746	421	905	1,347	3,450
Midland & South Western Junction	0	3	2	36	35	76
TOTALS	**31**	**749**	**423**	**941**	**1,382**	**3,526**
SOUTHERN GROUP						
London & South Western	16	829	183	359	0	1,387
London, Brighton & South Coast	0	308	132	256	30	726
South Eastern & Chatham	10	572	184	114	52	932
Isle of Wight/Isle of Wight Central	0/0	11/6	7/0	1/1	0/0	19/7
TOTALS	**26**	**1,726**	**506**	**731**	**82**	**3,071**
INDEPENDENT AND JOINTLY OWNED STANDARD GAUGE COMPANIES						
Cheshire Lines Committee	0	14	22	35	20	91
Midland & Great Northern	0	32	6	8	0	46
Somerset & Dorset	0	22	10	14	24	70
East Kent/Kent & East Sussex	0	1/4	0/0	0/0	0/0	1/4
Metropolitan/Shropshire & Montgomery	0	6/1	4/0	8/1	4/0	22/2
TOTALS	**0**	**80**	**42**	**66**	**48**	**236**

Bibliography

General

Gamble G, *British railway non-passenger rolling stock; Railways in profile series No 6,* Cheona Publications 1998.
Jenkinson D, *British railway carriages of the 20th century, Vols 1 and 2*, Patrick Stephens 1988 and 1990 and Pendragon (combined volume) 1996.
Johnson P, *The British travelling Post Office*, Ian Allan 1985.

LMS group

Bourne TW, *Operating non-passenger coaching stock*, pp 46-48, *LMS Society two notes*, LMS Society, 1985.
Casserley RM and Millard PA, *A register of West Coast Joint Stock*, Historical Model Railway Society 1980.
Dow G & Lacey RE, *Midland style*, Historical Model Railway Society 1975.
Geddes H and Bellass E, *Highland Railway liveries*, Pendragon and Historical Model Railway Society 1995.
Hunter DLG, *Carriages & wagons of the Highland Railway*, Turntable Enterprises 1971.
Jenkinson D & Essery RJ, *LMS coaches – An illustrated history 1923-1957*, Oxford Pub. Co 1969 and 1991-2000 (3 vol.).
Jenkinson D & Essery RJ, *Midland carriages – An illustrated review 1877 onwards*, Oxford Publishing Co 1984.
Jenkinson D, *An illustrated history of LNWR coaches (including West Coast Joint Stock)*, Oxford Publishing Co 1978 and Pendragon 1995.
Jenkinson D, *Historic carriage drawings – Vol 2, LMS and constituents*, Pendragon 1998.
Lacey RE & Dow G, *Midland Railway carriages – Vols 1 & 2*, Wild Swan 1984 & 1986.
Talbot E, Millard P, Dow G and Davies P, *LNWR liveries*, Historical Model Railway Society 1985.

LNER group

Campling NH, *Historic carriage drawings – Vol 1, LNER and constituents*, Pendragon 1997.
Harris M, *Great Northern Railway and East Coast Joint Stock carriages from 1905*, Oakwood Press 1995.
Harris M, *LNER standard Gresley carriages*, Mallard Books 1998.
North Eastern Railway Association, *North Eastern record, Vol 2*, Historical Model Railway Society 1997.

Great Western group

Atkins AG, Beard W, Hyde DJ & Tourret R, *A history of GWR goods wagons – Vols 1 & 2*, David & Charles 1975, 1976 and 1986.
Barnsley M, *Midland & South Western Junction Railway, Vol 3,* Wild Swan 1995.
Mountford ER, *A register of GWR absorbed coaching stock*, Oakwood Press 1978.
Russell JH, *A pictorial record of Great Western coaches – Part 1 1838-1903*, Oxford Publishing Co 1972.
Russell JH, *A pictorial record of Great Western coaches – Part 2 1903-1948,* Oxford Publishing Co 1973.
Russell JH, *Great Western wagon plans*, Oxford Publishing Co 1976.
Russell JH, *Great Western coaches appendix – Vol 2, specific duty coaches and the brown vehicles*, Oxford Publishing Co 1984.
Slinn JN, *Great Western way*, Historical Model Railway Society 1978.
Slinn JN, *Great Western Railway Siphons*, Historical Model Railway Society 1986.

Southern group

Gould D, *Bogie carriages of the London, Brighton & South Coast Railway*, Oakwood Press 1995.
Gould D, *Bogie carriages of the South Eastern & Chatham Railway*, Oakwood Press 1993.
Gould D, *Carriage stock of the SE&CR*, Oakwood Press 1976.
Gould D, *Southern Railway passenger vans*, Oakwood Press 1992.
Kidner RW, *Service stock of the Southern Railway*, Oakwood Press 1993.
Newbury PJ, *Carriage stock of the LB&SCR*, Oakwood Press 1976.
Tavender L, *HMRS livery register No 3 – LSWR and Southern*, Historical Model Railway Society 1970.